# P&C Insurance Claim Management

*A comprehensive manual for claim supervisors and managers in the property and casualty insurance industry*

**Authored by:**

**Michael T. Murdock, M.S., CPCU, ARM, ARe, ASLI, ACI**

Ins-Edu

**Ins-Edu Company**

Windsor Locks, Connecticut, 06096, USA
www.ins-edu.com

**First Edition 2018**
**Second Printing January 2021**

PRINTED IN THE UNITED STATES OF AMERICA

"This publication is designed to provide accurate and authoritative information in regard to the subject matter covered. It is sold with the understanding that the publisher is not engaged in rendering legal, accounting, or other professional services. If professional advice is required, the services of a competent professional should be sought."

— From a Declaration of Principles jointly adopted by a Committee of the American Bar Association and a Committee of Publishers and Associations.

Authored by:

**Michael T. Murdock, M.S., CPCU, ARM, ARe, ASLI, ACI**

**ISBN 978-0-9998885-0-6**

**Ins-Edu Company**
Windsor Locks, CT 06096
Tel (860) 698-0200
Fax (860) 920-7312
www.ins-edu.com

*Ins-Edu Company is a trade name of Insurance Consulting, LLC*

# TABLE OF CONTENTS

# Preface

*P&C Insurance Claim Management* was written as a guide for the claim supervisor and claim manager. The book focuses on key aspects of claim management from a technical claim oversight and administrative perspective. If you are a new to the industry, recently promoted to a supervisory role, or a seasoned claim manager, you will find this book useful. Balancing the management of claim files and people can be challenging, and having a relevant resource provides guidance, increases your confidence level, and makes the job a little easier.

The insurance industry is undergoing a shortage of available qualified and experienced claim resources at the professional and management levels. Within the next five years the industry will lose over 20% of its claim resources to retirement. With these retirements will be a significant loss of knowledge and experience which will take many years to replace. As a result, the industry will be challenged in not only filling positions and competing in the job market for the "best" resources, but also sustaining a claim quality level which will yield favorable financial results.

Companies which have traditionally recruited externally for qualified and experienced staff are now implementing internal training programs to develop their own claim staff, including supervisory training for both current and future claim supervisors and managers. These training programs are well structured and often administered by experienced claim professionals with learning and development skills.

Historically, the insurance industry has promoted adjusters to claim supervisors or managers based on their claim technical ability and not necessarily on the ability to manage people effectively. Promoting from within an organization is encouraged as it creates a positive work environment and a career path for adjusters who want to be a supervisor or manager; however, for the new supervisor or manager to be successful, they require fundamental claim management training and education.

Management training and education can be in the form of industry textbook readings, completing insurance designation programs, enrolling in undergraduate and graduate level management courses, taking internal and external training courses, and on-the-job (OTJ) training by working closely with other experienced supervisors and managers.

Management training and education can be structured over a specific time-period and include industry training on properly managing a claim unit or operation; or training in human resource issues such as recruiting, interviewing, hiring and firing, performance management and properly handling employee performance issues. Understanding and applying basics concepts such as coaching and mentoring, delegation, effective communication, critical thinking and problem solving, as well as the necessary skills to develop strategic and tactical plans, are essential for all managers.

Not all insurance professionals have the required leadership skills or the personality to manage other people. Leadership skills may be in our personality or cultivated over time and these skills may become more evident with increasing responsibility in an organization. Although a manager may have the characteristics of a leader, they will need to earn the respect of their staff to be an effective leader in motivating and challenging the staff to meet organizational objectives.

Advancements in technology are changing the claim operational landscape, the overall role of the claim manager, and how the claim manager handles daily claim activities. Managing claims and people in an electronic claim environment requires system knowledge and a comfort level working with intuitive modern architecture claim applications, document management systems and integrated external applications. Many of the *management controls* used by claim managers are now integrated within the claim system using dashboards, metrics, reports, business rules, work queues and advanced diary management processes.

The new claim manager must be disciplined to work in an electronic claim environment and manage claim activities electronically which may involve less personal interaction with adjusters. The environment is fast-paced and requires attention to detail in making sure the electronic claim file is properly documented by the claim staff with completion of structured and unstructured fields (including claim attributes and coding), as well as, electronic notes, investigation, adjustment activities and claim evaluations (e.g. reserves and settlements). Financial claim management requires ongoing review and oversight, including review and approval of claim reserves and payments.

This book was written for the new and experienced claim supervisor or manager working in the property and casualty insurance industry. It focuses on many fundamental technical and operational aspects of a claim operation and the challenges faced by many new and experienced claim managers.

Specifically, the book includes the following chapters:

## Chapter 1 – The Claim Manager Role

*Chapter 1* reviews the various claim organizations and structures, detailing the fundamental roles and responsibilities of the claim manager in each type of claim facility. The role of the claim manager may differ depending on the type of claim facility in terms of both claim technical and management responsibilities, as well the daily activities performed by the manager.

For example, a claim manager working for a self-insured entity may provide oversight to external independent adjusters, or a TPA, compared to a claim manager working at an insurance company managing internal claim resources.

The claim manager of the future will be much more focused on data and analytics – technology experience and analytics skills will be the new skillset for the future claim manager.

## Chapter 2 – Financial Operations

As a claim manager, it is critically important to understand how the claim operation impacts the insurance company's financial results, both from a loss and expense perspective.

*Chapter 2* examines insurance financial operations. In this chapter we review various insurance industry terms, as well as financial metrics and ratios (e.g. combined ratio, loss ratio, LAE, expense ratio, etc.).

There are illustrative examples of how the loss ratio is impacted by both increased losses and a reduction in earned premium. Reserve management is discussed both from a methodology perspective and the claim evaluation process.

We also review the monetary impact of case reserves (including redundancy and deficiency), the importance of a reserve philosophy, avoiding claim overpayments, expense control, operating budgets and vendor management.

## Chapter 3 – Managing Effectively

*Chapter 3* focuses on managing effectively. Being an effective manager is not necessarily measured by your specific technical expertise, but more importantly the ability to motivate your staff in meeting departmental and company objectives, including quality claim handling and outcomes.

Balancing technical claim management and administrative management responsibilities can be a challenging task. In this chapter we review key concepts on how to manage people including the various management styles. The chapter reviews both technical and administrative activities, the importance of claim guidelines and standards, managing to expectations, being an effective leader and delegating appropriately.

We also review the effective management of human resources and its impact on claim results (positive and negative), working with difficult employees and managing employee turnover.

## Chapter 4 – Management Controls

*Chapter 4* reviews *management controls* which are any processes, systems or tasks used to manage, control, or monitor business operations, including financial transactions.

As a claim manager, the use of management controls is a key responsibility to ensure consistent quality results, and compliance with company guidelines, standards and procedures. A primary management control used to effectively manage claim technical quality is the *claims quality review process*. We also manage and control adjuster workloads through productivity and workload management reports.

Management controls are used in claim technical activities such as extending claim authority (e.g. reserve, settlement and payment approval), reviewing and providing oversight on claims over an adjuster's authority using a dual diary process, and approving claim denials and coverage position letters.

## Chapter 5 – Managing Technical Claim Handling

The quality of claim handling directly impacts the claim outcome or result, as well as the overall *loss ratio*. As a claim manager, you need to establish expectations for quality claim handling. This is accomplished by having clear, concise and consistent *best practice* claim handling guidelines, standards and procedures.

*Chapter 5* examines various claim handling *best practice* categories in property & casualty (including workers' compensation) claims. In each *best practice* category, we review specific claim handling requirements and provide relevant recommendations and comments on effective supervision. We also review claim analysis and evaluation, reporting and documentation (including *Action Plans*), and litigation management activities.

In this chapter, we also introduce the framework for *Supervisory Best Practices,* including recommendations for management dual diary reviews at various intervals in the claim process.

## Chapter 6 – Claims Quality Review Process

The industry has evolved with respect to claim review or claim audit tools and methodologies which are detailed in this chapter.

*Chapter 6* provides an overview of the *Claims Quality Review Process*. The claims quality review process includes a methodology to review a sampling of claim files on a regular basis, without having to review, or dual diary, all claim files in the claim supervisor or manager's unit. Our objective in the claims quality review process is to review a sampling of claims from each adjuster on a monthly or quarterly basis to evaluate handling trends (positive and negative). We use the trending results to focus on claim handling improvement and as an input for adjuster performance.

In this chapter we review various auditing tools and methodologies, the claims quality review objective, an effective review framework and the audit format.

The end of the chapter includes ***Appendix I*** which provides a detailed list of claim *best practice* audit categories and the requirements in each category to meet an acceptable quality level standard.

## <u>Chapter 7 – Staffing & Resource Management</u>

*Chapter 7* discusses staffing and resource management in a claim organization. The financial impact of staffing can be challenging for claim management in achieving the balance between the staff necessary to meet quality claim expectations and the approved claim expense (staffing) budget.

Workload management is complex since there are many factors which impact staffing. These factors are discussed in detail including their effect on productivity and workloads.

This chapter reviews various *Claim Workload Models* which are used as the basis to develop workload and productivity standards. We also review *Claim Staffing Models* which apply the established workload standards to create appropriate adjuster staffing levels, by distributing the workload equitably based on standards for the claim type, role and responsibilities.

We review productivity reporting which is an important management control and requires ongoing review to be sure the claim staff is meeting productivity standards and requirements (e.g. closing ratios). The chapter includes comments on adjuster *capacity* and workload *balancing* which are important aspects of productivity management to be monitored closely.

## <u>Chapter 8 – Technology & Claim Systems</u>

*Chapter 8* examines the impact of the claim supervisor or manager working in an electronic claim environment including the need to be well organized and not lose sight of their primary function to achieve a quality claim work product by providing high quality supervision and oversight.

Modern architecture claim systems provide many features and benefits which can improve productivity, efficiency and supervision. After a decision has been made to explore purchasing a new claim system, it is important to establish a realistic budget for the project and get executive management approval. The development of comprehensive *business requirements* will help facilitate the selection process and achieve a better outcome.

In this chapter we provide a detailed review of various system features and benefits, and the impact on the claim operation. We review the system implementation process and the need to develop an organized project structure with the assistance of a consultant. System implementations are time consuming and require dedicated resources for the vendor selection process, vendor interviews, system demonstrations, and testing during the implementation phase. Dedicated project claim resources are necessary for a successful claim system implementation – which is often underestimated.

Technology is changing very rapidly with auto-adjudication of claims, mobile technology, telematics and UBI, autonomous vehicle technology (AVT), drone technology, predictive analytics, machine learning and robotics. The future claim operation will be very different for both the adjuster and manager.

## Chapter 9 – Claim Management Reports

*Chapter 9* reviews various financial and operational claim management reports available to the claim operation.

The types of claim management reports used, or have access to, will depend on your level in the organization. The higher your level in the organization the more you will depend on claim management reports to be effective.

To properly manage a claim unit or claim department, management reports should be relevant and useful. Reports need to be in a functional format to allow for customized reporting with a specific dataset. For example, management reports in an Excel® format with available pivot tables provide an excellent tool to tailor reports to a manager's specific needs.

The reports do not tell you everything. You are working with people – you need to get out of your office and know what is going on in the claim operation!

––––––––––––––––––––––––––––––––––––

I hope you find this book useful and interesting. By developing and improving the quality of claim management and supervision we will improve industry results through increased knowledge, skill and effective leadership. We will also improve the work environment with quality supervision and generate more interest in a career in the insurance industry.

Thank you.

Michael T. Murdock, M.S., CPCU, ARM, ARe, ASLI, ACI

April 2018

# About the Author

## Michael T. Murdock, M.S., CPCU, ARM, ARe, ASLI, ACI

Michael Murdock has worked in the insurance industry for over 35 years in various industry technical and management positions, including adjuster, supervisor, manager, and senior officer in insurance, reinsurance, risk management, and third-party administrator (TPA) firms.

With his diversified multiline insurance background, Mr. Murdock has adjusted, managed and audited many insurance claims – in property, casualty, workers' compensation and professional lines.

Mr. Murdock has worked in the traditional, specialty and alternative insurance markets. All these experiences have provided the framework for writing this book, from an insurance company, risk management and TPA perspective.

Mr. Murdock has authored many insurance articles and given presentations on insurance related topics. He also authored *Claim Operations: A Practical Guide*, published by the International Risk Management Institute, Inc., in 2010.

Mr. Murdock has a master's degree in Insurance Management from Boston University Graduate School of Management and holds the following insurance designations:

- Chartered Property Casualty Underwriter (CPCU)
- Associate in Risk Management (ARM)
- Associate in Reinsurance (ARe)
- Associate in Surplus Lines Insurance (ASLI)
- Associate in Captive Insurance (ACI)

Mr. Murdock grew up in Long Island, New York, and spent most of his career in the northeastern part of the United States. He is an Insurance Practice Director at *The Nolan Company*, a management consulting firm specializing in insurance, banking and health care markets.

---

**Michael Murdock** can be contacted at:
Tel 860.817.3080 | Email mikemurd@gmail.com

---

# CHAPTER 1
# THE CLAIM MANAGER ROLE

## Role of the Claim Manager

The claim management role is a critical role in any claim operation as the position manages and controls adjuster activities at the line level which has a direct impact on company financial results. The claim manager is responsible for subordinates who investigate and adjudicate claims working within established claim guidelines, standards and procedures. Any deviation from claim guidelines, standards or procedures, including mistakes or improper claim handling, may have a direct impact on company's financial results with increased loss and expense exposure.

The specific role in claim management will vary depending on the type of claims, line of business being managed, the volume of business, the number of staff subordinates, and the role of your direct report manager or executive. These roles include claim supervisor, assistant claim manager, claim manager, branch claim manager, home office claim manager, assistant vice president, claim director and vice president. For purpose of this book we will simply refer to the generic role of *claim manager* meaning any of the above positions or other variations in title.

The specific roles in claim management will vary by entity type and size of the claim operation. The various risk bearing and non-risk bearing entities outlined below have different claim operational structures which will impact the roles and responsibilities of the claim manager.

- Insurance Companies
- Third Party Claim Administrators (TPA)
- Self-Insured Entities
- Captive Insurance Companies and Risk Retention Groups
- Risk Pools
- Reinsurance Companies
- Independent Adjuster Firms
- Agencies and MGAs

## Insurance Companies

The largest structured claim operations are within *Insurance Company* organizations. Insurance companies can have a considerable number of technical and management claim personnel including claim support, adjusters, appraisers, SIU investigators, claim attorneys, supervisors, managers, claim directors and officers.

Each position is included in a functional group (e.g. claim support, automobile claims, casualty claims, property claims, appraisal unit, branch claim office, home office claims, etc.) which includes a supervisor or manager reporting to the next level in the management hierarchy.

Insurance company claim operations vary in size from a small group of 50 to well over 500+, depending on the premium volume, claim volume and type of business being written. High transactional insurance business such as automobile, property or workers' compensation will have larger claim operations due to a higher claim volume compared to a more specialized class of business such as professional lines which may have a lower claim volume.

Many insurance company claim operations have both branch and home office claim units. The branch claim manager may administratively report to a local general manager, but on technical claim matters report to the home office claim staff – on those claims which exceed the branch office claim authority or meet special claim reporting criteria such as complex coverage issues or allegations of "bad faith".

The claim manager role in an insurance company is a key line management position which has a direct impact on the company results (positive or negative). The primary responsibility of the claim manager is to manage and control the claim operation effectively in accordance with company guidelines, standards and procedures, as well as various *Fair Claim Acts* and insurance regulations.

The claim manager controls loss and expense reserves and payments up to a certain dollar authority level, and adjusters request claim authority from the claim manager on financial transactions over their own claim authority level. Claim managers at the line level are involved in claim technical oversight (file supervision) and personnel matters.

In an insurance company, actions by the claim manager affect the company's profitability. The insurance company is in the business of selling insurance and to be profitable the company must achieve a combined ratio under 100% (without investment returns). Included in the *combined ratio* are the *loss ratio* and *loss adjustment expense ratio* (LAE). These ratios are impacted by technical and administrative claim handling, which is under the direct control of the claim manager.

A claim operation provides claim services to its policyholders and the expense to operate an insurance company claim operation is funded from the insurance premium. These expenses are referred to as *Unallocated Loss Adjustment Expenses* (ULAE), which will be discussed in **Chapter 2 – Financial Operations.**

# Third Party Administrators (TPA)

*Third Party Claim Administrator* (TPAs) are companies which provide outsourced claim handling to insurance companies, self-insured's, captives and pools. Claim handling is provided to a client under contract for a specified time-period and fee schedule. TPA's handle and manage claims from the claim report date to conclusion. The size of a TPA will vary from a small operation with 25 employees to large national TPAs with over 1,000 employees.

TPA claim operations are very similar to an insurance company claim operation in how claims are reported, handled and managed – and the structure of the claim operation is very similar to an insurance company with multiple claim position levels and a management hierarchy. Claim systems are similar in functionality with integrated billing for claim service fees.

The primary difference between a TPA and an insurance company claim operation is that a TPA is in the business of selling claim services and its revenue is derived from the volume of TPA service fees sold. TPA service fee billing may be based on a percentage of written premium, annual fixed fees, fixed fees per claim or exposure, or on an hourly rate. In contrast, insurance company revenue is derived from earned premium and the internal claim operation is not a revenue producing business unit.

TPAs will have specialized claim units either by class of business, program or by client depending on the size of a client program. This distinction makes the TPA claim environment *client-centric* with each client potentially having customized special claim handling requirements and reporting. The claim manager must manage claim units with different special claim handling guidelines and protocols, requiring the manager to closely monitor the claim staff to be sure there is full compliance – as non-compliance could have financial consequences with a dissatisfied client cancelling the TPA contract.

A TPA will contract with the client to deliver claim services in accordance with industry *Best Practices*, which may incorporate the client's claim handling guidelines or the TPA's own internal claim handling guidelines. The TPA contract, commonly referred to as a *Claims Service Agreement*, may also stipulate certain service levels called *Service Level Agreements*, or SLAs. If the TPA does not provide the level of service required, there could be financial consequences.

The TPA will offer a variety of services to its client including access to the TPA claims system, loss fund account management, large loss reporting, claim file summaries, quarterly risk management meetings, as well as reporting and analytics. The client will audit the TPA claim operations periodically which may be at least annually. The TPA management staff may also work closely with the client's risk manager.

A unique aspect of being a claim manager at a TPA is the fluctuation in business volume due to loss of client business and the addition of new business. This creates upward and downward shifts in staffing requirements which can also adversely impact claim quality. As the claim staff is reduced due to the loss of an account (expense reduction), existing claim volume remains which needs to be handled and managed, yielding high adjuster caseloads.

If a TPA contracts for claim services with fees based on a percentage of written premium it can result in a problem when the program or client is terminated – with no more premium (or fees) being generated and continued claim activity. Under this fee structure, the TPA will no longer

earn income from the program (without any written premium). This creates an environment wherein the claim manager may be challenged in managing a claim operation in "run-off" with no service fee income to pay for adequate claim staff, resulting in a potential adverse impact on claim quality and employee turnover.

As in the insurance company claim operation, the claim manager role in a TPA is a key line management position which will have a direct impact on the TPA client's profitability and results.

The TPA claim manager will be responsible for specific clients and programs; requiring an additional responsibility of managing client's expectations and results. The claim manager must also manage the client audit process – since most TPAs are audited by the client, or a contracted third party on a regular basis. With multiple clients requesting claim audits, the claim manager spends a lot of time preparing for client claim audits and managing the process of complying with claim audit recommendations or claim handling remediation plans. Successful TPAs have internal quality review processes to control claim quality and meet client claim handling requirements. Achieving quality claim handling standards is critical for a TPA to maintain long-term client relationships.

When a TPA is involved in a program with an insurance company, the service fees paid to the TPA are paid by the insurance company as an *Unallocated Loss Adjustment Expense* (ULAE). If the TPA is providing claim services to a self-insured corporation, the service fees are paid as an operating cost or expense by the self-insured corporation.

## **Self-Insured Entities**

*Self-Insured* claim operations are usually part of large corporate entities which partially or fully self-insure various insurance coverages or exposures such as liability, workers' compensation, physical damage and property exposures. The self-insured entity may purchase excess insurance to cover the exposure above the self-insured retained limit or SIR (which is usually the predictable frequency layer of losses).

Depending on the size of the operation, the self-insured claim department may have internal claim support, adjuster and claim manager roles, but not be actively involved in the investigation and adjudication of claims. There may be more use of external vendors to assist in the claim handling and adjudication process, such as the use of independent adjusters and TPAs, with the self-insured claim operation providing oversight.

In certain lines of business, the self-insured entity may need to be licensed or file with the state or regulatory authorities to self-administer claims and will contract with a licensed TPA to handle and manage all claims within the self-insured retained limit.

The claim manager role in a self-insured claim operation may be different than an insurance company or TPA. The claim manager may have direct involvement in large exposure claims monitoring the TPA claim handling (over the TPA authority threshold) and reporting to the excess carrier, extending claim authority over a certain dollar threshold to the independent adjuster or TPA, and conducting periodic claim audits on the claim facility, or outsource this function to a third-party contractor.

In some self-insured internal claim operations, the authority to establish claim reserves and pay claims may rest with the claim manager, risk manager or finance manager. When a TPA is managing claims for the self-insured, the claims service agreement will stipulate claim authority and reporting criteria.

The claim operation in a self-insured entity is not a revenue producing unit and the cost of the claim operation is an operating expense to the self-insured company.

# Captive Insurance Companies & RRGs

A *Captive Insurance Company* is an insurance vehicle formed to insure the risks of the captive owner(s). There are several types of captive insurance companies; a captive owned by members having similar or homogeneous risks such as a *Group Captive*; an *Association Captive* insuring similar risks for members of a trade association; or a captive having one owner called a *Single Parent Captive* (also called a *Pure Captive*). Captives may also be formed by managing general agents to share in the risk and results (e.g. Agency Captive).

There are also *Segregated Account Captives* or a *Protected Cell Company* which segregate the assets and liabilities of each captive "cell" within a core captive – a more cost-effective approach to forming a captive. Captives may start out as a *Segregated Account Captive* and restructure into a fully operating captive later.

There are variations in captive structures depending on the captive domicile. Captives may be direct writers of insurance (e.g. general liability, automobile physical damage or property coverage) or formed as a reinsurance company and *fronted* by a traditional licensed insurance company (e.g. automobile liability or workers' compensation coverage). Captive insurance companies may have limited surplus and rely heavily on reinsurance

A "fronting" arrangement is when one insurance company (fronting carrier) allows another insurance company or reinsurer to use its "paper[1]" in insurance transactions in exchange for a fee, which is typically a percentage of the premium. In this arrangement the fronting carrier is responsible for the risk and regulatory compliance but transfers the risk contractually.

---

[1] This means the insurance policy issued to the policyholder will indicate the fronting carrier's name and domicile. All insurance transactions are under the fronting carrier's name and license.

The fronting agreement will transfer the risk to the insurance company or reinsurer, and stipulate responsibilities including the need for the insurance company or reinsurer to post collateral (which may be in the form of a *letter of credit* or LOC) to protect the fronting carrier's risk, as the fronting carrier is taking insurance, credit and regulatory risks. Depending on the fronting agreement, the fronting carrier may want to retain claim handling responsibility or require specific claim handling requirements for a contracted TPA, auditing the claim facility periodically.

*Single Parent Captives* are used by corporations to manage risk either as a direct writer of insurance (e.g. property, physical damage, extended warranty) or as a captive reinsurance facility. An example would be a corporation forming a captive reinsurance company to retain its workers' compensation exposures. The insurance policy(s) is issued by a fronting insurance company, and then reinsured by the captive insurance company up to a retained level of the risk, transferring exposure above the retention layer to another reinsurer, who may be the same company as the fronting carrier, or another reinsurer. In this captive structure, there may be a risk manager, or claim manager who provides oversight of a TPA, or other claim facility, including conducting periodic claim audits.

In the United States, there is a form of a group captive, called a *Risk Retention Group* (RRG) which are formed under the Federal Liability Risk Retention Act[2] (LRRA). The primary difference with an RRG is that the insurance vehicle is formed under the laws of one state – regulated as a captive or traditional insurance company – and may write liability insurance coverage direct without the need for a fronted insurance company. The RRG has direct access to the reinsurance market to transfer or cede risks beyond its own capacity.

The claim operations within Captive and RRG organizations will vary depending on the captive structure. If the captive is structured as a reinsurance facility, and there is a fronting carrier, there may be minimal claim staff in the captive facility depending on the claim services performed by the captive. When a fronting carrier is involved, the carrier may provide the insurance claim infrastructure including the claims staff, systems, and reporting – charging a fee for these services as a percentage of the premium.

Group Captives and RRGs may have claim operations similar to a traditional insurance company on a smaller scale but claims are often handled by TPAs. The claim manager role in a captive structure will vary depending on the captive type and the role the captive facility has in the claim handling process. For example, if the captive is a direct insurance writer or an RRG, with no TPA involved, then the claim structure may be similar to an insurance company with adjusters and a claim management hierarchy.

However, if the captive is a reinsurance facility with a fronting carrier, or there is a contracted TPA, the captive may have a limited role in the claim process but have a claim manager on staff

---

[2] This federal law was passed by Congress in 1986 to assist U.S. businesses in purchasing liability insurance which was difficult to obtain at the time.

who monitors the claim handling by the fronting carrier or TPA claim staff – to protect their financial interests. The claim manager may have the responsibility to extend claim authority and conduct periodic claim audits if a TPA has been contracted to handle claims for the group captive or RRG.

Captive and RRG claim operations provide claim services to the owners and the expense to operate the claim operation is funded from the insurance premium. These expenses are referred to as *Unallocated Loss Adjustment Expenses* (ULAE).

# Risk Pools

*Risk Pools* or *Pools* are member-based risk-sharing vehicles wherein organizations pool funds to finance risk exposure (e.g. liability or workers' compensation). Pools are formed by private entities and public entities – they have a limited capacity for risk and purchase reinsurance to cover the excess exposure over the retained layer.

Pools may have claim operations similar to a traditional insurance company on a smaller scale. Often, the claim services for pools are handled by TPAs, or a *Management Company* which provides claims and other services such as underwriting management, policy administration, marketing, finance and technology.

The claim manager role in a pool will vary depending on the pool structure. If the pool has its own claim staff, then the pool may be operated similar to an insurance company. If the pool is operated under contract with a management company or TPA, the pool may have their own limited claim management staff who monitor the claim handling by the management company or TPA claim staff – to protect their financial interests.

When pools are under contract with a management company, the claim manager role in the management company is very similar to an insurance company. The primary difference is that the management company is being paid for their services either as an annual fixed fee or a percentage of the premium with claim service fees included in the overall management service fee.

The claim management staff at a *management company* operating a risk pool are very focused on quality claim results and client satisfaction. The service contract may include service level agreements (SLAs) and specific claim handling requirements. The management company derives its income from the service fees (similar to a TPA) and must maintain an acceptable level of claim quality to retain or renew the contract. The risk pool will also conduct periodic claim audits on the management company using an external vendor.

Pool claim operations provide claim services to the pool members and the expense to operate the claim operation is funded from the pool insurance premium. These expenses are referred to as *Unallocated Loss Adjustment Expenses* (ULAE) and may be paid to a management company or a TPA.

# Reinsurance Companies

*Reinsurance Companies* provide protection to an insurance company by sharing in premium and losses either on an excess or pro-rata basis.

*Excess of Loss* reinsurance provides protection above a primary carrier's retained layer of loss. Excess of Loss reinsurance includes *Per Risk Excess* – a property treaty applying to each loss or risk; *Catastrophe Excess* – protection from aggregate property losses due to a catastrophe; *Per Policy Excess* – reinsurance applying to liability policies issued by the primary insurer; *Per Occurrence Excess* – reinsurance applying to liability on an occurrence basis without regard to the number of policies subject to a loss; and *Aggregate Excess* – or *Stop Loss Treaty* with the primary insurer's retention and limits based on a loss ratio.

*Pro Rata Reinsurance* is the proportional sharing of policy limits, premiums and losses between the primary insurer and the reinsurer. There are two types of Pro Rata Reinsurance: (1) *Quota Share* (property and liability) – the primary insurer and the reinsurer agree to share in policy limits, premiums and losses; and (2) *Surplus Share* (property) the retention of the primary insurer is based on a minimum retained dollar amount (line), with the amount above the limit (surplus) ceded to the reinsurer.

The reinsurance claims function is very different than the claims function at an insurance company or TPA and varies depending on whether the claim is an *excess* reinsurance claim or *pro-rata* reinsurance claim. Excess reinsurance claims focus on large losses which may impact the reinsurance excess layer and pro-rata reinsurance claims focus on the underlying claim activity since the reinsurers exposure may begin at first dollar as a percentage of each loss (e.g. risk prorated as 40% ceding company and 60% reinsurer).

The reinsurance claims staff manages claims submitted by the ceding company or reinsured. The ceding company reports claims to the reinsurer in the form of claim notices (reinsurance advices) involving large losses or other losses qualifying for reinsurance reporting. Depending on the exposure at the reinsurance level, the reinsurance claim staff may request claim documentation to support the reserves or payments and may also conduct onsite claim audits of specific claims, or a book of claims.

The reinsurance claim operation is much smaller than a typical insurance company claim operation as the reinsurance claim staff is not involved in the daily underlying claim activities (e.g. investigation, taking statements, claim adjudication and litigation management) or involved in daily claim operational issues as in a primary insurer operation. The claim manager role is limited to the managing claims with reinsurance exposure. The reinsurance claim staff are routinely recruited from primary insurance claim operations.

There is a management hierarchy in the reinsurance claim operation – which can range from a reinsurance claim analyst or account executive, to claim manager and officer level positions. The claim manager (which may be an officer level position) in a reinsurance claim operation is responsible for the reinsurance claim technical staff, which includes monitoring new reinsurance claim assignments, providing oversight on reinsurance claims, reviewing claim reports and audit results, and working with ceding companies (primary insurers) on claim related issues.

The reinsurance claim operation expenses are paid from reinsurance premium and referred to as *Unallocated Loss Adjustment Expenses* (ULAE).

# Independent Adjuster Firms

*Independent Adjuster Firms* are companies which provide outsourced adjusting services to insurance companies, TPAs and any other risk-bearing entities referenced above. These adjusters handle claims in the field and provide full adjustment services or task adjusting assignments requested by the insurance entity, or client. Many companies, including TPAs, use independent adjusters to supplement their own internal claim staff to handle an overflow, or handle field task assignments such as statements, scene photographs, inspections, property damage appraisals and witness canvasses.

Independent adjuster firms are structured similar to an insurance company with adjusters, supervisors and a claim management hierarchy. The independent adjuster handles the client's claims and prepares the necessary reporting which will include various exhibits such as photographs, statements, damage appraisals, official reports and other elements of the investigation and adjustment process.

Independent adjusters are "task oriented" and may have a different focus than an insurance company adjuster who manages claims at a desk to a conclusion making decisions on liability, compensability and damages, as well as expenses, reserve management and litigation management. The independent adjuster is rarely audited by the client carrier or TPA, unless the independent adjuster firm is operating as a TPA.

The claim manager role in the independent adjuster firm is to monitor the work product of the field adjusters and appraisers and be a liaison with the client. Their role is very different than that of an insurance company or TPA claim manager for the same reasons cited above. Typically, the independent adjuster working at an adjusting firm is promoted to claim manager.

The independent adjuster firm earns revenue based on fees billed hourly, task-based fees, or contingency-based fees (e.g. subrogation). The fees paid by the client (e.g. insurance company or TPA) to the Independent Adjuster firm are paid either as an *Unallocated Loss Adjustment Expense* (ULAE) or an *Allocated Loss Adjustment Expenses* (ALAE).

# Agencies and MGAs

*Agency* claim operations fall into two major categories – Retail or Wholesale Agencies and Managing General Agents (MGAs) or Program Administrators.

The claim operation in a *Retail* or *Wholesale Insurance Agency* is limited to taking first reports, providing status reports to policyholders, clients or other agents, and in some instances conducting insurance company reserve reviews particularly for workers' compensation claims. The claim manager role is limited and provides oversight of the agency claim staff which may include both claim support and desk adjusters. The claim manager in an agency claim operation has no claim authority to settle, pay or reserve claims, does not provide oversight of claim investigations or adjudication, and primarily represents the interests of the agency client, or policyholder.

*Managing General Agents* (MGAs) and program administrators have a contract with an insurance company, have some level of underwriting and claim authority, and benefit from the profitability of the program; therefore, very interested in a high-quality claim operation. These organizations may have an internal claim operation similar to a small insurance company, or may outsource claim services to an external TPA, or own a subsidiary TPA. The MGA contract with the insurance company will specify claim authority and outline claim handling requirements. This will include the right to audit claims handled by the MGA and TPA, by the insurance company and reinsurer.

MGAs manage program business which may include a homogenous group of risks. This requires special claim handling and expertise in the type of program business (e.g. contractors, taxi and limo business, waste management, tow trucks, etc.). The insurance company may allow the MGA to handle claims if the MGA has the claim expertise and proper licensing. The insurance company may require contracting with a TPA – either between the MGA and TPA or the insurance company and the TPA, or a three-party contract.

The claim manager role in an MGA or program administrator will vary depending on the structure. If the claim operation is an internal claim operation, or a subsidiary owned TPA, there will be a claim structure similar to a TPA or small insurance company with adjusters and a claim management hierarchy, including designated claim managers with claim and decision-making authority. If claim services are outsourced to a TPA, there may be an internal staff claim manager who monitors the claim services provided by the TPA and conducts periodic claim audits.

The expense of having an internal retail or wholesale agency claim operation is paid by the agency as an operating expense. The expense of an MGA or program administrator internal claim operation, or outsourced TPA, is paid from the premium as an *Unallocated Loss Adjustment Expense* (ULAE). When the MGA has a contract with the insurance company, the contract will stipulate the claim fee structure (e.g. fixed fee per claim or fees based on a percentage of premium) and claim handling requirements.

# The Future Claim Manager

For the last 30+ years the claim manager's job has not changed in terms of its role in the claim organization and overall responsibility.

The claim manager is responsible for budgeting, interpretation and application of coverage, assignment of claims, productivity and workload management, claim audits, managing claim reserves, claim analysis and evaluation, approving claim payments, reserves and extending authority, managing expenses, achieving quality claim handling and outcomes, analysis of claim trends, and managing the claim staff effectively (hiring, firing, recruitment, training and development, performance management, etc.).

What has changed is how these tasks and functions are handled today by various claim organizations because of technological advancements. Claim operations using modern architecture claim system technology have adapted a "claims workstation" environment converting many of the manual management tasks of the past to automated management tasks using system functionality, document management, flexible business rules, work queues, dashboards, and robust management reporting using a data warehouse with analytical reporting tools.

Claim organizations which operate in a manual or legacy technology environment are inefficient and adversely impacted by high expenses. Manual tasks impact the ability to manage caseloads effectively and meet compliance requirements (e.g. workers' compensation state requirements) – creating manual "work-arounds" which cause errors and inefficiency.

Technology is advancing very rapidly and companies which do not make the technological shift to a modern architecture claim system will be left behind. As technology continues to advance in the industry any delay in moving to a current technology platform will make the transition even more difficult.

The claim manager of the future will be much more focused on data and analytics – technology experience and analytics skills will be the new skillset required for the claim manager. The way we manage people and customer expectation is changing rapidly and the claim operation of the future will look very different than today.

**Chapter 8 – Technology & Claim Systems** discusses current technology in the claim operation, its impact on overall claim performance and the technology advancements we can expect in the future.

# Chapter Comments

The common thread to these various claim structures is that the fundamental role of the claim manager is similar; however, specific roles and responsibilities change depending on the claim facility.

Claim managers have opportunities to work in different claim environments such as insurance companies, TPAs, self-insureds, captives, RRGs, risk pools, MGAs, independent adjusting firms and reinsurance companies. Although the roles may be somewhat different, the similarity in all claim environments is the critical role of the claim manager to manage claims and people effectively to achieve the desired financial results.

We will discuss managing people in other chapters – claim managers need to train and motivate their technical claim staff to achieve a high-quality work product in any claim facility. High quality work translates into improved financial results with a positive impact on the company's overall profitability.

Technology is advancing rapidly, and the claim manager of the future will be much more focused on data and analytics – technology experience and analytics skills is the new skillset required for the claim manager.

# CHAPTER 2
# FINANCIAL OPERATIONS

This chapter will review the financial aspects of an insurance operation, including the impact of claim handling on an insurance company, or other risk-bearing entity.

A claim manager should be familiar with insurance financial terms, metrics and industry *ratios* to be able to properly evaluate claim financial results and its overall impact on the company. This includes understanding the potential shifts in the *loss ratio* and determining whether the loss ratio is being negatively impacted by the quality of claim handling or attributed to other causes. As you will read in this chapter, the loss ratio may not always be adversely affected by claim handling – the loss ratio may be affected by premium rates, fluctuations in earned premium volume, and the upward or downward movement of the policy count (with changes in premium volume).

To fully understand the financial aspects of an insurance operation, let's define some key financial terms we use in insurance.

## Key Insurance Terms

## Earned Premium

*Earned Premium* is the premium which is earned by the insurance company. Insurance *Statutory Accounting Principles* (SAP)[3] state the premium is not "earned" until each month of the policy period has ended. Many insurance policies are 12-months in duration and therefore earn premium on a $1/12^{th}$ basis, or pro rata over the term of the policy.

As an example, the policy begins on January 1st as its effective date with total premium at $1,200. When it reaches June 31st, it would have earned 6/12's ($600) of the premium which is the premium amount booked in the insurance company's financials on July 1st to calculate its ratio on a *statutory* basis. The policy premium does not become fully earned until the end of the 12th month in this example which would be on December 31st.

## Written Premium

*Written Premium* is expressed in terms of "Gross" and "Net" – Gross Written Premium or GWP includes reinsurance (the full premium without any ceded reinsurance transactions) and Net Written Premium or NWP is "net" of reinsurance. GWP is also referred to as Direct Written Premium or DWP or Gross Premium Written or GPW.

---

[3] Most insurers authorized to do business in the United States and its territories are required to prepare statutory financial statements in accordance with *Statutory Accounting Principles* or SAP (National Associaion of Insurance Commissioners (NAIC)).

Written premium is the premium booked within a specific time-period (e.g. monthly) and booked at the full amount when received – it does not *earn* over a period. Using the same example above – the policy begins on January 1st as its effective date with total premium at $1,200 – this is the premium amount booked in the insurance company's financials to calculate some of its ratios but using written premium as the denominator and not earned premium.

*Underwriting Expenses* are typically calculated based on net written premium (net of reinsurance) as the expense attributed to each written premium dollar is booked when incurred.

## Policies in Force or PIF Count

The *Policies in Force* or *PIF Count* is the number of effective polices an insurance company has in force at a given point in time. This is often used as a metric to determine whether the insurance company has booked additional new business (policy growth) or lost existing business (policy reduction). It is also used to measure policy renewal counts or policy retention.

If premium has increased but the PIF count remains constant, then the increased premium is more than likely due to rate increases.

Understanding PIF counts is important as a change in the PIF count may cause fluctuations in claim volume, and the potential need for adjustments to claim staffing (upward or downward).

## Losses

*Losses* are the amounts paid to or on behalf of a policyholder either as a *first party* loss – paid to the policyholder directly such as a property or automobile physical damage loss, or as a *third-party* loss such as a bodily injury or property damage liability claim paid to a third party on behalf of the policyholder.

*Direct* losses pertain to the actual damage and *indirect* losses pertain to loss of use because of the direct damage such as the cost of a vehicle rental, or business interruption and loss of income in a commercial property loss.

Losses include claim *reserves* and *paid losses*. Claim reserves are the funds set aside to pay losses and can be posted as a *case reserve* representing a reserve for an individual exposure or as a *bulk reserve* posted by the actuarial department to supplement or strengthen case reserves. Actuaries will also post IBNR or *Incurred But Not Reported* reserves for those claims which have occurred but not yet reported to the insurance company.

The claim manager should understand the impact of losses as it is the largest component of the *combined ratio* (see below). Losses include case reserves and payments which are controlled by the claim operation. If there is reserve redundancy or deficiency, or claim overpayments, the loss ratio will be adversely impacted.

Losses are controlled by adhering to *best practices* in claim handling including quality investigations, adjustments and evaluations. A quality claim operation can have a material impact on the claim (loss) results and overall loss ratio.

## Incurred Losses

*Incurred Losses* are case loss *reserves* plus loss *payments* less loss *recoveries*. The incurred loss calculation provides the most accurate measure of a complete loss and is used by underwriting when analyzing loss history on a policy.

Most claim systems provide a screen view of incurred claim activity at an exposure and claim level including reserves, paid(s), recoveries and total incurred (loss and expense).

As indicated above, losses are controlled by adhering to *best practices* in claim handling which includes recovery claim handling (see below).

## Recovery

*Recoveries* are those funds received as reimbursements due to *subrogation, salvage, third party deductibles* or *refunds* (e.g. overpayments) and applies to both loss and claim expense.

Under the insurance policy provisions, the insurance company has a *right of subrogation* meaning that after payment of a claim, the insurance company may pursue a claim against the responsible party to recover damages paid to the policyholder (including reimbursement of the policyholder's deductible). The insurance policy also provides for the right of the insurance company to retain salvage after payment of a total loss claim to the policyholder.

As in losses, managing the recovery process is an important function for the claim manager. Recovery dollars reduce the incurred losses which improves the loss ratio. If payments and case reserves remain constant, with each additional recovery dollar received, we will see a reduction in the incurred losses. Some managers describe subrogation recovery as dollars which fall directly to the "bottom line".

## Total Incurred

*Total Incurred* includes incurred losses (as indicated above) and incurred expenses (ALAE).

The calculation for incurred expenses includes Allocated Loss Adjustment Expenses (ALAE) case reserves plus ALAE payments less ALAE recoveries.

# Gross Expense (Operating Expense)

*Operating Expense* includes all the expenses of the company as illustrated below. These expenses are referred to as *Gross Expense* and include all departments with some expense allocated back to each department using some type of allocation method such as employee count, or a percentage of the overall operational budget (e.g. departmental costs as a percentage of the total company's expense). Examples of these charge-back expenses are shared services such as IT, Human Resources and Legal

Gross expense includes *underwriting expense* and *unallocated loss adjustment expenses* (ULAE). The typical operating expenses in an insurance company are illustrated below in **Exhibit 2-A.**

| OPERATING EXPENSES: EXHIBIT 2-A | | |
|---|---|---|
| Employee Salaries | Underwriting Reports | Entertainment |
| Employee Benefits | Agent Commissions | Rent |
| Advertising | Insurance | Printing |
| Boards & Bureaus | Travel | Telephone |
| Postage | Office Supplies | Legal |
| Accounting | Audit | Licenses |
| Directors Expense | Equipment | Information Technology |
| Payroll Taxes | Premium Taxes | Associations |

# Underwriting Expense

*Underwriting Expenses* are a component of the *Gross Expense* and include all policy acquisition costs such as agent's salaries and commissions, advertising, surveys and underwriting reports, premium taxes and other expense such as boards and bureaus (e.g. Insurance Services Office or ISO and Property Casualty Insurance Association of America or PCI, etc.).

Underwriting expenses are sometimes reflected on an insurance company income statement as *internal expense* representing *General Other & Administrative Expense* (GO&A) and *external expense* representing acquisition costs such as commissions.

# Loss Adjustment Expense

*Loss Adjustment Expenses* or LAE has two components: Allocated Loss Adjustment Expense (ALAE) and Unallocated Loss Adjustment Expense (ULAE). These are expenses related to the administration of claims, either specific to a claim or a claim operational expense.

## Allocated Loss Adjustment Expense

*Allocated Loss Adjustment Expenses* (ALAE) are those claim expenses which are attributable to a specific claim such as defense and litigation costs, the cost of experts, medical cost containment, and some adjusting expenses.

ALAE expense is also referred to as *Defense and Cost Containment* or *DCC* expense. These expenses include litigation, defense and medical cost containment expenses – similar to the ALAE definition above.

ALAE expenses may be case-reserved managed by the claim operation at the individual claim or exposure level, or bulk-reserved managed by the actuarial staff with a bulk reserve estimate based on historical paid expense and adjusted as needed.

Controlling expense is a primary responsibility of the claim manager. We control ALAE expense by managing claim vendors and litigation costs, effectively. We will discuss ALAE expense control in other chapters.

## Unallocated Loss Adjustment Expense

*Unallocated Loss Adjustment Expenses* (ULAE) are those claim expenses which are not attributable to a specific claim and include the overhead costs of the claim operation.

ULAE expense is also referred to as *Adjusting & Other* or *A&O* expense. These expenses include fees for internal and external adjusters/appraisers, the expenses related to the evaluation of coverage, and the cost of internal claim operations or TPA service fees if outsourcing claims to a TPA.

ULAE expense is not case-reserved unless the company or TPA want to track specific expenses such as adjuster or appraiser expense which may not be coded as ALAE.

As with ALAE, controlling ULAE expense is a primary responsibility of the claim manager. We control ULAE expense by managing the claim operation effectively. For example, decisions around workloads and staffing, as well as salary management, impact the ULAE expense. We will discuss ULAE expense control in other chapters.

## The Insurance Industry Cycle

The insurance industry has various economic "cycles" it goes through – which are commonly referred to as the *hard market* and *soft market*. The cycle is based on "supply and demand".

The *hard market* includes higher insurance rates, more stringent underwriting, less insurance capacity in the marketplace, and reduced competition. The *soft market* includes lower insurance rates, less stringent underwriting, more insurance capacity in the marketplace, and increased competition. These economic cycles are frequently brought on by significant catastrophic events such as major hurricanes or earthquakes where large losses are incurred.

Insurance companies want to write more business in a hard market (being more risk selective) as the premium rates are higher, thereby increasing premium volume and not necessarily increasing policies-in-force or PIF count. In a soft market insurance rates are lower and insurance companies need to increase premium volume but may need to write more policies (increasing the PIF count). If rates are too low, earned premium volume may decline which may have an adverse impact on the loss ratio since the loss ratio is calculated as incurred losses divided by earned premium.

From a claim perspective, in a *soft market* there may be an increased number of claims to handle, due to more policies being written (increase in PIF count) with the potential to generate additional claim activity.

If claims are being handled by a TPA and the claim service agreement was executed in a *hard market* (with service fees paid a percentage of premium), moving into a soft market may require hiring additional claim staff due to increased PIF count and claim volume, reducing the TPA's profit margin if there is no adjustment in the fee structure.

## Combined Ratio

The *Combined Ratio* is a measure of a company's profitability and includes all the expense attributed to each earned premium dollar – most, if not all, insurance companies want to achieve a Combined Ratio under 100% to be profitable.

If an insurance company has a 95% combined ratio, they are making five cents on each dollar of earned premium, or a 5% underwriting profit (gross margin). However, this does not include the investment income earned by the insurance company which can be sizable due to the interest earned on *Unearned Premium Reserves* (UPR) and claim reserves.

Insurance companies can remain solvent and continue operations with a combined ratio over 100% because of the investment income. It should be noted that achieving an overall *operating* profit without an *underwriting* profit is not a good long-term strategy – insurance companies need to allocate a portion of their underwriting profit back to surplus to facilitate growth and have funds available should the underwriting results deteriorate.

The *Combined Ratio* is the sum of *Incurred Losses + LAE* divided by *Earned Premium + Expenses* (Underwriting) divided by *Net Written Premium*[4] (premium *net* of reinsurance). The formula is illustrated below in **Exhibit 2-B.**

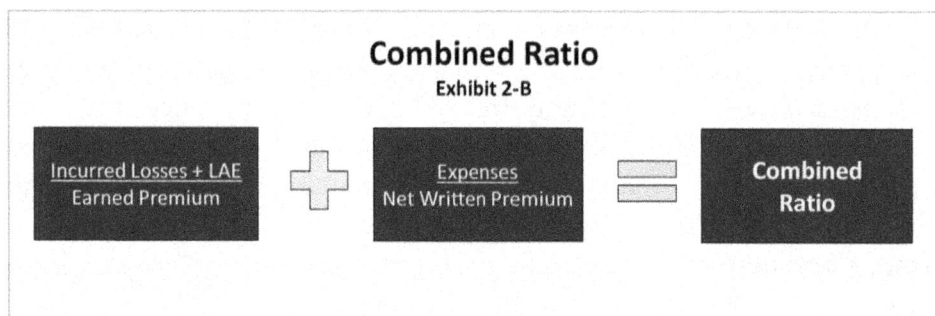

**Combined Ratio**
Exhibit 2-B

$$\frac{\text{Incurred Losses + LAE}}{\text{Earned Premium}} \; + \; \frac{\text{Expenses}}{\text{Net Written Premium}} \; = \; \text{Combined Ratio}$$

Understanding the individual components of the combined ratio provides the foundation to evaluate and analyze the financial impact of loss, expense (LAE and Underwriting Expense), insurance rates, policies in force (PIF) and premium on the insurance operation.

As a claim manager, you should be able to identify where the combined ratio is being affected to either establish a corrective action plan in your claim operation or advise others that the cost impact is not claim related. Incurred losses and LAE should be your primary focus to determine whether either are impacting the combined ratio results. This would involve a loss and expense (ALAE and ULAE) analysis.

Find your best source of data in the organization and use the ratios in your analysis of the data. The ratios will point you in a specific direction, but you may need to dig deeper to find your answer or solution. This could include a claim review, large loss review, budget variance analysis, expense analysis and crossing departmental lines to secure the necessary information or data.

**Exhibit 2-C** illustrates the components of the Combined Ratio at 100%. Boards, Bureaus & Taxes (BB&T) are included in the underwriting expenses but separated in the exhibit for illustrative purposes. The combined ratio may also include a separate line code for *policyholder dividends*.

In the illustration below, the total combined ratio is indicated at 100%, which means there is no underwriting profit. The company may yield an operating profit through investments. If the company wants to improve their combined ratio, they should look at all loss and expense components. For example, if the company can reduce their pure loss ratio by 3 points (%) to 56%, reduce the underwriting expense by 2 points (%) to 26% and the ULAE by .05 (%) to 8.5%, the company would be at a 94.5% combined ratio, making a profit.

---

[4] The expense ratio can be calculated by dividing the underwriting expense by *Net Written Premium* (Statutory Accounting method) or by dividing the underwriting expense by *Net Earned Premium* (GAAP or Generally Accepted Accounting Principles method).

## Combined Ratio of 100% - Exhibit 2-C

- ULAE, 9%
- BB&T, 2%
- Underwriting Expense 28%
- Pure Losses, 59%
- ALAE, 2%

Legend: ■ Pure Losses ■ ALAE ■ Underwriting Expense ■ ULAE ■ BB&T

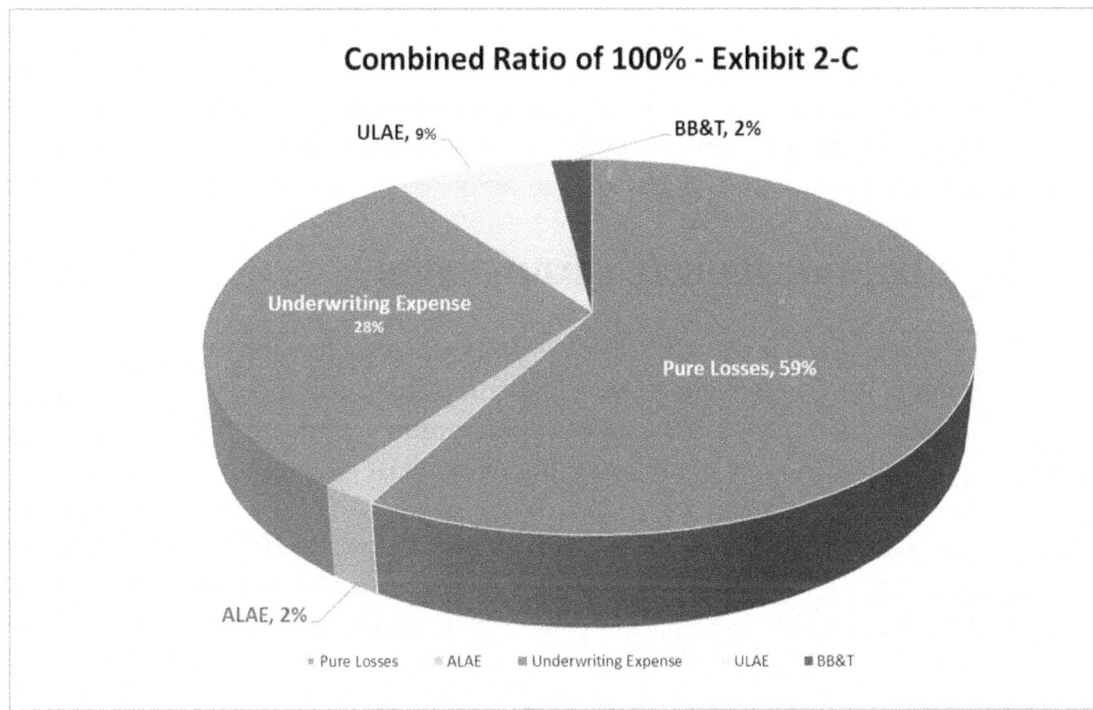

# Gross Expense Ratio (Operating Expense Ratio)

The *Gross Expense Ratio* is the sum of *Underwriting Expense* divided by *Net Written Premium* (or earned premium) + *Unallocated Loss Adjustment Expenses* (ULAE) divided by *Earned Premium*.

The acceptable gross expense ratio target varies by company and may be in the range of 30% to 38%. The most significant component of the expense ratio are the acquisition costs paid to insurance agents and brokers in the *underwriting expense*. Most insurance companies pay close attention to the *gross expense ratio* as it includes all its operating expenses which have a direct impact on financial results (including budget expense projections).

The gross expense ratio (operating expense ratio) includes *Underwriting Expense* and *Unallocated Loss Adjustment Expenses* (ULAE) which are explained below. The formula for the gross expense ratio is illustrated below in **Exhibit 2-D**.

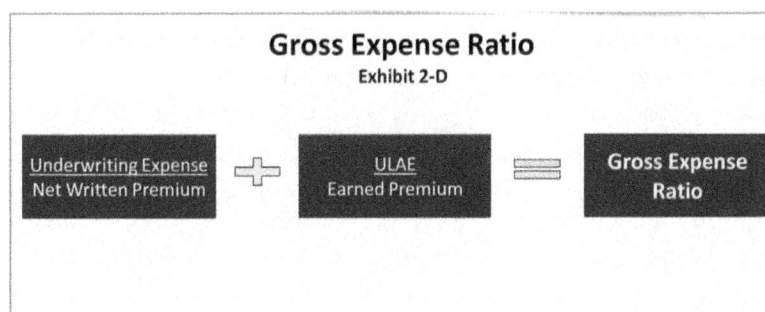

## Gross Expense Ratio
### Exhibit 2-D

$$\frac{\text{Underwriting Expense}}{\text{Net Written Premium}} + \frac{\text{ULAE}}{\text{Earned Premium}} = \text{Gross Expense Ratio}$$

The gross expense ratio may be artificially low if an insurance company is in a growth-mode. When an insurance company is in a growth mode written premium is increasing, but expenses may not be increasing as quickly. This could be attributed to not adding staff resources until the premium reaches a certain level. Since written premium is the denominator in the expense ratio calculation, any increase in written premium with limited corresponding increase in underwriting and ULAE expense, will result in a lower expense ratio.

## Underwriting Expense Ratio (Expense Ratio)

The *Underwriting Expense Ratio* is the sum of *Underwriting Expense* divided by *Net Written Premium* (or earned premium). When referring to the "expense ratio", the industry is referring to the [Underwriting] *Expense Ratio*, which is the gross expense ratio less the ULAE expense. This ratio measures the company's efficiency in underwriting its book of business.

The Underwriting Expense Ratio formula is illustrated below in **Exhibit 2-E** wherein the underwriting expense ratio is being calculated on a *statutory basis* (underwriting expense divided by net written premium).

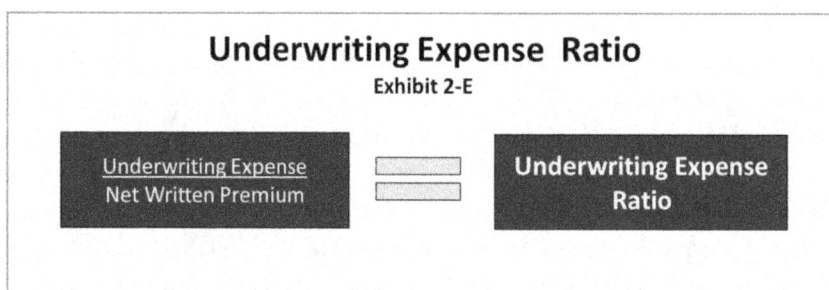

**Underwriting Expense Ratio**
Exhibit 2-E

$$\frac{\text{Underwriting Expense}}{\text{Net Written Premium}} = \text{Underwriting Expense Ratio}$$

It is important to note that underwriting expense is typically calculated by dividing the underwriting expense by the *Net Written Premium* (Statutory Accounting method).

*Underwriting Expense* is the primary component of the gross expense ratio and may be in the range of 24% - 30% of net written premium. These expenses are a measure of how much it is costing the insurance company to book premium, or its acquisition costs.

## Loss Adjustment Expense (LAE) Ratio

The *Loss Adjustment Expense Ratio* or *LAE Ratio* includes both *Allocated Loss Adjustment Expense* (ALAE) and *Unallocated Loss Adjustment Expense* (ULAE).

The ratio is calculated as *Allocated Loss Adjustment Expense* (ALAE) + *Unallocated Loss Adjustment Expense* (ULAE) divided by *Earned Premium* as illustrated below in **Exhibit 2-F**.

**Loss Adjustment Expense or *LAE* Ratio**
Exhibit 2-F

| ALAE Earned Premium | + | ULAE Earned Premium | = | LAE Ratio |

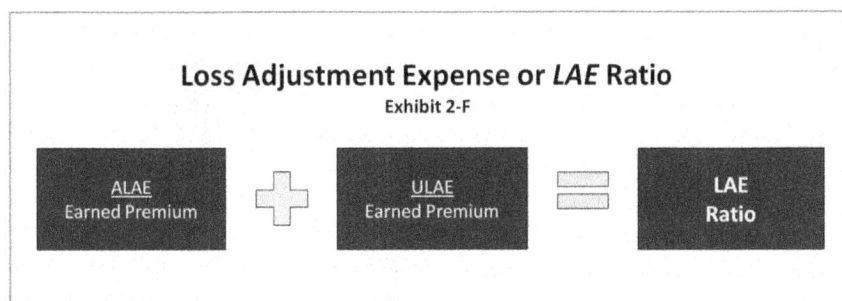

The total LAE Ratio will be in the range of 8% to 14% of the earned premium but can vary depending the line and class of business. Both ALAE and ULAE components are also expressed as separate ratios, being divided by earned premium.

The *Allocated Loss Adjustment Expense* (ALAE) is usually included in the loss ratio when we refer to the total loss ratio, but it is also expressed as a separate ratio as illustrated in **Exhibit 2-G**.

ALAE expenses may be in the range of 2% to 4% of the earned premium but can vary depending the line and class of business. For example, the ALAE ratio in professional lines may be much higher as legal costs are higher per claim than in an automobile line of business.

The *Unallocated Loss Adjustment Expense* (ULAE) is included as a component in the gross expense ratio, but is also expressed as a separate ratio as illustrated in **Exhibit 2-H**.

**ALAE Ratio**
Exhibit 2-G

| ALAE Earned Premium | = | ALAE Ratio |

ULAE expenses may be in the range of 6% to 10% of the earned premium but can vary depending the line and class of business.

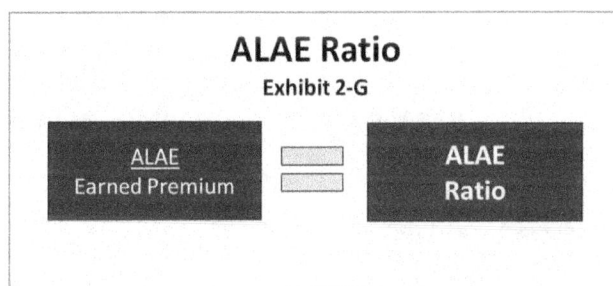

ULAE expense is primarily impacted by the staff resources necessary to maintain the claim operation. If ULAE expenses are low, it may not necessarily have a positive impact on the overall financial results. With low ULAE expenses adjuster workloads may be higher yielding lower salary costs, but it may negatively impact the quality of claim handling (and loss ratio) with high adjuster workloads.

**ULAE Ratio**
Exhibit 2-H

| ULAE Earned Premium | = | ULAE Ratio |

There is a direct correlation between claim staff adequacy and a favorable loss ratio. The quality of claim handling will be negatively impacted by inadequate staffing and be reflective in a higher loss ratio.

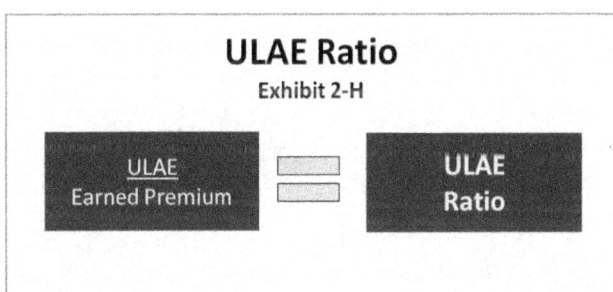

ULAE and ALAE ratios will be impacted based on how the claim department operates. If the claim operation primarily uses internal staff adjusters to handle claims (only outsourcing task assignments), most of the costs will be reflected in the ULAE expense. If the claim operation outsources most of its claim activities to external vendors (including full adjustment assignments), most of the costs will be reflected in the ALAE expense.

## Loss Ratio

The *Loss Ratio* is the sum of *Incurred Losses* (reserves + payments – recovery) divided by *Earned Premium* + *Allocated Loss Adjustment Expenses* (ALAE) divided by *Earned Premium*.

The loss ratio formula is illustrated below in **Exhibit 2-I**. In a pure loss ratio, the loss ratio only includes *Incurred Losses* divided by *Earned Premium* (without ALAE). This may also be referred to as the Loss Ratio excluding ALAE.

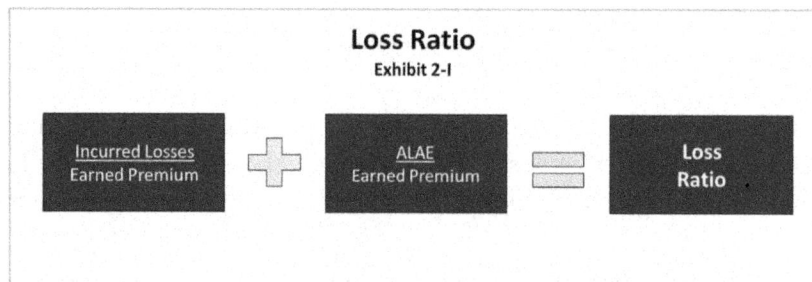

**Loss Ratio**
Exhibit 2-I

Loss ratios can be calculated on a *calendar year*, *accident year* and *underwriting year* basis. When evaluating a loss ratio, it is important to determine what methodology is being used to calculate the loss ratio.

*Calendar Year* data means all claim transactions which occur within the calendar year of 1/1 – 12/31 are included in the financials for that *calendar year*. For example, if a new reserve or reserve adjustment is posted on 12/15/XX, the financial data will be included in the current calendar year ("XX").

*Accident Year* data means that all claim transactions which occur are put back into the year the accident or loss occurred and are included in the financials for that *accident year*. For example, if an accident or loss occurs on 3/15/XX, all new reserves or reserve adjustments posted in any calendar year are included in the "XX" accident year.

*Policy Year* (also referred to as *Underwriting Year*) data means all claim transactions which occur are put back into the year the policy was effective and are included in the financials for that policy year. For example, if the policy was effective 6/15/XX, the policy year will be "XX". If an accident or loss occurs on 8/15/YY (the calendar year after "XX"), all new reserves or reserve adjustments posted in the "YY" calendar year are included in the "XX" policy or underwriting year.

What is an acceptable loss ratio? That depends on the line and class of business involved. A typical loss ratio in the automobile line of business may be in the 50% to 60% range inclusive of ALAE; however, in professional lines, the pure loss ratio may be low but correspondingly, the total loss ratio may be higher due to the impact of higher ALAE defense costs.

It is important to understand that a high loss ratio is not necessarily indicative of a company not being profitable. For example, a company may be operating at a lower gross expense ratio which may allow for a higher loss ratio and remain profitable with an acceptable combined ratio.

# Controlling Loss Costs

Controlling loss costs is the responsibility of both underwriting and claims. Underwriting controls loss costs by pricing the business properly with adequate insurance rates and proper risk selection – which has an impact on both *frequency* and *severity* of losses.

The role of the claim operation in controlling loss costs starts with managing the quality of claim handling and its impact on claim results through proper coverage analysis, timely claim investigations, effective litigation management, and timely and accurate claim evaluations (reserves and dispositions). The claim manger is responsible for claim quality which directly impacts the loss ratio.

The claim operation may not be able to reduce loss frequency, but they can control and mitigate loss severity from both a damage and liability perspective. The two claim examples below illustrate loss mitigation with proactive and effective claim handling of bodily injury liability claims.

---

### Claim Example 1

The adjuster evaluates *general damages* (e.g. pain and suffering, permanency, etc.) which is a subjective component and *special damages* (e.g. medical, hospital and wage loss) which is an objective component, to arrive at a *gross damage* exposure[5] (or gross value) of the claim. Due to the subjective nature of the general damage component, bodily injury claim evaluations will vary and are often expressed in a range.

In this example at 100% liability on the insured, the adjuster evaluated the claim in a range of $9,000 to $12,000, ultimately negotiating and settling the claim at the mid-range (e.g. $10,500). The negotiation effort by the adjuster yielded a mid-range settlement disposition, reducing loss severity by $1,500.

---

[5] The *gross* damage exposure is the full value exposure of a claim without any offsets for negligence of the claimant or contribution from a third party.

## Claim Example 2

From a liability perspective, the claim jurisdiction may have a *comparative negligence* statute allowing for damages to be reduced if the claimant is partially negligent. Our liability evaluation, based on the results of the claim investigation, will apportion negligence between the claimant and the policyholder, as well as any potential third-party.

In this example, the *gross* value of the damages is indicated at $10,000, and the liability on the policyholder is initially evaluated at 80%, with a *net* claim evaluation at $8,000. Thereafter, the follow-up claim investigation included locating a favorable witness. The same claim with a *gross* value of $10,000 is now reduced by a liability percentage of 50%, or a net claim evaluation at $5,000, yielding a $3,000 reduction in loss severity. The diligent follow-up claim investigation by the adjuster changed the net claim value reducing loss severity.

---

From a damage perspective, there are no specific written guidelines on ranges in evaluating bodily injury claims. Although there may be computer programs to assist in the evaluation process, there is no specific source that provides the evaluation of an injury claim by injury category. The same injury may be valued differently by a claimant, the claimant attorney, an adjuster, defense counsel, or a jury. Claim values are also affected by the jurisdiction or venue of the claim. Venues which have a poor economic climate may have higher jury verdicts and settlement values.

From an underwriting perspective, all the ratios we have discussed in this chapter are affected by movement in the earned premium.

The *pure loss ratio* (without ALAE) is calculated as incurred losses divided by the earned premium. As illustrated in **Exhibit 2-J**, if the incurred losses remain unchanged and the premium rates increase, then the loss ratio is reduced with the increase in earned premium and no change in incurred loss activity.

Correspondingly, if the incurred losses remain the same and the earned premium is reduced either by declining insurance rates or reduced PIF (policy count), the loss ratio will increase with the reduction in earned premium as illustrated in **Exhibit 2-K.**

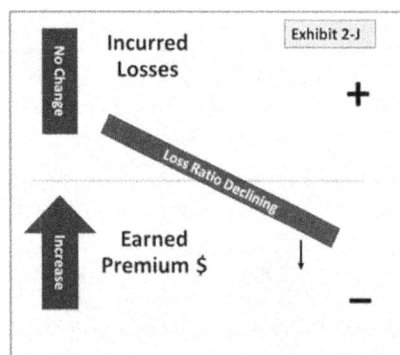

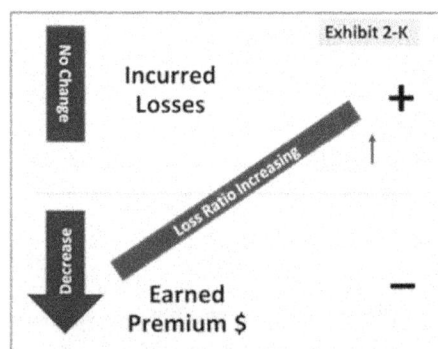

If the incurred losses increase and the premium rates and PIF count remain the same, then the loss ratio will increase with no change in earned premium and increased incurred loss activity (See **Exhibit 2-L**).

**Exhibits 2-M** and **Exhibit 2-N** below illustrate the loss ratio movements based on changes in incurred losses or earned premium.

In *Exhibit 2-M* if a company has $30M in incurred losses and $60M in earned premium, the loss ratio will be 50%. However, if the incurred losses are maintained at $30M and the earned premium reduces to $40M, the loss ratio will increase to 75%.

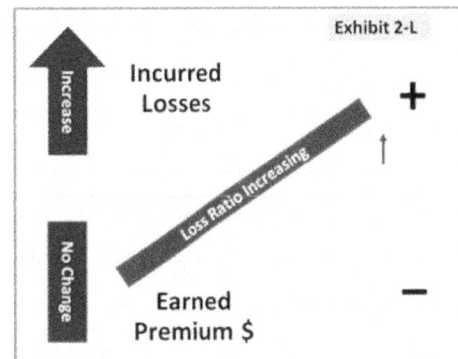

Exhibit 2-L

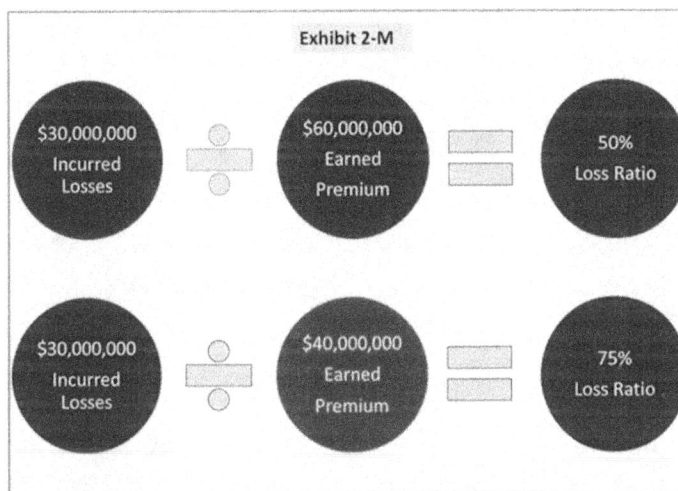

Exhibit 2-M

In *Exhibit 2-N* if a company has $30M in incurred losses and $60M in earned premium, the loss ratio will be 50%. However, if the incurred losses increase to $40M and the earned premium remains at $60M, the loss ratio will increase to 67%.

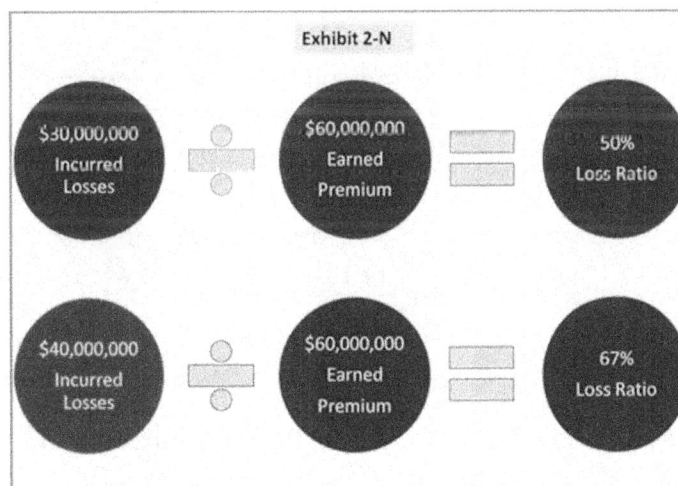

Exhibit 2-N

In looking at **Exhibit 2-C** above (under the *Combined Ratio* – page 35) at a 100% combined ratio you can see where the claim operation has responsibility for 68% of the total costs to the company – 58% in Pure Loss, 2% in ALAE and 8% in ULAE. These expenditures need to be controlled effectively by the claim operation for the company to achieve profitability.

As a claim operation, you cannot control all claim severity; however, you can have a material impact on financial results by handling and managing claims effectively.

A primary area where the claim staff can have a significant impact (positive or negative) on the company's financial results is in the claim *reserve* analysis and *disposition evaluation* process – in how we evaluate claims.

Over-evaluation of case reserves creates reserve redundancy (more reserves than needed) and over evaluating claims for settlement dispositions, results in over-payments – both having an adverse impact on the loss ratio with increased incurred claim activity.

# Financial Impact of Claim Reserving

We will also discuss claim reserving in other chapters as it is a primary fundamental responsibility of the claim technical and management staff.

## Types of Reserves

Claim reserves are the funds set aside by the company to pay future losses. There are several types of claim reserve methodologies which can be manually set or automated by a system business rule. Several reserve methods include *Individual Case Reserves*, *Average* or *Factor Reserves*, *Tabular Reserves*, *Bulk Reserves* and *Incurred But Not Reported Reserves* (IBNR).

## Individual Case Reserve

*Individual Case Reserves* are established on an individual exposure level for both loss and ALAE expense (some companies may bulk-reserve ALAE expense). The case reserve is entered by the adjuster or manager and adjusted as the claim progresses. Some companies have claim systems which automatically establish initial case reserves in certain types of claims or lines of business based on established business rules.

Case reserves is the most common loss reserve methodology in P&C claims. These reserves require continued monitoring by the claims staff to ensure that case reserves are adequate.

## Average or Factor Reserve

*Average* or *Factor Reserves* are reserves which are established manually or automatically at the claim exposure level based on an actuarial analysis. The base reserve is calculated by line of business and exposure by looking at the historical paid amounts for a prior period such as one year. Each year the base amount may change if the average historical paid amount for that exposure has changed.

Some companies use the *Factor Reserve* methodology for fast track claims which are only pending for a short period such as auto physical damage or property damage claims to avoid having to manually maintain case reserves.

However, the factor reserve methodology is also used for other claims as an initial reserve based historical paid amounts. For example, the initial reserves on bodily injury claims may all be established at $5,000 and then converted to a *terminal reserve*[6] within a specified period such as 90 days after the initial reserve entry. This provides the adjuster with more time to properly investigate the claim and secure the necessary special damage documentation – establishing a more accurate case reserve at the 90-day period.

The factor reserve methodology has its challenges in making sure the claims are converted at the 90-day period. This requires a diligent follow-up process and management controls.

## Tabular Reserves

*Tabular Reserves* are reserves established using tables such as *mortality tables* to determine the future life expectancy of a claimant. This reserve methodology is used in workers' compensation claim handling to determine the amount of benefits to be paid for injuries which result in partial or total permanency (or a fatality) to be paid over the claimant's (or surviving spouse or dependent's) life-time.

Sometimes life expectancy may be modified (reduced) due to the claimant have preexisting illnesses (comorbidities) such as diabetes, hypertension or cancer.

## Bulk Reserves

*Bulk Reserves* are established by the actuaries to supplement individual case reserves which may be inadequate, or there is a low confidence level in the aggregate case reserves based on a decline in reserve redundancy or increase in reserve deficiency.

Low confidence levels in case reserves is a reflection on claim management. As a claim manager you should understand bulk reserve adjustments and the reasoning behind the decision.

---

[6] A **Terminal Reserve** is the reserve which represents the amount you will ultimately pay on a claim unless the facts of the claim change (e.g. liability or damages).

## Incurred But Not Reported Reserves (IBNR)

*Incurred But Not Reported Reserves* (IBNR) are bulk reserves established by actuarial for claims which have occurred but have not been reported to the company yet, as indicated earlier in this chapter.

## Reserve Redundancy & Deficiency

Overly redundant case reserves (over reserving) and deficient case reserves (not enough reserve) can both negatively impact financial results. Overly redundant case reserves increase the incurred losses and corresponding loss ratio. When payments are made on redundant case reserves the incurred claim activity may have been overstated, and if insurance rates were based on overly redundant case reserves, the rates may have been too high and not competitive in the market (limiting premium growth).

As an insurance company, there needs to be some redundancy but too much redundancy will negatively affect financial results. Also, overly redundant claim reserves may artificially decrease an insurance company's taxable income and could cause concern with regulators, external auditors or tax authorities.

When paying claims on deficient case reserves there is an opposite effect – pricing or rates may have been negatively affected being based on the stated deficient reserves at the time the rates were filed and implemented – by paying over the case reserves, rates may have been inadequate. To cover the anticipated losses due to deficient case reserves, the actuaries may need to add a bulk reserve to make up the difference which some companies refer to as *reserve strengthening*.

The reserve responsibility rests with the adjuster and claim manager, but ultimately it is the claim manager's responsibility to maintain adequate case reserves within their unit or department. Due to the importance of reserve management and its financial-impact on the company the reserve management process is one of the most critical claim management responsibilities.

When handling P&C claims – e.g. property, liability, physical damage, and workers' compensation claims – the reserve process is a daily activity and because it becomes routine, we may lose sight of its financial-impact on the company. As we indicated above, both redundant and deficient claim reserves can negatively impact an insurance company's results. Monitoring the adequacy of claim reserves requires diligence and attention to detail.

Although it's the claim manager's responsibility to manage and control the reserve process to achieve an optimum reserve outcome, this can be a challenging task unless you want to review every new and adjusted claim reserve in your unit or department which is not practical. Alternatively, the claim manager can monitor the adjusters reserve activity to be sure they are following the company reserve philosophy and procedures (e.g. completing reserve worksheets or reserve screens), utilizing management controls to identify reserve issues or trends (e.g. claim management reports including a reserve redundancy & deficiency report[7]), implementing an effective claim authority structure, and using the claims quality review process.

## Reserve Philosophy

The *Reserve Philosophy* memorializes the reserve methodology and overall process for all employees – including non-claim personnel. It represents the foundation and guide for the claim operation in establishing new and adjusted claim reserves. The most critical aspect of the reserve philosophy and procedures are that they be applied consistently across the claim operation. The actuarial staff relies on the reserve philosophy when evaluating loss trends and projecting future results.

Deviations or exceptions from the reserve philosophy can create chaos in the claim operation and potential adverse financial results. For example, the reserve philosophy indicates that all liability claims must have a comparative negligence calculation applied to the gross damage exposure to arrive at a *net* case reserve. A new bodily injury claim is received and reserved at $2,000,000 x 5% = $100,000 based on the company reserve philosophy. The claim investigation indicates that liability is doubtful; however, there could be minimal exposure and the claim is reserved at $100,000. The underwriting manager puts pressure on the claim manager to reduce the claim reserve to $5,000 with the indication there is "no liability" – and the claim manager reluctantly agrees. The claim ultimately goes to trial, and the adjuster is pressured to contribute to the claim settlement. A payment is made at $100,000 and there is a $95,000 reserve deficiency due to not adhering to the reserve philosophy. An additional consequence in this example is that the adjuster may apply this same logic on lower value claims with the same negative results.

Using this same example, there could be a similar issue but resulting in reserve redundancy. For example, the adjuster and claim manager take the same claim above and simply reserve it at $500,000 due to the severity of the injuries (ignoring the reserve philosophy and application of comparative negligence based on the claim investigation). In this scenario, there would have been a reserve redundancy of $400,000 if the claim payment was at $100,000.

Although these are just some examples, there are many more examples wherein a deviation from the reserve philosophy, procedures or methodology, can have an overall adverse effect on the financial results, either in the form of reserve deficiency or redundancy.

For a claim operation to achieve optimum results there needs to be consistency and uniformity in claim handling by following established guidelines, standards and procedures. The reserve philosophy and procedures are critical protocols in a claim operation and the claim manager should not deviate from the reserve philosophy and established procedures.

Below is considered a *Reserve Philosophy* used by an insurance claim operation:

---

[7] A *Reserve Redundancy & Deficiency Report* compares the open reserve amount at the time of payment to identify payments within the reserve to calculate the redundancy and payments over the reserve to calculate the deficiency.

## *Sample P&C Reserve Philosophy*

*We establish case reserves on all claims at the exposure level for all lines of business. The responsibility to establish claim case reserves rests with the handling adjuster and claim management. All claim personnel must adhere to the reserve philosophy when handling company claims. Our reserve philosophy includes the following:*

- *We establish individual case reserves for loss and allocated loss adjustment expenses.*
- *Our case reserves will be based on the expected payout or most probable outcome, and not on a "worst case" scenario.*
- *The authority to establish individual case reserves is based on the authority granted by management which may be adjusted from time to time. Your claim reserve authority may have different limits for loss and allocated loss adjustment expense.*
- *Individual case reserves over a claim employee's authority level must be referred to the next management level for approval and entry.*
- *All new, reopened and adjusted claim reserves must have the reserve evaluation screen completed for each exposure prior to reserve entry – addressing damages, liability and compensability issues (including application of comparative negligence, contribution or other viable offsets).*
- *All individual case reserves must be established within 30 days after the claim is reported.*
- *All individual case reserves which require a reserve adjustment (upward or downward) must be changed within 30 days of recognition of the change in exposure (e.g. liability or damages) with receipt of new verbal or written information or documentation.*
- *At each diary review interval, the handling adjuster and claim manager must comment on the adequacy of the claim reserves.*
- *A Claim Analysis Report (e.g. captioned report) must be completed on all open claims at 26-weeks from the initial reserve entry, with claim manager review and approval of the current reserves and/or recommended reserve adjustments.*
- *It is anticipated that within 6 months of the initial reserve entry the claim exposure will be mostly developed, and the case reserve should not require any further adjustment unless the facts of the claim materially change (e.g. liability or damages).*
- *On all claims at $100,000 or over the claim manager should consider a claim committee to discuss the recommended case reserves in a group format to gain input on the recommended reserve from other claim professionals.*
- *All new reserves and reserve adjustments at $200,000 or over require a Large Loss Report with distribution to management at the time of reserve entry.*

We will find more redundancy and deficiency reserve issues in liability and workers' compensation claims vs. first party property or physical damage claims. The latter have more fixed damages to accurately establish a monetary reserve based on an assessment of known damages using an estimate or appraisal. However, there are potential reserve issues in first party claims when the adjuster or manager do not establish timely initial or inadequate case reserves, or do not react quickly enough in increasing reserves with receipt of additional information.

The damage component of a bodily injury liability claim is much more difficult to assess, particularly subjective *general damages* such as pain and suffering and permanency. The liability assessment may also be difficult as there are no published guidelines on what percentage of comparative fault to apply to each party in specific types of claims such as slip and fall claims and intersection accidents.

Another potential problem encountered in the reserve process is *Pattern Reserving* – using prior claims as the basis for new claim reserves. An example would be reserving all soft tissue back injury claims at $7,500, disregarding the individuality or unique characteristics of the claim which may impact general and special damages, as well as proper application of comparative negligence. This can result in both reserve deficiency and redundancy.

All claim reserves (new, reopened and adjusted) should include the completion of a reserve evaluation form or screen to support the recommended reserves as illustrated in **Exhibit 2-O** (auto liability), **Exhibit 2-P** (property), and **Exhibit 2-Q** (workers' compensation) below.

The claim manager should approve all reserve evaluations which exceed the adjusters claim authority. This is a good opportunity to review the reserves, as well as the overall quality of claim handling. It is important that the reserve evaluation is clear, concise and supported by file documentation before it is approved by the claim manager.

| ***SAMPLE* AUTO BODILY INJURY LIABILITY RESERVE EVALUATION EXHIBIT: 2-O** | |
|---|---|
| **Claim Number:** | 14BI-798234 |
| **Date of Loss:** | 6/15/XX |
| **Facts of Loss:** | Insured vehicle made left turn in front of claimant vehicle at an uncontrolled intersection. |
| **State/Jurisdiction:** | Connecticut |
| **Reason for Reserve:** | New: Adjustment: X |
| **Claimant Name:** | Peter Smith |
| **Claimant Status:** | Claimant Vehicle Operator |
| **Claimant Age:** | 38 |
| **Claimant Occupation:** | Plumber |
| **Wage / Salary:** | $50,000 / Year |
| **Injury:** | Lumbar Sprain |
| **Pre-Existing Injuries:** | None |
| **Treatment:** | E/R hospital; 6 orthopedic doctor visits; 8 PT visits; Follow-up X-rays and Rx. |
| **Continued Treatment (Yes/No):** | No - discharged |
| **Medical Bills:** | $1,200 |
| **Hospital Bills:** | $1,800 |
| **Physical Therapy:** | $1,200 |
| **Diagnostics / X-Rays:** | $900 |
| **Other:** | $250 |

| | |
|---|---|
| Total Medicals: | $5,350 |
| Disability Period: | 10 days (@ $192.35/day) |
| Total Wage Loss: | $1,924 |
| Total *Special Damages*: | $7,274 |
| Permanency: | $3,000 |
| Pain & Suffering: | $6,000 |
| Total *General Damages*: | $9,000 |
| Total All Damages: | $16,274 |
| (-) Comparative Negligence on Claimant: | 25% |
| Total Claim Value: | $12,205 |
| Recommend BI Reserve: | $12,000 – $13,000 |
| Adjuster Approval: | Date: |
| Manager Approval: | Date: |

| SAMPLE PROPERTY RESERVE EVALUATION: EXHIBIT 2-P | |
|---|---|
| Claim Number: | 15CF-892353 |
| Date of Loss: | 3/21/XX |
| State/Jurisdiction: | New York |
| Reason for Reserve: | New:  X            Adjustment: |
| Insured Name: | Carla Russo |
| Property Location: | 15 Timber Lane, Babylon, NY |
| Field Inspection/Scope / Photos: | Yes |
| Cause of Loss: | Kitchen fire caused by faulty stove |
| Coverage Issues: | No |
| Fire Report Requested: | Yes |
| Subrogation Potential: | Yes |
| Cause & Origin Expert Assigned: | Yes |
| Subrogation Investigation Underway: | Yes |
| Total Projected Loss: | |
| Building/Dwelling Loss: | $35,000 |
| Contents Loss: | $15,000 |
| Time Element Loss: | $5,000 |
| Inland Marine Loss: | $1,500 |
| Other Loss: | $0 |
| Recommended Loss Reserves: | $56,500 |
| Adjuster Approval: | Date: |
| Manager Approval: | Date: |

| *SAMPLE* WORKERS' COMPENSATION RESERVE EVALUATION: EXHIBIT 2-Q | |
|---|---|
| Claim Number: | 32WC-987232 |
| Reason for Reserve: | New:  X            Adjustment: |
| Insured/Employer: | Peterson Carpet Company, Inc. |
| Date of Loss: | 4/18/XX |

| Facts of Loss: | Claimant tripped and fell on debris while entering a customer's premises. |
|---|---|
| State/Jurisdiction: | Utah |
| Subrogation: | Yes |
| Claimant Name: | Dana Fitzgerald |
| Claimant Status: | Employee |
| Claimant Age: | 32 |
| Claimant Occupation: | Field Sales Representative |
| Wage / Salary: | $44,200/ Year |
| Average Weekly Wage: | $850 |
| Compensation Rate: | TTD - $566.70 \| TPD - $266.68 \| PPD = $545 (max.) 18% |
| Injuries: | Fractured right arm with open reduction and internal fixation. |
| Pre-Existing Injuries: | None |
| Treatment: | Hospitalization for 3 days; surgery and orthopedic treatment; x-rays; diagnostic testing; anesthesia; physical therapy and prescriptions. |
| Continued Treatment (Yes/No): | No - discharged |

## COMPENSATION INDEMNITY PROJECTIONS

| Benefit | Compensation Rate | Disability Period | Indemnity |
|---|---|---|---|
| Temporary Total Disability (TTD) | $566.70 | 10 Weeks | $5,667.00 |
| Temporary Partial Disability (TPD) | $266.68 | 4 Weeks | $1,066.72 |
| Permanent Partial Disability (PPD) | $545.00 | 33.66 Weeks / 18% | $18,344.70 |
| Permanent Total Disability (PTD) | $0.00 | 0 | $0.00 |
| | | TOTAL COMPENSATION: | $25,078.42 |

## MEDICAL COST PROJECTIONS

| Medical Type | Treatment | Unit Cost | Medical |
|---|---|---|---|
| Physician | 10 Ortho Visits | $250 | $2,500 |
| Hospital - Inpatient | 3 Days | $4,000 | $12,000 |
| Diagnostic / Radiology | 3 X-Rays | $450 | $1,350 |
| Surgery | 1 | $8,500 | $8,500 |
| Anesthesia | 1 | $3,500 | $3,500 |
| Physical Therapy | 12 | $150 | $1,800 |
| Chiropractic | 0 | $0 | $0 |
| Prescriptions | Multiple Rx | $900 | $900 |
| Durable Medical Equipment | 1 Arm Brace | $250 | $250 |
| Ambulance / Transportation | 1 | $450 | $450 |
| Travel & Mileage Expense | 300 | $00.55 | $165 |
| Funeral Costs | 0 | $0 | $0 |
| Other Costs | 0 | $0 | $0 |
| | | TOTAL MEDICAL: | $31,415 |

## OTHER COST PROJECTIONS

| Type | Details | Cost | Other |
|---|---|---|---|
| Vocational Rehabilitation (VR) | 0 | $0 | $0 |
| | | TOTAL OTHER: | $0 |

## RECOMMENDED RESERVES

| | |
|---|---|
| Total Indemnity Reserve: | $25,078 |
| Total Medical Reserve: | $31,415 |
| Grand Total Reserves: | $56,493 |

| Adjuster Approval: | | Date: | |
|---|---|---|---|
| Manager Approval: | | Date: | |

To manage the claim reserve process, there needs to be both "front-end" and "back-end" management controls. For example, *Management Controls* consist of designated claim authority levels with system security and automatic referral process, controls and processes (manual and system) to monitor claim transactional activity, use of management reports and metrics, adjuster periodic reporting requirements, claim manager dual diary, quality review processes, and system business rules "fired" with entry of transactions over a certain dollar threshold triggering an email notification or work queue for the claim manager. We will further discuss management controls in **Chapter 4 – Management Controls.**

Case reserves are established when a new claim is reported to the company – entered at the time the claim is set up or within a specified period from the claim report date such as within 15 or 30 calendar days. Case reserve adjustments (increases and decreases) are usually changed within 30 days of recognition of the change in exposure (e.g. liability/compensability or damages) with new verbal or written information.

It is very important to clarify in your reserve guidelines and philosophy that you do not necessarily need written documentation of an increase in exposure if the new verbal information is credible. Large reserve adjustments on claims which have been pending for an extended period will get the attention of senior management – and senior management may question why it has taken so long to adjust the reserve and when was the change in exposure first recognized. Invariably, the adjuster or claim manager will indicate they were waiting for further written documentation (for a long time) on the claimant's injuries before making a reserve adjustment – this will not result in a favorable response from management.

Let's review some fundamental basics in reserve management – such as *claim authority*. We will talk about this in other chapters. In the context of management controls, establishing and maintaining claim authority is critical to managing the reserve entry and approval process, for both loss and ALAE reserves. Each employee has an established claim authority – and any recommended claim reserves above the established authority level should be referred to the next supervisory or management level for approval either manually or through a system referral work queue. The process should be documented in a claim manual to maintain uniformity and consistency in the reserve process.

In most claim operations, the claim manager will delegate the initial reserve entry process to the adjuster based on their claim authority – and the reserve authority may be based on either the net recommended reserve or the gross exposure of the claim. For example, if an adjuster completes the investigation of a liability claim and the claimant has sustained a fractured arm with open reduction and internal fixation, they may establish a gross claim exposure of $75,000, but the claim is reserved at $49,000 based on 65% liability on the policyholder. If the adjuster has claim authority at $50,000, the net reserve of $49,000 is within their authority; however, the *gross* exposure exceeds their authority. It is recommended that claim authority be based on *gross damage exposure* and not the *net* reserve recommendations.

We will further discuss the claim reserve process in **Chapter 5 – Managing Technical Claim Handling.**

# Impact of Claim Settlements

Mishandling liability claim settlement evaluations can have a material impact on the loss ratio and should be a key focus for the claim manager.

Some of the issues we discussed in the prior section on reserving also apply to claim settlements, particularly in how claims are evaluated – we should use the same format as a reserve evaluation form or screen when we evaluate claims for settlement disposition. The claim manager should approve settlement evaluations when the *gross* value of the claim exceeds the adjuster's settlement authority.

For liability claims, the proposed settlement should be explained in detail in terms of the liability and damage assessment with a settlement range. It is important to establish ranges for settlement evaluations – it provides structure to negotiate the claim and the framework to achieve a target settlement amount.

Liability and damage evaluations may not always be that precise. For example, if the adjuster evaluates the claim at 30% negligence on the claimant and the claim manager evaluates the claim at 40% negligence on the claimant – who is right? But if the gross value of the claim is $100,000, the difference in the evaluation is $10,000, which is material. The same concept applies to damages in a liability claim. For example, if the adjuster evaluates the gross value of the claim at $60,000 and the claim manager evaluates the claim at $50,000 – who is right?

Require the adjuster to prepare their own detailed settlement evaluation with the claim manager providing guidance and direction when warranted, but don't criticize the adjuster if their liability or damage evaluation is different due to slight variations in liability percentages or the gross value – give the adjuster some latitude. Insist on a detailed analysis in how the adjuster arrived at the settlement evaluation including the general and special damage calculation. This calculation will provide the basis for the gross claim evaluation.

The point to remember on claim settlements (liability) is that ultimately if the claim is tried to a conclusion, the jury (lay people) will decide the claim value and percentage of liability on each party. The objective in negotiating settlements is to make a fair and reasonable offer based on the claim investigation and evaluation of the claim documentation.

Loss payments impact the loss ratio – and claim settlements is an area which will overpayments. Overpayments are costly and preventative, but often caused by inexperience, lack of knowledge, being unprepared, lack of negotiation skills, as well as poor quality investigations and documentation. As a claim manager, making sure there is compliance with company claim *best practices* and settlement evaluation procedures will reduce poor settlement evaluations and improve the quality of claim dispositions.

# Claim Leakage

When a claim is paid beyond what the payment should have been, we call it "leakage". *Leakage* is an industry-wide problem and will vary in severity by company. It is a known fact that leakage will be materially reduced with effective claim management and oversight.

Claim operations which are well organized with a reasonable span of control (e.g. no more than 1 manager to 6 adjusters), have manageable adjuster workloads, and a claim staff with quality technical skills will have a lower claim leakage rate. Conversely, claim operations which have an unreasonable span of control, high adjuster workloads, inexperienced adjusters, and poor management oversight will have higher leakage rates.

*Leakage* is caused by many factors and is often not recognizable without conducting a formal leakage study or review. Leakage can be subtle and affect many areas in the organization. Some potential leakage issues are the result of:

- Poor management oversight
- Inexperienced technical claim staff
- Poor or inadequate claim investigations
- Poor negotiations skills
- Improper interpretation of coverage or paying beyond coverage limits
- Not inspecting first and third-party automobile damage claims – relying on submitted repair estimates for payment
- Inaccurate damage appraisals or total loss evaluations on first party and third-party automobile claims
- Not controlling automobile rental claims (first and third party)
- Inaccurate damage appraisals or estimates on first party property claims
- Not taking depreciation when warranted
- Mishandling or not controlling salvage
- Exaggerated assessment of bodily injury general damages
- Inappropriate application of comparative negligence
- Failure to collect third party deductibles
- Ineffective medical management in workers' compensation claims including not using nurse case management, IMEs, utilization review and medical bill review (Medical Management)

- Not controlling claimant disability periods and return to work target dates in workers' compensation claims (Disability Management)
- Fraud – internal and external
- Employee turnover (with increased workloads on the remaining staff)

All companies have claim leakage and leakage rates will vary by company and line of business. Generally, leakage rates will range from 3% to 15%. An acceptable leakage rate is what the company can tolerate in terms of its impact on the loss ratio.

In **Chapter 6 – Claims Quality Review Process** we will discuss effective management of technical claim handling using a comprehensive quality review process which can also assist in identifying potential leakage areas.

# Controlling Claim Expenses

Claim expense, whether it is ULAE or ALAE will have a material impact on financial results if not controlled properly. We will also discuss controlling these expenses in other chapters.

The primary ULAE expense is the cost of the claim operation, but also includes some external adjuster and appraiser expenses, as well as legal costs which pertain to coverage analysis. The cost of the claim operation will be included as line items in the claim department *operational budget* which will include claim employee salaries and benefits, travel and entertainment, as well as other claim departmental expenses.

The claim manager is involved in the annual budgeting process which includes making expense projections for the upcoming year, establishing a budget for each line item and projecting claim staff resources for the upcoming year. *Operating Budgets* are discussed further below.

The total cost of claim staff resources, including salary and benefits, will be in the range of 50% - 60% of the total claim budget expenses. The cost of benefits or employee relations expense are calculated as a percentage of the total salary. The balance of the claim budget includes expense items specific to the claim department such as the cost of ISO ClaimSearch®, claim estimating software, automobile expense, travel and entertainment, office supplies, training and education, memberships, periodicals and other miscellaneous expense. The claim department will also be allocated a percentage of the other shared department expenses for accounting, IT, legal, physical plant, human resources, mail and administrative support (e.g. scanning and document management) and other departmental expense.

The claim manager has the responsibility to control budget expenses to make sure the department meets its ULAE budget goals. Exceeding the budget will require a remediation plan which would consist of expense reduction in the areas being affected. Staffing and salary administration are the primary areas which require tight expense control – as they both have a material impact on the budget.

Controlling budget expenses requires a diligent effort by the claim manager to monitor closely. This is a challenging task especially when it comes to resource management. For example, if your budget only allows for six adjusters then you need to be sure each adjuster is contributing 100% toward the productivity standard, or you will have a workload management issue and a potential claim quality problem. The weak adjusters in a group may handle less claim volume, be less productive and potentially make costly mistakes. This in turn increases the workload for the other adjusters and may cause a morale problem, and potential turnover.

Always be sure to match the adjuster experience and knowledge with the job grade and salary level, and more importantly with the tasks being performed. Do not hire a higher salary level employee to handle claims which can be handled by a lower salary level employee. A manager may think it is an effective use of resources, but it is a waste of resources, and impacts expense.

As a claim manager, you may be challenged with limited staff to handle a variety of claims which are routine or simple versus complex. The key is how you staff the department and your hiring practices. If you have an approved vacancy for a property damage adjuster, then you should not hire an experienced bodily injury liability adjuster thinking you are "bolstering" the departmental experience. This type of decision adds salary expense to your budget and may eventually cause a negative variance in your salary budget due to the higher salary level. Also, the more experienced adjuster may not pay attention to the lower value claims and focus more on the complex claims – negatively impacting the quality of the lower value claims.

By hiring inexperienced staff to handle complex claims, thinking you are going to train that person and save salary dollars, may be a mistake, as well. A primary cause of claim leakage is having inexperienced staff handle complex claims – this will have a direct impact on loss leakage. Unless you are hiring a new trainee (without any claim experience) to handle small dollar claims, you should always match the necessary experience and knowledge with the position needed.

A critical challenge for the claim manager is achieving the balance in properly managing adjuster workloads – which has a direct impact on ULAE and ultimately loss costs. Increasing workloads will have a positive impact on total adjuster compensation costs (included in ULAE) – by increasing workloads you need less staff which will reduce your salary and benefit costs. Unfortunately, an increase in workloads may negatively impact loss costs. With higher workloads, the adjuster has less time to handle claims properly, and may take short-cuts resulting in inadequate claim investigations, redundant or deficient case reserves and potential claim overpayments.

Adjusters who have excessive workloads have less time to take quality statements, conduct proper claim investigations, evaluate and negotiate claims effectively, manage medical cost containment, and control litigation costs through effective litigation management. This all results in increased loss costs and ALAE (see below), and potential employee turnover.

Workload management will be further discussed in **Chapter 7 – Staffing and Resource Management**.

# Claim Operating Budgets

To control ULAE costs effectively, particularly the ULAE costs associated with running the claim operation, there needs to be an established departmental budget with financial targets and variance reporting. All insurance companies have internal operating budgets with the claim operation having a separate budget which rolls up to the total operating budget along with underwriting, accounting & finance, legal, sales and marketing, IT and other departments.

Budgeting is an annual task and management participates in the annual budgeting process starting in September through year-end. The objective of the budgeting process is to develop a total operating budget for the entire organization, which is the basis for the organization to meet its financial objectives. Most companies use either a comprehensive spreadsheet budget tool or budgeting software – and the budget process is facilitated by the accounting and finance department.

The budget process begins with a "top line" projection which is revenue or premium projections. In an insurance company, the revenue target (premium) is developed by projecting premium for the upcoming year. Management looks at existing business to determine if any increase or decrease in policy count (PIF) is expected, along with projected new business growth and increased insurance rates. In a TPA, revenue is derived from clients paying service fees for claim handling; therefore, revenue is projected based on current client revenue and new business growth projections.

Accuracy of the revenue target projection is critical for budgets to be achievable and realistic. The departmental budgets are all based on revenue projections – if the revenue targets are missed and the projection is inaccurate, the expense budgets will need to be adjusted. This may result in a company having staff reductions, downsizing, and hiring and salary adjustment freezes.

As an example, if the company budgeted for annual premium at $500M and had an expense budget (all expenses including loss and LAE) of $460M, they are budgeting for an 8% gross profit, or $40M. If that same company was only able to book $475M in annual premium, it would have a shortfall of $25M in premium. The impact on the financial results using the current expense budget of $460M, would yield a reduced gross operating profit of 3.2% ($15M), or a reduction in profit of 4.8%. This would be a huge operating loss and would result in a budget readjustment, yielding the need for material expense reductions (e.g. staff, salary, etc.).

Once the operating budget is finalized and approved it is used as the foundation for the operating *Profit & Loss* (P&L) model used by management to monitor financial performance. The P&L will include *month-to-date* (MTD) and *year-to-date* (YTD) financial data by expense category with columns for variance reporting adjacent to the MTD and YTD columns. There may also be a column which compares MTD and YTD for prior years.

*Variance Reporting* provides the ability to measure actual vs. budget achievement on a detail and summary level. This allows executive management to monitor whether management is meeting the established financial targets (budgets).

For example, if the annual budget for claim salaries is $3,000,000, then you may allocate or budget $250,000 for salaries each month (the specific monthly allocation method may differ if you plan to add or reduce staff during the upcoming year). At month-end for June, your budget would allocate $1,500,000 for salaries; however, if you hired additional staff between January and June, or had salary adjustments which exceeded the budget, your actual salaries may be at $1,650,000 – this would represent a negative variance of $150,000, or 10% for the first six months of the year.

When there is a negative variance, senior management will want feedback from the department manager on the cause of the variance including comments on whether the variance will improve or continue to deteriorate, and the proposed remediation plan.

Managing to a claim operating budget is not an easy task. Every expense dollar impacts your budget results. A budget is not a "guide" – it is intended to provide management with an indication of costs so that financial reporting can be consistent and accurate. When departments exceed budgets, the expense dollars must be reallocated to pay expense which will negatively affect company profitability if not recouped during the year.

As a claim manager, it is important to understand and be familiar with the budget process and your role in controlling expenses. Your biggest challenge in the budgeting process will be budgeting for staff resources. You will have an opportunity to propose a salary budget based on the number of approved FTEs (Full-Time Equivalent Employees), but if you need additional staff you will need to provide support for your request. Companies look at both the salary costs and FTE count, which is why it is important to hire staff resources commensurate with the position roles and responsibilities.

## **Vendor Management & ALAE**

Vendor management is critical in controlling *allocated loss adjustment expenses* or ALAE. The primary ALAE expenses are defense and litigation costs, experts, medical cost containment and some adjusting, and appraisal expense not coded as ULAE.

Controlling ALAE expenses is the responsibility of both the adjuster and claim manager, but the claim manager has the ultimate responsibility to control all departmental expense. To manage ALAE expense properly there needs to be annual projections in each ALAE category by claim business unit and company, with the ability to monitor performance by using ALAE expense management reports.

Just as in ULAE expense, the claim manager should monitor and control ALAE expense by having an annual budget by ALAE category with *month-to-date* (MTD) and *year-to-date* (YTD) financial reporting. This financial information will be necessary to provide feedback to management on upward and downward variances in ALAE expense.

We control ALAE expense by having agreed fee structures with vendor partners and making sure we control the expense at the individual claim exposure level. Adjusters can control expenses by making sure the expense is reasonable and necessary, confirming vendor assignments in writing specifically outlining the work to be completed, the duration of the assignment and the agreed upon fee schedule. This will avoid being over-billed for work not requested or unnecessary.

Attorney and associated legal costs have the biggest impact on ALAE expense and the most difficult to control, particularly when litigation is involved. There are several methods of controlling attorney and legal costs, and it starts with a comprehensive *Litigation Management Program* – which is discussed further in **Chapter 5 – Managing Technical Claim Handling**.

Litigation management starts with providing specific instructions to the handling attorney using a referral letter, or email, attaching a copy of the company's defense counsel litigation management guidelines, development of a litigation plan, requesting a legal budget commensurate with the litigation plan, requesting a timely acknowledgement of the referral and timely reporting. A collaborative approach with the adjuster and the attorney both having responsibility for specific handling activities, results in a better claim outcome. As you will read in **Chapter 5**, poor management of litigation will adversely affect both ALAE expense and loss costs.

Legal bill review vendors provide *legal bill review* services for the insurance industry. As legal bills are received, they are routed to the legal bill review provider or vendor who adjusts the legal bills based on industry billing practices and business rules. The legal bill review provider works directly with the law firm to facilitate the bill adjustment process, and is paid as either a percentage of savings, a fee per bill, or a combination of both.

Many legal bill review providers have integrated their review process into insurance carrier claim systems and document management applications to streamline and expedite the legal bill review process. Some legal bill review providers have web portals which include the legal bill review process (including the budget process) and a repository for litigation documents.

# Chapter Comments

As a claim manager, it is critically important to understand how the claim operation impacts the insurance company's financial results, both from a loss and expense perspective.

The claim manager should be familiar with common industry financial terminology, and how to calculate various financial ratios such as the combined ratio, loss ratio, ALAE and ULAE, and the expense ratio. These ratios measure the company's financial performance, including claim performance. The loss ratio may also be impacted by the quality of underwriting, insurance rate changes, and movement in policy counts resulting in upward or downward shifts in premium. It is important to understand the basis for the ratio and the specific reasons for changes (e.g. ratio impacted by claim handling or due to some other reason).

If the insurance company generates $500M in annual earned premium with a 50% loss ratio and a 10% LAE – this is equivalent to total incurred losses at $250M and LAE at $50M – with the claim operation having the overall responsibility to manage $300M in loss and expense costs. As a claim manager, your share of that critical responsibility will depend on your level in the claim organization – with the fiduciary responsibility to manage loss and expense (ALAE and ULAE) costs of the insurance company to achieve its financial objectives.

Controlling loss costs is the responsibility of the claim manager and the adjusting staff. Although the claim department cannot specifically control the frequency and severity of claims as they occur, they can impact claim severity by managing the damage aspect of the claim effectively (e.g. appraising damages, proper claim evaluations and reserving, quality claim dispositions, etc.), as well as proper application of comparative negligence (e.g. effective negotiations) and appropriate compensability decisions based on a timely and thorough claim investigation.

Controlling expenses, both ALAE and ULAE, is achieved by managing vendor costs (e.g. adjuster, expert, attorney and legal costs) and claim department budget expenses effectively (including staffing, compensation, travel, automobile, etc.). This is accomplished with the implementation of cost control programs (e.g. legal bill review) and managing departmental costs (e.g. staffing and workloads) effectively.

# CHAPTER 3
# MANAGING EFFECTIVELY

## Managing People

A simple definition of *management* is controlling resources and making business decisions. Managers organize, plan, control and direct company resources – and the degree to which the manager is involved in these functions depends on their level in the organization. Claim managers can hold various levels in an insurance organization including line, staff, and executive levels.

Executive and senior level managers establish organizational goals, develop overall strategy and operating policies. Middle Managers have direct responsibility for line management and supervisory staff. These managers are responsible to execute strategy and operating policies, including claim policies and procedures – with line managers providing direct supervision of technical claim employees such as adjusters.

It is important to understand that not all managers are *leaders* – leaders inspire and motivate the staff to achieve company objectives, but leadership must be earned. Leadership may be inherent in our personality but may also be developed and improved over time. Managers who have effective leadership skills are more successful in their roles as they can motivate their staff to achieve productivity goals, quality results, timeliness and company objectives.

Remember, employees are a company's most important asset – without employees there is no company. Managers should treat their staff with respect and when guidance is necessary, it should be done constructively without criticism of the employee personally – only the work product, if necessary.

Employees want to be heard and successful managers have developed the important skill of *listening*. It sounds easy and routine, but managers get busy and sometimes lose sight of their organizational role of directing and managing people. If you are not listening effectively you will not develop relationships with your staff nor will you know what issues are developing in your department. By listening you will also keep current with the *informal* work environment which often provides valuable information for you to understand and resolve departmental issues.

One of the biggest challenges faced by a claim manager is balancing their time between technical claim oversight and overall administrative management. When a claim manager places too much emphasis on technical claim oversight, they may be spending too much time directing claim file development to the detriment of their responsibility as a manager to mentor, train and develop, provide oversight, guidance and manage "people issues". On the other hand, if a claim manager spends too much time on administrative management, they may not know the quality of the work being produced by their staff (good and poor) or potential problems developing in claim files. The manager may also not be able to respond to senior management inquiries concerning individual claims (e.g. large losses) or developing claim trends.

We tend to gravitate toward our comfort zone – so if we prefer technical claim file reviews vs. managing people, we will spend more time reviewing claim files. If we prefer managing people, we will spend less time in the claim files and more time with the staff having discussion and meetings. If you have good quality claim results, few employee issues, minimal turnover and a well-run claim department or unit, you may have achieved the necessary *balance*.

Oftentimes, claim managers are promoted because of their technical claim skills, and the new claim manager may spend more time providing technical claim supervision which may be their comfort zone. For the claim manager to be successful, they will need to make the transition by balancing their time with technical file reviews and managing people – this is not always an easy transition for some managers.

Managers are responsible to plan, organize and control daily activities. If you are not controlling your day and consistently "putting out fires", quality will suffer, and you will be ineffective as a manager. Don't let your employees plan your day – plan your own day and prioritize the tasks and projects which are most important to accomplish during a specific time-period.

We all have required daily activities, but quite often a good part of our day is taken up by employees who visit our office with routine questions or just want to "chat". Be selfish about your time and don't let employees control your day. Ask employees to schedule time with you at pre-determined time periods you establish throughout the day – with specific allocated times, unless there is an emergency, or there is something that cannot wait.

When you do schedule time with your employees, ask the employee to be prepared for the discussion and come to the meeting with proposed solutions – not just problems or issues. When your discussion is complete, close the discussion so that both you and the employee can get back to work.

> ### Be Selfish
> ### About Your Time
> #### Exhibit 3-A
>
> Managers need to be selfish about their time. It's okay to occasionally close your door, or ask people to come back later, if you need uninterrupted time to get something done. This is an effective way to let people know you are busy. However, you should never keep your door closed all the time – its sends a message to the employees that you are not accessible and don't care.

Where you spend, your time may also be driven by your role in the organization and your direct manager's requirement. Your direct manager may insist that you provide technical supervision in every claim file in your unit – which is unrealistic. If you look at every claim file, you are micromanaging your staff and stifling their professional growth and development. Your staff needs to have a reasonable claim authority level to handle claims without the claim manager's active oversight. Claim managers who micromanage will find it difficult to move into the next level of management – the higher level in an organization, the more reliance on delegation.

The more personnel reporting to the manager, the less time available for the manager to provide substantive direction and input in claim files. The maximum span of control for a claim manager should not exceed six employees to one manager to be effective. If the average open caseload per adjuster is 125 claims, then the total open claims in the unit will be 750, if the claim manager has six direct reports. At least 40% - 50% of the claims should not be on the claim manager's active diary (e.g. handled within the adjuster's authority level or *charged back* to the adjuster for handling without active supervision).

Managers with a staff of six will spend more time supervising claim file development vs. administrative activities.

# Management Style

Management styles are the characteristics of the way we make decisions and relate to subordinates as managers and defines the way you manage and interact with your staff. There are different management styles, and as a manager becomes more experienced their style may or may not change over time.

Your style of management has a direct impact on how decisions are made in your business unit, upward and downward communication, the ability to motivate the staff, employee turnover and your overall results. Some managers may have a combination of management styles depending on the specific situation.

There are a broad range of management styles, but for purpose of this book we will focus on the following six management styles (Cardinal) illustrated in **Exhibit 3-B** below:

| Six Management Styles (Cardinal) - Exhibit 3-B | |
|---|---|
| 1. **Directive Style (Coercive)** | • Primary objective of immediate compliance from employees<br>• Close control of employees / micromanaged<br>• Motivate by threats and discipline<br>• Sets high-standards<br>• Disciplines those who do not meet standards |
| 2. **Authoritative Style (Visionary)** | • Primary objective of providing long-term direction and vision for employees<br>• A "firm but fair" manager providing employees with clear direction<br>• Motivates by persuasion and feedback on task performance |
| 3. **Affiliative Style** | • Primary objective of creating harmony among employees and between employee and manager<br>• People first and tasks second |

| | |
|---|---|
| | • Avoids conflicts with emphasis on good personal relationships among employees<br>• Motivates by trying to keep people happy |
| 4.  Participative Style (Democratic) | • Primary objective of building commitment and consensus among employees<br>• Encourages employee input on decisions<br>• Motivates by rewarding team effort |
| 5.  Pacesetting Style | • Primary objective of accomplishing tasks to a high standard of excellence<br>• Performs many tasks personally to set an example<br>• Motivates by setting high-standards and expects self-direction from employees |
| 6.  Coaching Style | • Primary objective of long-term professional development of employees<br>• Helps and encourages employees to develop strengths and improve performance<br>• Motivates by providing opportunities for professional development |

Some management styles simply do not work in a claim operation when used exclusively. An effective manager knows which style works best to achieve the desired results, which may include the use of multiple management styles. However, if a manager is unable to be flexible and adapt the management style suitable to the circumstances, problems may develop, including employee resentment, lack of employee motivation, poor morale, stifled creativity, low production, poor claim quality and turnover (especially the talented employees).

Remember, whatever management style you use, you need to get the job done and meet organizational objectives.

Employees require both *positive* and *negative* feedback and reinforcement. Consistent negative feedback will result in a negative work environment. Positive feedback and reinforcement creates a pleasant work environment and improves employee morale and retention.

> ## Management Style
> ## What Works Best for You?
> ### Exhibit 3-C
>
> Your management style defines what type of a manager you are and how you interact with your employees. Treat employees as you would like to be treated in a work environment. Lead by example – this builds trust and respect.
>
> Adapt a management style that best fits you personally and the management situation. The same management style will not work in every situation – and may not work with certain employees.

# Technical Claim Management

The claim manager provides oversight of claim technical issues, customer service and overall people issues. Managing the quality of technical claim handling is the primary responsibility of a claim manager. The claim manager establishes the level of quality required and defines the work product expectations.

A claim operation can have a material impact on the loss ratio and cause it to deviate by 2% to 4% – positive or negative, depending on the quality of the claim operation. As a claim manager, you should be cognizant of your financial-impact on the company results, particularly when approving claim evaluations for reserve management and claim dispositions, as well as, overall control of loss and expense costs.

Managers require different skills including technical skills, interpersonal skills and conceptional skills. Technical skills are the specialized skills necessary to manage technical claim handling. In a claim operation the line management staff requires technical skills to be able to monitor and control the claim tasks performed by adjusters.

Technical claim supervision refers to the direct supervision of the adjuster's claim activities in the claim file – in the form of extending claim authority (settlements and reserves), reviewing reports, providing instructional and commentary notes on claim file development, monitoring entry of relevant data fields and screens, recommending revisions to letters and reports, diary reviews and file development discussion.

Providing technical claim supervision or oversight should be selective and substantive. The level of detail in your supervisory comments depends on the claim complexity and severity, impact of the issues involved, as well as the adjuster's experience, knowledge and claim authority. The reality is that you cannot be current and fully apprised of every claim file in your unit and need to rely on your staff to handle the details and decisions within their own authority. If an adjuster consistently relies on the claim manager for help the adjuster may need training or may be in the wrong position or role. You may want to consider reducing the adjuster's claim authority to a more appropriate level.

For some claim managers, not being involved in every claim file is a difficult environment, feeling the need to review every claim file to be sure it is being handled properly. Managers should provide supervision where and when it is necessary – don't look for perfection. The objective is to direct the claim toward a fair and equitable resolution in compliance with *best practice* claim handling guidelines, standards and *Fair Claim* acts, not create a masterpiece.

Outlining a detailed "to do list" for an adjuster is a waste of management resources. Don't waste time outlining a punch list of items to be completed by the adjuster – a more effective method is to request the adjuster to update the claim file notes with a current *action plan*. The claim manager can then review the *action plan* to determine if it is appropriate, adding to or modifying the plan as needed. Another approach is to meet with the adjuster to discuss the claim details, with the adjuster documenting the discussion and agreed upon action plan in the claim file notes.

When the adjuster proactively documents the *action plan* in the claim file notes for review by the claim manager, the process becomes less time consuming for the manager. It also allows the claim manager to understand the adjuster's thought process and knowledge level of the issues (e.g. liability and damage evaluations), and the claim manager's comments on the proposed action plan would then be documented in the claim file notes.

It is appropriate to provide guidance and direction in the claim file notes, even commenting on occasional mistakes or tardiness when necessary; however, it is not appropriate to criticize handling using the claim notes as a communicative tool to document poor-performance. This is particularly true when the same poor-performance issues are in multiple claim files. Take the performance issue out of the claim file and work with the Human Resource department to develop an employee performance plan to address any claim handling deficiencies. Poor-performance can be a temporary isolated incident or continuous. Obviously, continuous poor-performance is more serious and requires more attention, and documentation.

> **Claim Manager Technical Activities**
> **Exhibit 3-D**
>
> - Claim assignment
> - File direction & supervision
> - Action Plan reviews
> - Summary Report reviews
> - Quality assurance
> - Adjuster report reviews
> - Diary reviews
> - Monitoring and managing claim reserves
> - Extending claim authority
> - Approving loss and expense payments
> - Input on coverage issues
> - Handling large loss reviews
> - Management reports and metrics
> - Managing customer service concerns or complaints.

The claim manager's typical technical claim file activities include the claim assignment, technical claim file direction and supervision, *action plan* reviews, summary report reviews, diary reviews, monitoring and managing claim reserves, extending claim authority, approving loss and expense payments, providing input on coverage issues, handling large loss reviews, reviewing claim management reports, and managing customer service concerns or complaints.

Reviewing claim files and providing guidance and direction is important but be selective in where you provide the management support based on need and impact.

When managing technical claim files, it is important to focus on *claim trends* – this is where you will have the biggest impact as a claim manager. We cannot expect the quality of a claim file to be "perfect", but issues which evolve into trends can and should be addressed quickly to avoid any potential adverse financial-impact. Identifying claim trends may be difficult for some claim managers if they do not make effective use of dashboards, management reports, metrics and analytics tools, or do not have an effective claims quality review process in place. See **Chapter 6 – Claims Quality Review Process**.

Many companies have implemented claims quality review processes to monitor the quality of claim handling and validate adherence and compliance with claim technical guidelines, standards, and procedures, or *Best Practices*.

The primary objective of a claims quality review process is to identify and evaluate claim handling *trends* – positive and negative – and to enhance the effectiveness of the claim operation. By identifying claim handling trends, we become more focused on performance issues and less focused on claim review methods which only address individual claim file issues, and not overall claim trends which have a much larger financial-impact. Individual claim file issues are important and cannot be ignored but claim trends (particularly adverse trends) represent a bigger challenge for claim management.

To achieve consistency in claim handling the claim operation should have established and documented best practice *Claim Handling Guidelines and Standards* and *Litigation Management Guidelines*, as well as copies of the *Fair Claim Acts* for all states wherein claims are handled. These guidelines and standards provide the foundation for acceptable work performance and serve as the basis for the claims quality review process.

We use guidelines and standards for adjuster training, establishing expectations, documenting claim procedures, as well as the need to achieve uniformity and consistency in the handling of claims. For example, the claim operation should have consistent reporting guidelines and reserve management procedures to ensure proper reporting of claims to management and timely and adequate case reserves. Periodic training on claim handling guidelines and standards should be considered, particularly if there are new adjusters in the company.

In a claim operation, it is inevitable that adverse quality claim handling issues will develop for a variety of reasons such as inexperience, improper training, poor-performance, or just an isolated mistake. We cannot expect technical claim handling perfection in a claim operation, but we do want to achieve consistency, and at minimum, claim handling at a satisfactory level. When claim handling issues do develop, the claim manager needs to implement appropriate corrective actions plans for improvement, and training if necessary.

There are two critical procedural philosophies which can have a material effect on a company's financial results, the *Reserve Philosophy* and *Settlement Philosophy*. Both should also be well documented, understood and be included in the claim guidelines and procedures. Deviating from these philosophies can develop into problems including inadequate claim reserves and inappropriate closing of claims (e.g. not closing claims, closing too quickly, claim overpayments, etc.).

## Reserve Philosophy

The *Reserve Philosophy* documents reserve procedures, methodology and overall process for all claim employees – and non-claim personnel. It documents the reserve management guidelines and standards for the claim operation in establishing new, adjusted and closing claim reserves.

As a claim manager, you are responsible for the adequacy of claim reserves in your area of responsibility. Large swings in reserve development cause concerns for management and the actuaries. The reserve development can be caused by newly reported large losses or reserve adjustments. If large reserve adjustments are not timely, it will impact prior underwriting or accident year results, causing concern by senior management. With a well-documented reserve philosophy, adverse reserve development can be minimized.

The most critical aspect of the reserve philosophy is that it is applied consistently across the claim operation without exception. The actuarial staff relies on the reserve philosophy when evaluating loss trends and projecting future results. **Exhibit 2-O in Chapter 2 – Financial Operations** provides a sample illustration of a *Reserve Philosophy*.

## Settlement Philosophy

The settlement philosophy provides guidance and direction to the adjuster to allow for decision making in directing claims toward a settlement disposition. The objective for the claim adjuster is to investigate or adjust the claim and bring the claim to closing by settlement, denial, award, or jury verdict. **Exhibit 3-E** provides a sample illustration of a *Settlement Philosophy*.

---

### Sample Settlement Philosophy
#### Exhibit 3-E

We handle all claims fairly, equitably and ethically in compliance with our best practice claim handling guidelines and *Fair Claim Acts*, as well as other statutes. When handling liability claims, we evaluate liability on our insured by conducting a claim investigation to determine the degree of fault on each party (e.g. application of *comparative negligence*).

Once we have determined the degree of fault, indicating the insured is partially or fully responsible for the loss, we should secure the special damages, evaluate the general and special damages being claimed, and attempt to direct the claim toward a settlement disposition.

If the claim cannot be settled, the claim should be prepared for defense of the insured, including completion of all outstanding investigation and requests for documentation.

---

## Claim Handling Guidelines & Standards

*Claim Handling Guidelines & Standards*, sometimes referred to as *Claim Best Practices*, provide the framework for how claims will be handled consistently throughout the organization. The guidelines include instructions and requirements and establish expectations as to how claims should be handled and managed.

The guidelines and standards may include litigation management guidelines, fair claim act summaries, and process and workflow details.

Claim handling guidelines and standards should be comprehensive, indexed for ease of use and readily accessible to the staff for review and reference (e.g. ability to access documents electronically). Claim management establishes claim guidelines to achieve consistency in claim handling and compliance with state *Fair Claim Acts*. Your job as a claim manager is to make sure the staff complies and follows the established guidelines, standards and procedures.

There are two *schools of thought* on the detail necessary when developing claim guidelines. Some claim management feel too much detail or specificity may yield potential *bad faith* claims if adjusters do not strictly adhere to all the claim guidelines, while others feel the lack of detailed comprehensive claim guidelines has the potential to create organizational chaos, inconsistency and mistakes. It makes sense to have claim guidelines and standards in place, but there may be exceptions to the guidelines which should be understood by the claim manager.

Claim guidelines may include technical claim handling requirements for specific claim functions or processes and reference information such as:

- Claim organizational structure
- First notice of loss (FNOL) process
- Claim acknowledgements
- Coverage verification and analysis
- Investigation requirements (e.g. contacts, taking statements, scene investigations, action plans, ISO ClaimSearch®[8], etc.)
- Claimant attorney engagement and attorney allegations
- Medical management procedures (nurse case management, utilization review, vocational rehabilitation and medical bill review)
- Recovery (subrogation, salvage and loss refund)
- Automobile and property appraisals/inspection requirements
- Claim authority
- Reserve management
- Reserve philosophy
- Settlement philosophy
- File documentation
- Claim Evaluation
- Reporting requirements
- Diary management
- Large loss reporting
- Litigation management procedures

---

[8] ***ISO ClaimSearch®*** is an industry tool used by many insurance companies and third-party claim administrators for the review and exchange of claims history information between subscribing companies. It provides important data to claim professionals on property, casualty, and automobile claims, including physical damage, theft, and salvage information (Verisk Analytics, Inc. | Verisk Analytics® | ISO ClaimSearch®).

- Claim handling by specific line of business
- Auto physical damage claim handling
- Reinsurance reporting
- Fraud claim handling / special investigative unit (SIU)
- Closing documentation (e.g. releases, proofs of loss, etc.)
- Use of experts
- Claim correspondence and forms
- Payment processing
- Complaint handling
- Use of vendors
- Claims quality review process

As a claim manager you need to be very familiar with the claim guidelines and procedures. When there is a technical problem in a claim unit, it is usually attributable to non-compliance with a claim guideline or procedure, particularly best practices. Your role as claim manager is to manage this process. Don't allow adjusters to take shortcuts or not follow claim guidelines because they are "experienced" – this is how problems develop. The guidelines are in place for a reason and your focus on all types of claim reviews should always include making sure there is full compliance with claim guidelines and best practices.

## Litigation Management Guidelines

A comprehensive litigation management program provides a consistent handling approach and creates an environment wherein the adjuster and defense counsel are engaged in working toward a common goal.

A successful litigation management program includes clear and concise expectations for both defense counsel and the adjuster to ensure that both parties understand the handling objectives. Roles and responsibilities are clearly defined with projected time frames for completion. Expectations are well documented so there are no misunderstandings with defense counsel and the adjuster collaborating to achieve a favorable claim outcome.

The litigation process is a team effort between the adjuster and defense counsel; however, it is important to note that defense counsel has a professional and ethical responsibility to protect the policyholder's interests. This includes settling claims promptly and equitably when it is in the best interests of the policyholder.

*Litigation Management Guidelines* provide the claim operation with a specific protocol for the handling of litigation claims, including the defense of policyholders and the handling of coverage issues. The guidelines also serve as the company's instructional framework for defense counsel to handle claims, on behalf of the company and the policyholder.

Litigation management guidelines should include at minimum the following:

- Initial review of the litigation
- Selection of approved defense counsel
- Use of extensions of time to answer (when appropriate)
- Referral letter to defense counsel with outlined defense counsel and adjuster activities
- Development of a collaborative litigation plan
- Defense counsel submitting a legal budget consistent with the litigation plan
- Control of the litigation process
- Timely and quality reporting by defense counsel
- Motion practice guidelines
- Trial activity guidelines
- Appeal process
- Legal research guidelines
- Legal billing (requirements and procedures)
- Issuance of excess letters (when required)

Claim managers should be involved in monitoring litigation claims, which represent the costliest claims in the organization. As a claim manager, your dual diary on litigation claims will provide oversight of reserve adequacy and legal expense. Also use available claim management reports to monitor litigation claim activity.

Providing claim oversight on a litigation claim is no different than a non-litigation claim, other than the litigation component (e.g. litigation management). The same best practice guidelines and standards apply for the underlying claim. Retaining defense counsel is not an opportunity for the adjuster to tender claim handling activities to defense counsel which should be handled by the adjuster.

Litigation management requires specialized claim handling skills to achieve high-quality claim outcomes and control legal expense. The same specialized skills are needed at the management level if the claim manager is providing direct supervision of litigation claims.

Litigation management will be further discussed in **Chapter 5 – Managing Technical Claim Handling**.

## Process and Workflow Manuals

Many companies have established process and workflow manuals including the use of *workflow* diagrams prepared in Visio®.

These manuals document guidelines and procedures for non-technical claim activities, workflow, claim support processes, entry of financial transactions (reserves and payments) and document management (mail and scanning) processes.

For example, detailed workflow and processes may include (but not limited to):

- New claim set-up
- Claim acknowledgements
- Reserve and payment transactions
- Entry of a claim payables (loss and expense)
- Check issuance and printing
- Vendor management (including W-9 requirements and 1099 issuance)
- System data corrections and updates
- Medical bill review
- Medicare reporting
- OFAC reporting
- ISO ClaimSearch®
- Document management (mail management and scanning)
- Faxing documents
- Correspondence process (claim forms and form letters)

The manuals provide the claim operation with consistency in process and workflow including OFAC[9] and Medicare CMS compliance reporting[10].

As a claim manager you should be very familiar with claim process and workflow even if the claim support unit does not report to you directly. This area impacts adjuster productivity particularly if the adjuster is handling claim support functions detracting from technical claim handling – which may need to be reassigned to the claim support unit.

---

[9] "The Office of Foreign Assets Control (OFAC) of the US Department of the Treasury administers and enforces economic and trade sanctions based on US foreign policy and national security goals against targeted foreign countries and regimes, terrorists, international narcotics traffickers, those engaged in activities related to the proliferation of weapons of mass destruction, and other threats to the national security, foreign policy or economy of the United States. OFAC acts under Presidential national emergency powers, as well as authority granted by specific legislation, to impose controls on transactions and freeze assets under US jurisdiction. Many of the sanctions are based on United Nations and other international mandates, are multilateral in scope, and involve close cooperation with allied governments". Non-compliance can result in substantial fines and prison. (Department of the Treasury)

[10] "Section 111 of the Medicare, Medicaid, and SCHIP Extension Act of 2007 (MMSEA) added mandatory reporting requirements with respect to Medicare beneficiaries who have coverage under group health plan (GHP) arrangements as well as for Medicare beneficiaries who receive settlements, judgments, awards or other payment from liability insurance (including self-insurance), no-fault insurance, or workers' compensation, collectively referred to as Non-Group Health Plan (NGHP) or NGHP insurance." (U.S. Centers for Medicare & Medicaid Services)

Claim managers should be able to recognize process and workflow issues and know when there is a critical path breakdown. Sometimes, a change in workflow, or roles and responsibilities, can have a material improvement on a claim operation.

In **Chapter 5 – Managing Technical Claim Handling** we will review specific categories of P&C technical claim handling and how the claim manager can monitor claims using effective management techniques to achieve the most desired results.

# Fair Claim Acts

*Fair Claim Acts* exist in many states and are based on statutes and insurance regulations. Fair Claim Acts are enacted to protect consumers (claimants and policyholders) from unfair insurance claim practices including compliance with statutory timeframes to contact and respond to parties to a claim, timely inspection of damages, extending settlement offers or denying claims, and issuing claim payments.

Fair Claim Acts establish the standard for fair and equitable claim handling. There are some comprehensive *best practices* claim guidelines which take into consideration the requirements of various Fair Claim Acts; however, you need to review each state to be sure claim handling complies with state requirements, which may not be outlined in the claim guidelines or best practices.

The state insurance departments provide oversight of the Fair Claim Acts and insurance regulations. Periodically, the state insurance department will audit a representative sampling of claim files handled by an insurance company or TPA. The claim audit measures compliance with the Fair Claim Act and insurance regulations, and the insurance department has the power to levy fines against the insurance company for non-compliance with insurance regulations.

As the claim manager you need to be familiar with the various state Fair Claim Acts and make sure your staff understands the requirements in each state and complies with the regulations. Some states have stringent claim handling requirements in certain lines of business such as automobile claims. For example, handling automobile physical damage, property damage and no fault (PIP) claims in New York requires compliance with specific statutes which includes timely issuance of letters and forms at certain intervals in the claim process.

# Administrative Claim Management

Administrative claim management refers to managing people – the staff who report directly to the claim manager.

Administrative claim management responsibilities include staffing, workload management, quality review processes, management reporting, metrics analysis, performance management, salary administration, hiring and firing, compliance, training and development and other miscellaneous duties.

One of the most challenging aspects of management is to embrace the concept of *delegation*. Delegation is both an art and science, and for some managers a difficult transition. Merriam-Webster defines *Delegation* as "the act of giving control, authority, a job, a duty, etc., to another person" (The Merriam-Webster Online Dictionary).

> **Claim Manager Administrative Activities**
> **Exhibit 3-F**
>
> - Managing people
> - Staffing & resource management
> - Workload management
> - Productivity reporting
> - Quality assurance
> - Performance management
> - Salary Administration
> - Hiring & firing
> - Compliance
> - Training & development
> - Management reporting
> - Metrics & analytics

When a manager delegates a task, they are delegating the responsibility to complete the task in accordance with their instructions; however, the manager is still accountable for its completion – and this is where some managers are uncomfortable with delegating. Some managers may perform the task themselves to avoid an error or mishandling because the manager thinks this results in a better outcome and avoids any potential criticism.

If a claim manager does not delegate, they become ineffective and waste valuable management time and resources on performing tasks which should be performed by subordinates. It also stifles organizational growth in that subordinates are unable to make decisions on their own – preparing them for their next level in the organization.

Managers who do not delegate effectively work long hours, have a staff who lean on the manager for most decisions, and foster limited growth in their business unit. Employees become frustrated with the lack of ability to make their own decisions and the manager becomes frustrated with working long hours while subordinates do not. Managers who do not delegate will have excessive employee turnover.

A *cautionary note* on claim managers who have supervisory subordinates. It is important that the claim manager not provide direct oversight and supervision of adjusters who report directly to the claim supervisor. If there is an issue involving an adjuster, the claim manager should work directly with the claim supervisor and not bypass the supervisor. Bypassing the supervisor creates organizational confusion, disrupts the management hierarchy, and erodes the effectiveness of the supervisor. It also creates a supervisory morale issue creating an environment wherein the supervisor may resent their manager's direct involvement with their subordinate, questioning their own performance.

If you are a claim supervisor and your manager is involved in your area of responsibility, you need to find out why. Do you have unresolved technical or administrative issues in your unit? Does your manager have concerns about your supervision? Does your manager have problems with delegating effectively? If you are concerned with your manager being too involved in your area of responsibility it is worth a discussion with your manager.

## Making a Difference

An effective claim manager will make a difference by having a positive impact on their unit staff members and the organization.

Some tips on *making a difference* as a claim manager:

- Focus on *People, Process & Technology* – adapt a modern management model.
- Be selfish about your time but be available or accessible to your staff – never push the staff away, because whatever you are working on is never more important than people issues.
- Be a *change maker, change facilitator* or *change champion* – the claim function is changing rapidly, and the industry needs claim managers who can "think out of the box" and adapt rapidly to change.
- Know your limitations and seek help particularly with Human Resource (HR) issues.
- Address human resource issues promptly – do not let them fester – it deteriorates morale with the other staff.
- Set realistic and consistent goals with clear expectations.
- Hold the staff accountable to departmental and company goals – set goals which are measurable and achievable.
- Not all adjusters are above average – strive for satisfactory or above performance
- Do not encourage long working hours – it will cause resentment and turnover.
- Not having knowledge of a claim technical issue doesn't mean you are not supervising or managing properly.
- Know your staff – be personal and approachable.
- Do not micromanage – it will cause resentment and turnover.
- Stick up for your people if they are right – be bold!
- Be ethical in everything you do and set an example for your staff.

## Strive to be a Leader

*Leadership* is defined as "the time when a person holds the position of leader or the power or ability to lead other people (The Merriam-Webster Online Dictionary)".

Strive to be a leader - not all managers are leaders – leaders inspire and motivate the staff to achieve company objectives, but leadership must be earned. Some people have personalities which are amenable to leadership roles, and others don't.

Leaders earn respect from their subordinates by being fair, supportive, honest, ethical, empathetic, consistent, and have a vision for success. Being knowledgeable about claim technical issues does not necessarily mean you are a good manager or have leadership characteristics or skills.

Lead by example – employees respect their managers because of their leadership characteristics and will emulate their behavior and want to do an excellent job because of a positive work environment.

Great leaders know their staff and can identify the unique characteristics in a person which will benefit the organization. This requires a special skill.

## Manage to Expectations

It is important to establish realistic expectations for your staff, so the staff understands what is expected of them. Know your staff – not everyone is exceptional, nor do you want to have a staff of all exceptional performers. Be demanding but not unrealistic. Being *fully acceptable* or *satisfactory* should never have a negative connotation.

Employees follow their manager's queue – set a positive example. Don't work late every night and expect your staff to do the same – family is important and giving a solid 8+ hours of work per day should be acceptable, unless there is a special project or circumstance. Working late on a consistent basis causes organizational fatigue and "burn-out", and ultimately employee turnover.

Establishing clear-cut expectations creates a productive and consistent work environment. If expectations are not being met, reevaluate whether the expectations are realistic and achievable. Make sure your staff understands your expectations as their manager and the overall company expectations – do not establish unrealistic goals or workloads which will generate a morale issue and turnover. Establishing unrealistic expectations creates employee stress, uncertainty and job dissatisfaction.

Expectations should be translated into performance goals for the business unit as a group and for each individual employee. This allows the manager to periodically review the performance goal results and progress in meeting expectations.

## Be an Effective Communicator

Communicate with your staff effectively and regularly – be visible and do not always communicate by email. Get out of your office and engage in discussion. Walk around the office and talk with employees – you'll be surprised what you hear! Hold meetings regularly to keep your staff informed and working as a cohesive group, but don't make the meetings too long.

When a subordinate does an excellent job, give positive reinforcement in front of others. Use motivation to produce better results and drive positive behavior. Manage by example.

Communicate company information regularly and encourage an open communication environment. Highlight successes in the department or unit and communicate the details to the staff and senior management. Celebrate employee personal and work-related successes.

Your mode of communication is important. Direct verbal communication and written communication are both effective. Know when to communicate verbally vs. in writing – particularly on performance issues.

## Delegate Appropriately

Micromanagement stifles employee development and creativity. The staff become disengaged and resent being managed so closely. Some employees will leave the company and others will tolerate the environment but lose motivation and enthusiasm.

Employees do not like being micromanaged – delegate and check on results but do not re-check all work and re-do work which is unsatisfactory to you. Unsatisfactory work should be referred to the employee for resolution but used as a learning tool to avoid the same issue in the future.

As a claim supervisor or manager, you cannot look at every claim file – if you do not delegate authority to your staff, you will end up doing more work than your staff – and stifle your own career development – as effective delegation is a key management tool you need to use throughout your career. Delegation also provides the employee with an opportunity to further develop their own skills and knowledge. You may be surprised at the excellent work produced by subordinates when they made their own decision and are responsible for the outcome. Proactively delegating is the sign of a good manager and will be recognized by other managers and your direct manager.

A manager can "over-delegate" by attempting to delegate tasks to an unprepared or inexperienced employee. This could have a negative financial-impact on the company and should be avoided. As a condition precedent to employee delegation, the manager needs to be sure the employee has the requisite basic knowledge level to handle the task either through training and development, or experience.

We will talk more about delegation in **Chapter 4 – Management Controls**.

## Foster Teamwork

Breakdown business unit barriers – work as a team toward a common goal. Teamwork requires management by example – and starts at the top of the organization. Teamwork results in better results and reduces costs – it also creates comradery in the organization which yields positive attitudes.

It sometimes takes effort to develop a "team environment" through group activities, team building exercises and an effective reward and recognition process. Be proactive and participate – if you stand on the sidelines, don't expect the team to be built around you. Be active and lead by example.

## Be a Change Champion

*Change Management* refers to the ability of the organization to effectively make organizational change with minimal disruption to the staff and operations. Change can include implementation of new systems, process and workflow, and company culture.

The extent of the change management effort is driven by the type of change being considered and the staff involved. A change involving 10 people has far less impact on a company than a change involving 500 people. The primary issue is delivery of the change and making sure the change is being implemented properly and accepted by employees. Many projects have failed due to employees never embracing or accepting the change, due to management not implementing a change management plan as a component of an underlying project.

Change management is a topic far too comprehensive for this book; however, as a manager you should understand the critical need for change management in any organization and that your role as a change *champion* will have a material impact on the success of the project and the change being considered.

## Manage Claim Files Effectively

Review of claim files is an important claim manager responsibility, but the manager needs to be selective in the type of files reviewed, how often reviewed, and the review format.

Simply placing your dual diary on all claims within a certain dollar threshold which can clearly be handled by an adjuster within their authority, is a waste of your critical management time. You need to be selective in monitoring claims requiring your management input which may involve claims over an adjuster's authority, coverage issues, claim complaints, litigation claims and large loss claims. Use the claims quality review process as a method to review claims to identify claim handling *trends*, including a review of claims handled by the adjuster within their claim authority.

Give claim file direction – but don't criticize work in the claim file. Take performance issues out of the claim file – and remember that not every claim file is going to be perfect. There will be occasional mistakes – focus on claim trends and not individual isolated mistakes – address the mistakes but drive organizational effectiveness using *claim trending* with a comprehensive claims quality review process. Know your staff – their strengths and weaknesses – work on improving their weaknesses but also compliment their strengths.

## Focus on Priorities

Put your time where it is necessary – work hard but be smart. Be selfish about your time. Successful managers know when to deviate from routine tasks and projects to address critical or emerging issues.

Know where you are spending your time, focus on priorities and on what is important. As a manager you should never be uncertain about what are considered priorities – if you are not sure speak with your manager.

People issues, large losses, coverage issues, adverse claim handling trends, adverse reserve development, and regulatory complaints are some examples of priorities.

## Be Strategic

As a claim manager, you may have an opportunity to participate in the development of a claim departmental strategy or even an overall corporate strategy. Development of strategies is a key management function and becomes more prevalent as you assume increasing responsibility in an organization. Often, strategy development crosses multiple departments to develop a company-wide strategic plan.

The development of a strategic plan includes defining the strategy itself, or strategic direction, and then determining the resources necessary to implement the strategy. Strategic plans are written plans and may be incorporated into larger overall business plans.

A *Strategic Plan* is a general framework for a company outlining organizational strategy for a specified period (e.g. 5 years). It may include individual strategic plans by functional department (e.g. claims, underwriting, etc.). *Tactical Plans* are the processes designed to execute the strategic plan to meet organizational goals and objectives.

An example of a *strategic plan* (or strategy) would be an overall information technology strategy for an organization, including the claim operation. It may include short-term and long-term plans to improve system functionality including moving to a new system application or platform, development of a data warehouse and replacement of computer hardware.

The strategic plan provides an overview of the strategy and may include a **SWOT** analysis – which is stands for **S**trengths, **W**eaknesses, **O**pportunities and **T**hreats. The SWOT analysis includes a detailed situational analysis of internal strengths and weaknesses of an organization, and external opportunities and threats faced by the organization, which are examined using a strategic chart to plot information and data for review and analysis (Web Finance, Inc.).

Another type of situational analysis may include a **PEST** analysis which is a type of situational analysis wherein **P**olitical, **E**conomic, **S**ocial and **T**echnological factors are examined to chart an organization's long-term plans or strategy (Web Finance, Inc.).

Have a strategy – know where you are going and develop a plan. Strategy can be short-term or long-term. As a claim manger you can develop your own departmental or unit strategy so that you and your staff have a roadmap for the future.

## Achieve the Balance

At times, you may need to spend more time on claim file reviews due to technical claim performance issues or special projects, or on administrative issues due to people, or performance issues. The key is to understand that the balance may shift back and forth depending on the circumstances.

As a line claim supervisor or manager, your balance may be more toward the technical file reviews; however, a branch claim manager may have more administrative responsibility and be less involved in technical file reviews.

Achieving the balance is not always easy. Recognizing when you are out of balance is the first step in making an adjustment based on need. For example, if you are heavily involved in reviewing claim files and the unit or department has extensive turnover due to workloads, you need to move your primary focus to the turnover and workload issues.

## Managing Upward Effectively

Protect your staff and be their advocate when communicating upward in the organization. Be supportive of employee requests, suggestions and opinions. Above all, be honest and truthful. Being honest and forthright gives you credibility as a manager and an effective leader.

Communicate honestly to your direct manager and above all – don't simply communicate what you think your manager wants to hear from you. Effective managers learn how to deliver both good and unwelcome news to their manager. Take responsibility for issues requiring attention but be proactive in offering your resolution plan at the same time.

An example of a management discussion which is often avoided by an inexperienced manager (or reluctant manager) is the request for additional staff. If you feel additional staff is needed, then proactively conduct a *staffing analysis* to support your request and then discuss staffing with your direct manager. Staffing is critical to a successful claim operation and inadequate staffing levels can negatively impact financial results and is a primary cause of employee turnover.

**Chapter 7 – Staffing and Resource Management** discusses the impact of staffing on a claim operation.

# Understand Organizational Dynamics

Managers need to understand the Company's organizational dynamics, including organizational *politics* which exists in every organization. The politics in an organization may be subtle or outward. You can't avoid it and it is prevalent in every organization – the key is to understand that it exists and how you manage around it.

Organizational dynamics or politics comes in many forms – from the manager who is perceived to be "protected" from any performance issues due to their relationship with executives to cultural norms which have developed over time into informal "rules". For example, a company's expectation that you as a manager will contribute annually to a specific charity. Although the request is not outwardly stated – you contribute to avoid any effect on your good standing in the company.

Although organizational politics can be frustrating it is prevalent in every organization. The key to survival is to recognize it exists and try to work it to your benefit by being neutral. Don't get caught up in organizational politics – management personnel are always changing. You do not want to be a casualty of politics when your manager leaves the company and new management comes into the organization – you may be considered part of the "old regime" and be pushed out of the organization.

Part of organizational politics is the "rumor mill" which can run rampant in an organization. Try to stay out of it – it is unproductive! Also try to steer your employees away from it.

# Use Management Reports & Analytics

The use of claim management reports and analytics tools are critical in a claim operation. These reports include production reports, financial reports and operational reports.

Reports and analytics tools provide management with the ability to manage workflow, productivity, and financial results such as analysis of loss ratios an LAE. Trending of results allow the manager to identify organizational strengths and weaknesses and identify areas which require corrective action or training.

See **Chapter 9 – Claim Management Reports** for more detail on management reporting.

# Manage Staffing & Workloads Effectively

A critical challenge for the claim manager is achieving the balance in properly managing adjuster workloads – which have a direct impact on ULAE and ultimately loss costs. Increasing workloads will have a positive impact on total adjuster compensation costs (included in ULAE) – by increasing workloads you will require less staff which will reduce salary and benefit costs.

Unfortunately, an increase in workloads will have a negative impact on loss costs. With higher workloads, the adjuster will have less time to handle claims properly, and may take short-cuts resulting in inadequate claim investigations, redundant or deficient case reserves and claim overpayments. Adjusters who have excessive workloads have less time to take quality statements, conduct proper claim investigations, evaluate and negotiate claims effectively, manage medical cost containment, and control litigation costs through effective litigation management. This all results in increased loss costs and ALAE.

Workload standards should be established and enforced with standards by position, job grade, class of business, and line of business. For example, there should be an established workload for a senior claim representative inclusive of new claim exposures per month, closed claim exposures per month and exposure closing ratio for each month. The workload management report should include a rolling 12 month by employee, unit and company, for comparison purposes.

Workload management tips:

- Evaluate productivity and workload by *exposure* and not by occurrences – exposure counts are more relevant and provide an accurate assessment of workload.
- Don't overload the high performers because they can handle the increased workload and then give less work to marginal performers – this can result in morale problems and you are not addressing the underlying problem of poor-performance. It can also cause employee turnover.
- Match the assignment of claims to the adjuster skill level – assigning complex claims to an inexperienced adjuster can result in costly mistakes and assigning an experienced adjuster to simple claims increases expense with a higher salary grade employee handling a lower value claim which should be handled by a lower salary grade employee.
- Be transparent and always provide production or workload management reports to your staff monthly and communicate productivity trends.

Know when to request more staff – adverse staffing issues can develop quickly or subtly over time. Workloads can increase with staff reductions (temporary or permanent) and changes in claim volume caused by increased premium volume and/or policy count, new products, as well as storm and catastrophe losses.

Increased workloads can impact claim quality with less staff to manage the claims effectively. Increased workloads are also a contributing cause of employee turnover, compounding staffing issues even more.

See **Chapter 7 – Staffing and Resource Management** for more detail on the impact of staffing on a claim operation and how to staff appropriately.

# Work Effectively with Other Departments

As a claim manager, you will work with other departments on a regular basis – including underwriting, loss control, marketing & distribution, finance/accounting, compliance, legal and actuarial. Interactions with other departments may involve the following issues:

- Claim Reserves
- Claim Payments
- Coverage Issues
- Agency Complaints
- Customer Service Issues
- Exgratia[11] Payments
- Payment Errors
- Errors and Omissions Claims
- Claim Trending (e.g. reserve development)
- Insurance Department Complaints
- Compliance (e.g. adjuster licensing)

The claim department should work effectively and cooperatively with all departments in the organization. The financial results in the claim operation impact many departments in the organization; therefore, an obvious interest in results. Develop relationships with the management staff in other departments and meet regularly – these relationships will be helpful when a problem develops.

As a claim operation, our daily activities center around establishing and maintaining claim reserves and making claim payments, as well as coverage decisions. It is important that the other departments understand the procedures and philosophies for reserving claims and settlement of claims. This will reduce the number of questions and criticisms.

Over-payments or improper payments, as well as overly redundant case reserves (over reserving) and deficient case reserves (not enough reserve) can all have an adverse impact on financial results. Be prepared to respond to questions by the underwriting and senior management staff on reserve issues and payments. If the adjuster made a mistake or used poor judgment, admit it, and move on, don't try to defend a position which is improper or a mistake – you will lose credibility as a manager.

Work as a team with other departments – be cognizant of their role in the organization and their roles and responsibilities. The information being requested from you is part of their job requirement.

---

[11] **Exgratia Payments** are claim payments which are not within the policy coverage – and are paid as an accommodation.

# Human Resource Management

## Recruitment

The *recruitment* process is normally handled by the Human Resource (HR) department in conjunction with the claim manager – recruiting for new and the replacement of existing positions.

The key to effective recruitment is to understand the position, role and the experience level required to handle the job properly; and recruit staff who meet the job requirements outlined in the *Job Description.*

Job descriptions are an important control in an organization used in the hiring process – they outline the key aspects of position or role in the organization, and generally include the following:

- Job Description
- Position
- Department
- Job Code
- Job Grade
- Role, Duties and Responsibilities
- Job Requirements (skills, ability and knowledge)
- Education & Experience Requirements
- Claim Authority

As a claim manager, you should hire (or promote) candidates based on the required knowledge and experience level as outlined in the job description (e.g. job grade level). Don't upgrade the position to a higher job grade level to hire a candidate who may be over-qualified for the vacant or new position.

A common mistake made by a claim manager is to recruit for a lower level adjuster position (2 – 4 years' experience) and then hire an adjuster who is over-qualified to have more handling flexibility (and experience) in the unit. Two problems may develop: (1) you have increased your ULAE costs with the higher salary and may have exceeded your salary budget; and (2) the new employee will become dissatisfied with a less challenging role and may leave resulting in turnover.

Identifying qualified candidates can be challenging especially in certain areas of the country. Companies recruit for staff using a variety of methods including internal job posting, company website, online job posting, trade press advertising, job fairs, college campuses, employee recommendations and recruiters. The claim operation must have an effective recruitment program in place due to the transient nature of the business, especially in areas of the country where there is a concentration of insurance job opportunities.

Be proactive in the recruitment process, particularly if you have a vacancy or expect to have a vacancy in the future. It takes time to recruit, interview and hire new employees – including requirements for drug screens, reference checks and background investigations. The longer it takes to fill a vacant position the more increased workload for your staff to handle the vacant position claim volume (new and pending claims). This impacts employee morale and can cause turnover if the position remains vacant for an extended period.

# Interviewing

The *interview* process is the first step in bringing new potential employees into the organization. It starts with submission of a resume and completion of an employment application.

It involves a process of bringing a candidate into the organization for a series of interviews to determine whether the candidate has the experience and knowledge necessary to handle the job, the demeanor and personality to work effectively with employees in the unit or group and whether the candidate can be integrated into the corporate culture.

Conducting interviews requires training and experience. It is an important management function as you are identifying and interviewing candidates who will have a key role in the organization contributing to its overall success. You want to hire staff who are committed to a long-term career at the company.

Unfortunately, some managers are not trained in proper interview techniques and end up hiring staff who "they like" or feel a connection with, overlooking key attributes necessary to handle the job effectively. Having *chemistry* with a candidate is not an indicator of the candidate's ability to handle the job effectively.

If you need training on how to interview effectively ask the Human Resource department for assistance. There are many tools on the market which can assist in developing or enhancing interview skills.

The key to effective interviewing is *preparation* – outline the core questions you want to ask each candidate during the interview process, including some of the key attributes you feel are necessary to handle the job. Ask open-ended questions and look for specific examples. It is important to ask questions around claim technical proficiency using claim scenarios or examples, to understand the depth of the candidate's technical knowledge and expertise.

It is important to be truthful about the job and the company during the interview. Don't oversell the job to the candidate because you desperately need to fill the position. Be up front about the job challenges and emphasize both strengths and weaknesses. Being untruthful during the interview process may ultimately end up with the employee leaving the company.

Work with the Human Resource department to gain an understanding of what you can and cannot ask during an interview. Have the candidate interview with multiple interviewers to get a broader view on their potential integration into the organization, including being a good cultural fit with both the department and organization.

# Hiring & Termination

The *hiring* of new employees is a relatively easy task. After the interview process, reference checks, agreement on compensation and benefits, and projected start date, the job offer will be communicated to the candidate verbally by telephone – through the Human Resource manager or the hiring manager.

After the candidate formally accepts the job offer, a letter will be provided to the candidate confirming the job details including the position and title, compensation package, benefits, vacation, and start date. Prior to the offer letter being sent to the candidate, the company may require a drug screen and/or background investigation.

There are two types of employee terminations – *voluntary* termination wherein the employee voluntarily terminates from the company based on their own decision, and *involuntarily* termination wherein the employee is terminated by the company for cause.

The involuntarily *termination* of an employee can be a challenging task, with the authority to terminate only granted to certain individuals in the organization. Termination is the end-result of an ongoing performance plan, or an act, commission or omission, by the employee which results in immediate termination (e.g. theft, drugs/alcohol, insubordination, job abandonment, etc.).

Terminating an employee is never an easy task and can be an emotional situation. It is important to be prepared for the termination meeting with documentation and always have a human resource professional present. Termination may result in the employee being escorted from the building with the need to clear out the employee's personal things after the employee has left. During the termination meeting, be respectful and empathetic toward the employee recognizing the potential emotional impact, and do not prolong the meeting debating the termination decision.

Some companies may ask the voluntary terminating employee to complete an *exit interview*. These types of interviews, or even completion of an exit employee survey, can be helpful to the company to better understand why employees leave the organization.

# Performance Management

*Performance Management* is the ongoing process of managing employee performance, which may include quarterly coaching sessions with the employee and an annual written performance review.

Performance management includes monitoring, coaching and mentoring employees throughout the year – and providing feedback to the employee along the way. To achieve high quality claim results, it is critical to utilize an effective performance management program – by implementing consistent individual and company performance objectives for every claim employee at the beginning of the review period.

For example, performance management objectives for an adjuster may include:

- Quality of claim handling based on *Quality Review* process scoring and the manager's claim file reviews
- Productivity management (e.g. closing ratio)
- Teamwork
- Financial metrics (Loss Ratio)
- Expense control (ALAE and ULAE)
- Professional development
- Company goals and objectives

SMART goals should be established for each employee as part of the goal setting process. SMART goals are used to assist managers and employees in communicating and documenting specific goals established during the performance review process. **SMART** stands for:

- **S**pecific
- **M**easurable
- **A**chievable
- **R**elevant
- **T**ime-Bound

The manager and employee should have periodic performance review discussions (e.g. quarterly) throughout the performance review period to provide progress reporting. This process will provide consistency in documented objectives and substantive performance feedback to each employee throughout the year. It is important to document performance discussions as it will make the final performance review an easier process.

Many companies have implemented an annual performance review process which has a common anniversary date for all employees to simplify the process.

Performance management also includes the process of handling *performance issues* such as marginal or unsatisfactory employee performance which may result in a performance warning or a formal action plan. Performance issues require the involvement of the Human Resource department to assist with the process including review of proposed performance action plans or written warnings which will be provided to the employee. Depending on the performance issue, the Human Resource department may involve internal or external legal counsel.

See **Chapter 7 – Staffing and Resource Management** for more detail on performance management.

## Working with Difficult Employees

When working with people, you will encounter many types of personalities and behaviors with distinctive characteristics, demeanors and work ethic – with both positive and negative personality traits. Not everyone will be cooperative and agreeable, and you will encounter staff members who are irrational, contradictory, emotional, sarcastic, argumentative, negative, moody or even miserable.

As a manager, your job is to work with all the staff effectively and consider the impact of human behavior. You may need a different approach for some people – as the same management approach or style may not work for all your staff. Some staff require more monitoring and oversight than others – including additional oversight due to personality traits.

At some point in your career as a manager you will encounter a *difficult employee*. What makes the employee "difficult"? This can range from a personality trait which impacts the work product, such as being argumentative or uncooperative with your instructions or directives or being disruptive to the entire unit with negative behavior impacting others (e.g. consistent complaining, spreading rumors, being insulting or rude, undermining, etc.), or just a poor attitude. These behaviors are unacceptable and need to be dealt with to avoid any negative impact on claim results, and departmental morale and group cohesiveness.

The most effective way to handle a difficult employee is to be direct and communicate with the employee. This type of behavior can be temporary caused by a work issue (e.g. passed over for a promotion or salary increase) or a personal issue which you may be unaware of; or may be due to the employee's overall personality which may be difficult to turn-around or correct.

At minimum, you need to meet with the employee to discuss the behavior and why it is unacceptable. After the initial meeting takes place, record your notes outlining the discussion, expectations and any next steps. If the behavior continues, you may need to develop a written action plan (warning) with the assistance of the Human Resource department. The action plan should be specific with objectives, expectations, time frames and consequences of not meeting the objectives, inclusive of probation or termination.

You will find that non-technical personnel issues involving employees are more difficult to handle than issues involving unacceptable technical claim handling. Technical claim handling issues are more objective with evidence to support the issue documented in the claim file record. Non-technical personnel issues can be subtle, need to be witnessed or brought to your attention by others, have the potential to have a broader impact on the unit and company, and can be reversed (either way) by the employee temporarily without much effort.

Do not delay in addressing and resolving difficult employee issues – it has a material effect on coworkers and the entire department. Remember, attitude is just as important (if not more) than technical claim proficiency.

## Salary Administration

Most claim managers have salary administration responsibilities for new hires and existing employees. A salary budget is established as a component of the overall claim operating budget, which establishes a maximum salary pool for the department and salary adjustment ranges based on performance. It will also include a specific percentage increase of the total salary budget for salary adjustments for the upcoming year

Salary adjustments may vary depending on where the employee is in the salary range for the position and job grade. If you only have a certain salary adjustment percentage for your department (e.g. 3%), this translates into 3% of the total salary budget at budget inception. As an example, if the annual salary budget is $1,000,000 with a staff of 15, the maximum amount available for annual salary adjustments is $30,000 (3%) for the total staff of 15 employees. This means that some employees may receive 4%, with others at 2% or even 1%, depending on performance and contribution to the company.

In certain situations, depending on the employee's annual salary level, you may only be able to give a small salary percentage adjustment because the percentage increase has a higher dollar impact on the total salary adjustment dollars available (e.g. $30,000).

Salary administration should be tied to performance – reward top performers with higher compensation. Salary increases should not be guaranteed – employees who are low performers and do not contribute to the unit or company should not be rewarded with a salary increase. Spend your pool of salary dollars wisely so that you get the most impact on the departmental results you need.

Salary administration requires training and should be a structured process. For some managers salary administration may be a challenge. If you have a 3% salary adjustment budget pool, you can't give each employee 3% to make the process easier. You will erode the concept of *paying for performance* and send a clear message to the staff that everyone receives the same salary adjustment, whether you are a marginal, average or outstanding performance employee.

Transparency is important in salary administration – the employee should be advised as to the salary range for the job grade and where they are in the salary range. This can be expressed in terms of quadrants (e.g. four quadrants in the salary range), for example, advising the employee they are in the second quadrant for the job grade and salary range, which may be considered the mid-point. It should be noted that some companies will not disclose this information to employees.

## Training and Development

Training and development is a function handled by the Human Resource department and individual business units or departments. Training should be useful, informative and geared toward the audience which requires the training. All claim operations require ongoing training, including both the inexperienced and inexperienced claim staff.

Training and development may include the following:

- Monthly internal training sessions with the claim staff focusing on claim trends developed during the claims quality review process or key areas which have been recognized by management as deficiencies. A claim manager should have a minimum of 2 – 4 hours of departmental training monthly.
- Training conducted by the Human Resource department on assorted topics such as interviewing, performance management, salary administration and supervision.
- Training conducted by external resources such as consultants (or vendors) providing training on effective negotiations, application of comparative negligence, claim supervision and taking recorded statements.
- Training at various industry schools which may provide education on automobile and property estimating, casualty claim handling, etc.
- Training by taking formal educational coursework, including courses leading to an insurance designation such as an *Associate in Claims*[12] (AIC™), *Senior Claim Law Associate* through the American Educational Institute[13] (SCLA) or *Chartered Property Casualty Underwriter*[14] (CPCU®).

## Managing Employee Turnover

Most companies have employee turnover, which may be healthy for an organization if it does not exceed 8% - 10%.

Turnover can seriously impact an organization financially and operationally. Turnover in a claim operation can be critical to the overall financial results of the company. Turnover causes

---

[12] Associate in Claims (AIC™). (American Institute for Chartered Property Casualty Underwriters).
[13] Senior Claim Law Associate (SCLA). (American Educational Institute).
[14] Chartered Property Casualty Underwriter (CPCU®). (American Institute for Chartered Property Casualty Underwriters).

increased workloads with reduced emphasis on quality – case reserves tend to be understated due to lack of detailed quality claim investigations and evaluations. Claim payments may be excessive due to lack of detailed disposition evaluations and the need to reduce the open claim count to reduce workloads to be able to handle the volume of new incoming claims. Customer and regulatory complaints increase with delays in claim handling.

These together will have a negative impact on the loss ratio as claim quality deteriorates with inadequate case reserves and overpayments. LAE will also suffer with the ULAE component being adversely affected with increased costs for recruitment, temporary help and potentially higher salaries being paid to replace critical positions quickly to avoid any material disruption in the claim operation.

So, what causes turnover and how does it get resolved? First, without exception, turnover is a management problem and caused by management decisions and/or company direction.

Employee turnover can be caused by many varied factors, but the factors below are some of the primary causes of turnover:

- **Workloads:** High workloads is a primary cause of turnover – employees want to do a decent job, but if workloads are excessive, claim quality suffers, and employees are overworked creating a stressful and negative work environment. Becoming dissatisfied, employees leave the company for another job – and other employees follow based on positive feedback from the departing employee. The situation worsens when the departing employee's workload is redistributed to the remaining staff until the vacant position can be filled.

> ### What Causes Turnover?
> #### Exhibit 3-H
>
> Employee turnover is caused by management decisions and/or company direction. Unfortunately, turnover may cause more turnover as individual workloads are increased with the redistribution of new and open pending claim activity.
>
> Sometimes the only solution to correct turnover is to intentionally overstaff until staffing becomes stabilized.

- **Compensation and Benefits:** Companies which have competitive salary and benefit packages can retain employees longer creating a more stable workforce. Reducing or eliminating compensation or benefits will also impact turnover. If salary levels are not market-competitive, you will also risk the potential for turnover.

- **Company Stability:** If the financial stability of the company is perceived to be in jeopardy, turnover may occur as employees become concerned with position and job stability. For example, if the company AM Best rating was reduced from an A- to a B, agents may place business with another more financially stable insurance company causing a reduction in premium (revenue) necessitating the need to reduce expenses including staff reductions.

- **Company Direction or Action:** Mergers, acquisitions, and change in products may cause concern with employees relative to company stability.

- **Communication:** Companies which do not communicate effectively with their employees may experience turnover – employees not knowing the future and feeling uneasy about potential problems not being communicated.

- **Work Environment:** A positive work environment, including the condition and location of the physical plant, are important to most employees. A poor work environment will contribute to turnover.

- **Lack of Training & Development:** Employees want training and development to improve their skills and advance in their careers. This includes being reimbursed for external educational programs leading to a degree or an insurance designation. Companies which do not offer training and development risk the potential for employee turnover.

- **Personality Conflicts:** Personality conflicts between employees and management (or other employees) may develop into an aggravated or hostile work environment causing turnover.

- **Lack of Opportunity or Promotion:** Lack of future career opportunities for both advanced technical and managerial positions – including being passed over for a promotion, may cause turnover.

Turnover also has other critical impacts – including a loss of company knowledge, experience and skills which may take years to replace, development of a poor workplace reputation adversely impacting future recruitment efforts, a negative impact on professional relationships with agents and vendors, and overall loss of continuity in the organization.

Turnover has the potential to "breed" more turnover if not properly and timely addressed – which can have a material impact on the organization operationally and financially. It is the claim manager's responsibility to identify the root causes of turnover and work with the human resource department to reverse any trends.

## Compliance & Ethics in Claim Management

Compliance (legal, regulatory, etc.) and ethics in claim management represent a topic beyond the scope of this book; however, we will focus on the critical areas impacting claim managers.

As a claim manager, you will be faced with ethical, moral and legal issues throughout your career – always maintain the utmost integrity and never compromise your integrity to appease others internal or external to the organization. If you are being pushed into a situation you feel uncomfortable with, consult with human resources and/or legal counsel.

As a claim manager, you have a *fiduciary* and *ethical* responsibility in handling and managing claims. Unfortunately, there are industry professionals at all levels who are unethical or lack integrity in the handling of business transactions such as hiding or not disclosing financial or operational mistakes, lack of transparency with the Board of Directors on the financial health of the organization, personal financial gain from business dealings, and asking employees to do things which may be in violation of company procedures, best practices, the law, or insurance regulations.

Your integrity is far more important than breaching your *fiduciary* duty or *ethical* responsibility. If you sense, there is a possibility that the situation is a potential breach of your fiduciary duty or is unethical – it probably is! Rely on your instinct and don't put yourself in a situation which you may regret later. If the situation involves your direct manager, or even an executive, you need to bring it to the attention of the human resource manager, or even corporate counsel if there are potential violations of the law or regulations.

You should never ignore the situation. People can get into trouble by turning their head. Be proactive in making sure the appropriate executives are aware of the situation, and that you are not being pulled into something you will have difficulty explaining later. The situation can be overt in that the issue is obvious to anyone who has knowledge, or subtle in that the situation is moving toward a potential problem. If you are going to report the issue to human resources or corporate counsel, make sure you have all the relevant facts and details including the timeline, any written documentation or evidence, names of witnesses, and documented verbal discussions.

Below are some examples of unethical behavior or potential breaches of fiduciary responsibility:

- Intentionally failing to disclose a catastrophic loss to executive management at year-end to improve your bonus potential.
- Having confidential knowledge of the management team intentionally not disclosing material financial information to the Company Board of Directors, and not taking any action.
- Suppressing claim case reserves to yield more favorable results (e.g. improving the loss ratio) – by intentionally establishing inadequate new case reserves or improperly reducing or closing pending case reserves to improve results.
- Reducing reserves, or paying or not paying a claim, based on a request from another department (e.g. underwriting, general manager, etc.) unless it is warranted, and you agree with it – these types of requests should always be in writing. If you feel uncomfortable with the request, chances are that the request may not be appropriate.

- Agreeing with you manager (at your manager's request) not to report material case reserve deficiency to executive management due to the potential consequences on your manager. This will make you an accomplice and will surely catch up with you later!

- Changing financial transactions in a management report (to make it more favorable) which is going to be included in company financial reporting.

- Entering *quid pro quo* arrangements with a vendor or attorney by promising additional work to the vendor or attorney in exchange for a favor or financial gain (e.g. a weekend trip to Las Vegas, sports season tickets, cash, etc.).

- Being dishonest or unethical with a reinsurer. For example, intentionally applying coverage to a loss which may not be covered to satisfy the agent and/or insured – knowing the reinsurer will pay most of the loss if covered, and not disclosing relevant information and investigation on the coverage issue to the reinsurer.

- Condoning the settlement of bodily injury claims with an unrepresented claimant at a very low amount, knowing the claim has a settlement value at a much higher level – being dishonest and deceitful, and potentially violating the Fair Claim Act.

- Complying with your manager's request to help a friend or relative in a physical damage claim by paying more than warranted or allowed according to company procedures.

- Being dishonest with employees by making promises which can never be fulfilled, to prevent them from leaving the company.

There are sources which can provide guidelines on professional and ethical conduct. The American Institute for Chartered Property Casualty Underwriters publishes a Code of Professional Conduct called *The Canons, Rules, and Guidelines of the CPCU Code of Professional Conduct* (American Institute for Chartered Property Casualty Underwriters) which is a thorough source on professional and ethical conduct. The *Society of Registered Professional Adjusters* also publishes ethics guidelines.

## Chapter Comments

Managing people is not easy and not for everyone! Being an effectively manager is not necessarily measured by your specific technical expertise, but more importantly the ability to motivate your staff in meeting departmental and company objectives, including quality claim handling and outcomes.

Balancing technical claim management and administrative claim management can be a challenging task, particularly when the claim manager has a smaller claim unit. A claim manager can't look at every claim file – in the alternative the claim manager should manage people and selectively review claims and use of a claims quality review process to evaluate claim trends.

Be involved in claim files which require your attention and have the most impact on the company. Extend claim authority to your staff so they can work autonomously handling claims within their level of knowledge and experience.

Adapt a management style which best fits your role in the organization and most effective to achieve the desired objectives. Establish realistic expectations and delegate appropriately. Use claim and litigation handling guidelines, standards and procedures to achieve compliance and consistency in *best practice* claim handling.

Strive to be a leader and communicate effectively – focus on priorities and be strategic. Human resource management is a critical responsibility including performance management and compensation management. If you need training in human resource issues, work with the Human Resource department – they are there to help you.

Above all, be ethical in everything you do in your professional career. Don't let anyone put you in a position which has the potential to tarnish or damage your integrity or reputation. Be cognizant of situations which are, or have the potential to be, unethical, a violation of insurance regulations, or even illegal.

# CHAPTER 4
# MANAGEMENT CONTROLS

## Definition of Management Controls

*Management Controls* are any processes, systems or tasks used to manage, monitor and control business operations, including financial transactions. Without management controls in place there would be no "checks and balances" in the claim operation.

Since the claim operation is involved in many daily financial decisions and transactions, it is critically important that every claim operation have appropriate management controls in place. Management controls will vary by industry, but the primary reason for management controls is universal among all organizations – control of business operations to achieve financial and operational objectives, including maintaining an acceptable level of quality results.

As a claim manager, utilization of *Management Controls* is a key responsibility to ensure consistent quality results, and compliance with company guidelines, standards and procedures.

Management controls will vary by management level and responsibility. Executives have different responsibilities than line management and will also have different management controls. For example, a primary management control for an executive may include monitoring the company profit and loss report, or P&L, to evaluate compliance with the operational budget (variance reporting). In contrast, line management may have multiple management controls revolving around technical claim handling, quality control processes and compliance.

As a claim manager, you cannot and should not look at every claim file; however, the use of management controls allows the claim manager to focus on critical claim areas which require their attention or have the potential to develop into a problem or issue.

> ## Management Controls
> ### Exhibit 4-A
>
> Management controls are any processes, systems or tasks used to manage, monitor and control business operations, including financial transactions.
>
> Without management controls in place there would be no "checks and balances" in the claim operation.
>
> Management controls can be *formal* and used daily, weekly, or monthly; or *informal* used on an ad-hoc basis in a special project or upon request.

Management controls often prevent problems or issues from developing just by being in place. For example, maintaining a *Lawsuit Log* requiring the tracking of new incoming lawsuit activity, and the details of the referral to defense counsel, provides a management control to avoid any potential default judgment.

The measurement of the management control's effectiveness is that by being in place, it avoided a mistake or problem which could have adversely impacted the company, either financially or operationally.

Management controls can be deployed using various formats including:

- Process and workflow controls (e.g. approval processes, validation stages, authority levels, etc.).
- Metrics reporting (e.g. average paid loss and expense, average reserves, contact times, average lost time days, and appraisal assignment date to inspection date, etc.).
- Dashboard reporting (e.g. claim trending, claim volume, workload balancing, and productivity reporting).
- *Quality Review Process* (e.g. quality review programs, reinspection programs, etc.).
- Management reports (e.g. loss runs, productivity and workload management reports, departmental P&L budget variance report, large loss reports, etc.).
- Diary management controls (e.g. mandated diary review dates and system generated diary dates at specified intervals).
- System-based *business rules* which trigger action or the need for action by an adjuster or manager (e.g. claim payment or reserve above the adjuster's authority will be referred to the managers work queue for approval, large loss report trigger, etc.).
- Random review of various claim processes such as incoming mail processing and attributing, scanning and document management, checking printing, FNOL, outgoing correspondence (e.g. adjuster letters and claim forms), error reports, new claims set up, etc.

Generally, management controls for a claim manager will include routine tasks performed on a daily, weekly and monthly basis, including monitoring and controlling the outcome of special projects. Management controls are essential and an integral part of the claim manager's routine job responsibilities.

Unfortunately, some claim managers choose to ignore fundamental management controls, or only use those controls which are required for a transaction to be finalized (e.g. payment and reserve approval) – potentially resulting in adjuster errors or an operational failure depending on the severity of the issue.

For example, the following could occur if management controls were not in place:

- Exceeding authority on payments or reserve transactions.
- Inadvertently, letting a lawsuit go into default by not tracking the suit answer due date and filing a timely response pleading or answer (in some states this could have a significant financial-impact if the *default judgment* cannot be vacated).

- An improperly written and unapproved coverage position letter sent to the insured which waived certain rights under the policy increasing the company's exposure.
- Failure to properly dual diary a complex and serious loss which resulted in the claim being mishandled by the adjuster.
- A late reserve adjustment and large loss report to management.
- Decline in the quality of claim handling by not conducting periodic file reviews. Routine quality file reviews on each adjuster monitor technical claim performance by focusing on claim trends, positive and negative. Failing to conduct routine quality claim reviews can result in poor-quality claim handling financially impacting the company.

Some managers may develop their own management control as a method to check work or avoid a mistake. The key in developing and implementing a management control is to make sure the control is needed and that it addresses the underlying issue. For example, you have an adjuster who is always late on diary and recently had a late large loss report (and late new reserve) – causing you embarrassment with senior management. You immediately implement a new management control by having your dual diary automatically placed on <u>all</u> bodily injury claims at the 15-day period, in addition to your 30-day management diary – for all adjusters.

Due to this action, you increased your management oversight workload by having to look at all adjuster diaries at the 15-day period, when you should be addressing the problem with the individual offending adjuster with implementation of a performance plan to correct the late diary management problem.

It makes sense to look at management controls to confirm that the control is effective and necessary. If the management control is no longer necessary or ineffective then eliminate it. Some management controls will have developed over time and may have served a purpose in the past when the transactions or claim tasks were performed manually but may now be ineffective and outdated (particularly with a modern architecture claim system). Eliminate the management control and if it is required by your manager, meet with your manager to discuss why you want to eliminate it (e.g. waste of your management resources).

Included in this chapter are examples of *Management Controls*. The management controls reviewed below are not all inclusive – there are other management controls developed by managers in a claim operation.

## New Claim Assignment

The new claim assignment initiates the claim process and starts with the first report to the claim department which may be referred to as the *First Notice of Loss* (FNOL) or in workers' compensation, a *First Report of Injury* (FROI). Both reports provide initial accident or incident details to allow the claim department to establish a file record, an initial case reserve and acknowledgement to the parties to the claim (e.g. insured, claimant, agent, etc.).

The first notice of claim is the initial point in the claim process which provides the claim manager with an opportunity to review the claim details for complexity and severity, coverage issues, any special claim handling requirements, assignment level based on experience, and the specific adjuster to be assigned to handle the claim. This would be considered the first management control in the claim process as it provides the claim manager with initial notification of the claim and the basis for a decision as to whether the claim will be diaried by the claim manager for follow-up review or oversight.

Newer claim systems have automated the new claim assignment process including the development of business rules to identify claims which require review and diary by the claim manager, automatically setting a management diary for the day after the claim has been set up and assigned to the adjuster (and other future diary dates). The types of claims reviewed by the claim manager will depend on the operation but may generally include claims with complexity and severity (e.g. serious injury or fatality), coverage issues, litigation claims, total losses, etc.

## **Claim Authority**

*Claim authority* is the primary management control in a claim operation. Claim authority levels should be well documented, recorded with the Human Resource department, and provided to the adjuster in writing. The claim system should have the appropriate security levels (and controls in place) to preclude any claim transaction which exceeds the adjusters claim authority level either based on an individual claim transaction or in the aggregate (or both).

Claim authority may be based on an individual claim exposure (e.g. BI, PD, PIP, etc.), on an incurred activity level (reserves + payments – recoveries), or on a claim aggregate level (e.g. one claim event).

A claim operation will have system security-controlled claim authority levels which prevent the adjuster from exceeding the authority level without supervisory intervention and approval. Many claim systems will automatically refer any claim transaction above the adjuster's authority to the next level of direct supervision for approval using a work queue and designated activity with a diary date.

The claim authority control process allows for the layering of authority levels by claim position or role. For example, a payment transaction of $200,000 may require several authority levels for final approval of the payment. The handling adjuster may have payment approval authority of $50,000. The adjuster enters the claim payable and provides the initial approval of the claim transaction. Thereafter, the $200,000 payment transaction will be referred to the first management level which may have $150,000 in authority. This referral may be in the form of an email or internal to the claim system by having the claim payment transaction automatically referred to the first level manager in a work queue with an activity.

After the first management level approves the payment transaction of $200,000, the payment transaction will then be referred to the next management level (e.g. $500,000 and over authority) for final approval to release the payment or payable at $200,000. It should be noted that the claim manager would have already extended claim authority within the claim file electronic notes prior to the adjuster's preparation of the payment or payable.

Authority levels include loss and allocated loss adjustment expense (ALAE) and pertain to reserve transactions, payable approval process, check signing and settlement dispositions. Adjusters should be required to work within their designated claim authority working autonomously and claim managers should not be required to "dual diary" most claims within the adjuster's authority. See comments below under *Management Dual Diary*.

In the claim authority structure the adjuster handles and manages claims within their designated claim authority without active supervision by the claim manager. The claim authority and diary by the claim manager should be based on the *gross value* of the claim and not the *net value* (e.g. in a liability claim the amount offset by comparative negligence and other contribution). The claim manager should supervise all claims over the adjuster's claim authority (based on the *gross value* of claim) and claims within the adjuster's authority which require supervision such as coverage issues, unusual or complex exposures, potential fraud, or litigation claims (if the adjuster is not a *litigation specialist*).

All reserve adjustments and payments over the adjusters claim authority should require the claim manager's approval which also provides an opportunity for the claim manager to review the claim and add their dual diary, if necessary. It also allows the claim manager to extend claim authority to the adjuster above the adjuster's authority (e.g. settlement authority) fostering an environment wherein the claim manager is delegating authority to the adjuster. The ideal claim operational structure is to extend claim authority to each adjuster (or claim role) which is based on the adjuster's level of knowledge and experience.

If a claim exceeds the adjuster's claim authority and is being handled properly, the claim manager should consider allowing the adjuster to handle the claim on their own without active supervision. This is called a charge back – the manager *charges back* the claim to the adjuster with specific instructions. The instructions should be documented in the electronic notes and may include comments such as: "*I am charging this claim back to you for direct handling. Please refer the claim back to me if the liability and/or damage exposure, or current claim assessment changes. You have up to the current reserve amount of $50,000 as authority to settle this claim. Thank you.*"

Claim authority is a critical management control in that it provides the basis for authority for financial transactions and/or claim dispositions. Having levels of claim authority within an organization provides control of loss and expense transactions which impact the Company's financial results. By limiting claim authority to certain levels in the organization based on organizational role or position, claim authority provides a controlled and structured financial security level, precluding any claim transaction above the employee's claim authority.

Claim authority levels vary by organization and line of business. The key to developing an effective claim authority structure is to have documented claim authority levels by organizational role or position; and the ability to modify claim authority for specific individuals, if appropriate.

**Exhibit 4-B** illustrates an example of claim authority levels in a claim organization. In this authority structure the claim authority to approve a claim payable or enter a reserve transaction is limited to the designated authority, which in this illustration is the same for reserve, payable approval and settlement authority. Claim organizations may designate different claim authority levels for reserves, settlement, and payable approval transactions, and may also include authority levels for ALAE, which is an effective method to control expense costs.

| Claim Authority Levels: Exhibit 4-B | | | | |
|---|---|---|---|---|
| Role or Position | Claim Authority | | | |
| | Reserve | Payables | Settlement | ALAE |
| Adjuster I | $10,000 | $10,000 | $10,000 | $2,000 |
| Adjuster II | $20,000 | $20,000 | $20,000 | $5,000 |
| Adjuster III | $40,000 | $40,000 | $40,000 | $10,000 |
| Claim Specialist | $75,000 | $75,000 | $75,000 | $25,000 |
| Claim Manager | $150,000 | $150,000 | $150,000 | $75,000 |
| Regional Claim Manager | $250,000 | $250,000 | $250,000 | $150,000 |
| Vice President of Claims | $1,000,000 | $1,000,000 | $1,000,000 | $1,000,000 |

Authority for claim transactions above the adjuster's authority level are referred to their direct report manager for approval and then the next management level for approval depending on the dollar level of the transaction.

During the claim process, the adjuster will request approval for various claim transactions which exceed their individual claim authority. Examples of these transactions are outlined below.

## Reserve Approval

Reserve approval involves a request for approval to enter a reserve transaction above the adjuster's claim authority – either as a new reserve or reserve adjustment. This process may involve the adjuster requesting approval via email, electronic note or with an automatic approval request using a work queue referral and activity process in a modern architecture claim system. The claim manager should use this process as an opportunity to provide substantive feedback to the adjuster on the reserve request, claim evaluation and overall claim handling.

The claim manager should always require the adjuster to provide a detailed basis for the reserve request inclusive of an analysis of liability and damages (if applicable), and the reason for the reserve change. For example, if an adjuster is requesting approval to increase a case reserve from $50,000 to $100,000, a brief analysis should accompany the request including an evaluation of the damages (gross value), the basis for liability (as a percentage), and the projected net value of the claim. The reason for the reserve adjustment should also be included (e.g. new medical report received indicating surgery or a new witness discovered changing the liability analysis). If the reserve adjustment is not timely (e.g. reserve not adjusted within 30 days of the change in exposure), an explanation should be included.

A *reserve evaluation worksheet* (either as a form or claim system screen) is an excellent tool to provide relevant details for a new reserve and reserve adjustments in all lines of business. See **Chapter 2** which includes sample claim evaluation formats.

In workers' compensation claim handling, a *reserve evaluation worksheet* includes an itemization of the projected costs for indemnity or compensation (e.g. TTD, TPD, PPD, etc.) and medical related costs (e.g. physician, surgery, hospital, diagnostic, therapy, prescriptions, etc.).

For reserve purposes on liability claims, the claim manager may require the adjuster to use the *gross value* of the claim as the basis for authority over the adjuster's claim authority – or in seeking authority for settlement disposition purposes. For example, the adjuster who has claim authority at $50,000 may be precluded from adjusting a claim reserve from $25,000 to $50,000 if the *gross value* (without offset for comparative negligence or contribution from others) of the claim is $100,000, even though the reserve transaction (increase) is within the adjuster's authority level. This is an effective management control to avoid serious or complex exposure claims from being handled by the adjuster (at a reserve level within the adjuster's authority level) without supervision or management oversight. However, it may be difficult to control these transactions as some claim systems may not be able to track the gross claim value.

When *allocated loss adjustment expenses* (ALAE) are reserved as an expense case reserve, the adjuster should provide a detailed and documented explanation for the requested adjustment. If the claim is pending in litigation, a detailed *litigation budget* by defense counsel is helpful to support the adjustment, particularly material expense reserve adjustments.

As a claim manager, you have the responsibility to approve claim reserves and must avoid both *reserve redundancy* (too much reserve) and *reserve deficiency* (not enough reserve) – both potentially having a negative financial-impact on the company. Proposed reserve transactions which may be redundant or deficient should not be approved – and may require further discussion with the adjuster as a training opportunity.

The reserve approval process should also include an evaluation and comment on whether the adjuster is "step-ladder" reserving – incremental reserve increases over time to accommodate payments, instead of a proper and timely reserve for the *life of the claim* based on the known facts. "Step-ladder" reserving contributes to reserve deficiency.

Some claim managers may avoid reserve reductions or not process reserves timely. Reserve reductions, when warranted, prevent reserve redundancy and should be processed timely. Over-reserving adversely affects financial results and should be avoided.

It is important to note that certain case reserves have subjective components such as bodily injury case reserves involving general damages (e.g. pain and suffering, permanency, etc.). Therefore, it may be difficult to establish precise reserves on the claim. When providing a claim evaluation, a recommended reserve *range* may be helpful in arriving at the final recommended bodily injury reserve. This also helps close the gap in minor differences of opinion in the claim evaluation. For example, the adjuster may have evaluated the claim at $50,000 with the claim manager's evaluation at $60,000. Perhaps a $55,000 reserve may be appropriate.

Claim reserving is both an *art* and a *science*. There may be a difference of opinion in establishing certain types of case reserves such as bodily injury reserves. For example, an adjuster and claim manager may recommend the same bodily injury claim reserve at $30,000 but both have a different liability and damage analysis. To illustrate, the adjuster may have evaluated the gross value of the claim at $40,000 with liability assessment at 75%, resulting in a *net* recommended reserve at $30,000. The claim manager may have evaluated the gross value the claim at $45,000 with a liability assessment at 65%, resulting in a *net* recommended reserve of $29,250. Both net recommended reserves are basically the same; however, the damage and liability assessments are different. When these differences in evaluations occur, it presents an opportunity for the claim manager to discuss the adjuster's thought process in their evaluation and share their own thought process as a training opportunity.

## Settlement Approval

Settlement approval involves a request for authority to settle a claim above the adjuster's claim authority. This process may involve the adjuster requesting authority via email, using an electronic file note, or meeting with the claim manager to discuss the claim details. It is important to utilize a settlement evaluation form or screen to document the basis for the settlement evaluation, with documented approval by the claim manager.

The claim manager should use this process as an opportunity to provide substantive feedback to the adjuster on the authority request, claim evaluation and overall claim handling. As in the reserve evaluation process, the claim manager should always require the adjuster to provide a detailed basis for the settlement approval request inclusive of an analysis of the claim in terms of liability and damages (if applicable).

Settlement authority should always be documented in the claim file record. To evaluate the effectiveness of negotiations, and provide some flexibility in the settlement discussions, the claim manager should extend settlement authority using a range. For example, if the claim value is about $25,000, the claim manager may want to extend settlement authority in the $22,500 – 27,500 range. This provides some negotiation flexibility for the adjuster and an opportunity for the claim manager to evaluate the adjuster's negotiation skills

## Payable or Check Approval

The adjuster will request payment approval by preparing the check or payable using a check request form or within a payable entry screen in the claim system, or integrated check issuance module.

Payments or payables within the adjuster's claim authority may be released without claim manager co-approval. Releasing payables (or checks) above the adjuster's claim authority requires approval by the claim manager (for both loss or expense). This process may involve the adjuster requesting approval via email (for the claim manager to take action) or with an automatic approval request using a work queue and activity referral process in a modern architecture claim system – as indicated in the reserve approval process above.

The adjuster would have received approval for the transaction prior to the request to approve the payable, which would be documented in an electronic note in the claim file (e.g. settlement authority). Comments from the claim manager may have included substantive feedback to the adjuster on the request, the claim evaluation and overall claim handling.

# Management Dual Diary

The claim manager maintains a dual diary on the adjuster's claim to monitor its progress and provide substantive supervision and direction. The time span between diary dates and the duration of the diary will depend on the type of claim, complexity and its overall exposure.

Dual diary by the claim manager may be used to monitor claims above the adjuster's claim authority (e.g. *gross exposure* of the claim) and claims within the adjuster's claim authority meeting specific criteria such as claims pending in litigation, coverage issues, potential fraud and claim handling complaints.

Management *dual diary* is a tool used by the claim manager to monitor the progress of the claim and provide substantive supervision when warranted. Supervision can be in the form of written communication by the claim manager to the adjuster or a documented discussion between the adjuster and claim manager recorded in the electronic file notes by the adjuster. A claim manager may also want to delegate claim authority above the adjuster's authority with specific instructions and then remove their dual diary (e.g. charge back).

Management dual diary does not mean that every diary review date requires comments by the claim manager; however, when action is required, the claim manager must provide relevant comment and instruction. If the claim manager requires periodic *action plans* by the adjuster, the management diary review is an easier process. Action plans include a brief description of the claim, analysis and evaluation, reserve comment, what has been accomplished and what needs to be done. It provides a quick analysis and update on the claim and used by the claim manager to determine whether the claim is on the right track or requires further management input.

An *Action Plan* commonly referred to as a *Plan of Action* or *POA* should be required at various intervals in the claim process and include relevant details such as:

## Liability Claim Action Plan

- Coverage
- Facts of Accident
- Liability Analysis
- Damage Evaluation
- Third Party Involvement
- Investigation Completed & Outstanding
- Litigation Status
- Settlement Evaluation (Settlement Discussions)
- Reserve Analysis
- Next Steps

## Property Claim Action Plan

- Coverage
- Facts of Loss
- Cause Determination
- Scope of Damages
- Damage Estimate
- Subrogation
- Use of Experts (e.g. construction or building consultant, engineer, cause & origin, etc.)
- Investigation & Adjustment Activities Completed & Outstanding
- Reserve Analysis
- Next Steps

## Workers' Compensation Action Plan

- Coverage
- Facts of Accident
- Compensability Issues (Course and Scope of Employment)
- Injuries (Diagnosis, Prognosis and Treatment)
- Disability Management (RTW plan & disability status, availability of light or modified duty, etc.)
- Current WC Rate, AWW and Classification (e.g. TTD, TPD, PPD, etc.)
- Medical Management (IME, NCM, UR, VR, etc.)

- Investigation Completed & Outstanding
- Subrogation
- Litigation Status
- Settlement Evaluation
- Reserve Analysis
- Next Steps

Management dual diaries can be established automatically at certain intervals in the claim process or manually by the claim manager. System generated manager diaries may include a diary date at critical intervals such as:

- 15 days to evaluate the progress of the initial investigation or adjustment process, and a determination of exposure.
- 30 days to evaluate the initial investigation or adjustment process and adequacy of the current case reserves, as well as review of the adjuster's *Action Plan.*
- 45 days to evaluate to evaluate the initial investigation or adjustment process and adequacy of the current case reserves, as well as follow-up review of the adjuster's *Action Plan.*
- 90 days to evaluate completion of outstanding elements of the claim investigation or adjustment process, adequacy of the current case reserves, and review of the current *Action Plan.*
- 180 days to evaluate file direction and adequacy of the current case reserves.

## Adjuster – Claim Manager Discussion

In most claim operations, there is an ongoing dialogue between the adjuster and claim manager relative to technical claim and non-claim issues. Technical claim issues involve adjuster-claim manager discussions on specific claims which may include discussion around coverage, reserving, evaluation (liability/compensability and damages), investigation and case strategy.

As a claim manager, you want to be sure all relevant discussions involving technical claim issues are posted to the electronic file notes, if appropriate. For example, if the claim manager had a detailed discussion with the adjuster concerning the analysis and evaluation of a bodily injury liability claim, the specific details of that discussion should be documented in the claim file, preferably by the handling adjuster. Discussions which are not documented, cannot be verified or reviewed later, if necessary.

The documented discussion between the adjuster and claim manager serve as a control to document claim manager instructions. When the claim manager reviews the claim on diary, electronic file notes documenting the previous discussion between the adjuster and claim manager will be helpful in providing further file direction.

The claim manager may also want to specifically document the claim file concerning the discussion, if necessary, particularly if you have determined that the adjuster has not documented prior discussions.

## Management by "Walking Around"

It is important for the claim manager to be visible in the department by "walking around". Getting out of your office and being visible creates a more positive and team-oriented work environment. As a manager, you don't need to spend hours walking around your department, but routine visits to the adjuster's work area provides for more adjuster engagement, including social engagement. It allows the claim manager to participate in group discussion and gain a better understanding of the dynamics within the business unit. It also provides an opportunity to listen to adjusters on the telephone, including taking statements, to evaluate customer service and investigation proficiency.

Although this would be considered an informal management control, it is necessary and should be a part of a claim manager's daily routine. A word of caution, it is recommended that you do not use this type of activity to berate or criticize adjusters in front of their peers (e.g. praise in public and criticize in private); however, it is a perfect opportunity to publicly congratulate an adjuster for a job well done.

Some managers have used this activity inappropriately. For example, it is not recommended that the claim manager engage in the same discussion every time you visit an adjuster's work area or ask the same questions to each adjuster you visit. Be sincere in your interactions with your subordinates – you will get a much better result.

## Approval of Claim Denials

Depending on the line of business, claim managers may want to approve claim denials. For example, in workers' compensation claims the claim manager may want to review all claims with a compensability denial recommendation. This is prudent in that you may lose control when denying the claim and incur legal costs for workers' compensation hearings or protracted litigation.

Claim managers may also want to approve liability claim denials involving claims which exceed the adjuster's authority level. Generally, claim denials with attorney represented claimants will result in litigation which is costly. A fresh look at the claim may result in a sharp compromise to avoid costly litigation.

## Approval of Coverage Position

Coverage issues may be known at the time of the initial claim report or may develop during the claim investigation or adjustment process. Claims which involve coverage issues may range from policy exceptions, exclusions, definitions and conditions to policy violations. The complexity and severity of the claim and coverage issue will determine whether a claim manager will become involved or monitor the claim.

Coverage related issues should be handled properly and timely. Any delays in handling coverage issues may result in a situation wherein the company will have waived its rights under the policy if it took too long to respond or take a firm coverage position. This is referred to as "waiver and estoppel" and could result in having to accept the financial-impact of a claim which is not covered or only partially covered under the policy. Therefore, it is imperative that the claim manager have a short dual diary on claims which involve complex coverage issues.

When a claim manager follows a claim, which has a coverage issue, the claim manager will provide file input and direction, and approve the coverage position letter. As a manager, you should request that the adjuster prepare the *draft* coverage position letter for your review and approval (if the letter is not prepared by coverage counsel). This provides an opportunity to evaluate the adjuster's knowledge of coverage issues and writing skills. The claim manager can review the draft letter and make any necessary changes prior to the letter being released. If the coverage position is being documented in a *non-waiver agreement*, the claim manager would only need to be involved in reviewing the non-waiver agreement if it deviates from the established company approved format or includes custom language.

In some claim operations, coverage issues may trigger the need to report the claim to the home office claim operation, or a reinsurer. This may be done by the adjuster with a copy of the transmittal notice (e.g. email or report) to the claim manager or sent directly by the claim manager for review and transmittal to the home office claim operation or reinsurer.

Approval of coverage letters, as a management control, is an example of managing those areas which may have a critical impact on the claim operation and company.

## Periodic File Reporting

Periodic file reporting is fundamental to any claim operation. As a claim manager, file reporting is a critical management control – with the expectation that periodic file reporting by the adjuster is required at various intervals in the claim process, including referral of the report to the claim manager for review and comment.

We use file reporting to outline the facts of the claim, the details of the claim investigation and adjustment process, liability or compensability analysis, damage evaluation, reserve or settlement recommendations, what has been accomplished to date and what needs to be done. Periodic file reporting may include all the above, or just several reporting elements depending on the timing and reason for the reporting.

File reporting can be facilitated using an electronic claim form, memo, email, electronic file notes, claim screen, or an uploaded document. With the advancement of modern architecture claim systems, file reporting has been incorporated into the electronic claim file using fillable web-based forms, or screens for ease of entry. Many of the forms are prefilled with relevant claim file information with the ability to add various fields and free-form notes.

The adjuster will prepare status reports or claim file reporting at various intervals in the claim process based on the type of claim, complexity and severity including the extent of the damages (e.g. injury or property damage), the stage in the claim process, the incurred amount level, how long the claim has been open, and whether the claim qualifies for home office reporting.

Examples of periodic status reports include:

- 15-day and 30-day investigation reports
- Action Plans
- Captioned claim reports
- Case analysis reports
- Home office referral reports
- 30, 60, 90 and 180-day reserve reviews
- Settlement authority requests
- Reserve adjustment authority requests
- Excess carrier reporting
- Reinsurance reporting
- Pretrial reporting
- Trial reporting
- Closing reports

The claim manager will review the adjuster's reports to monitor the quality of the adjuster's work product, provide substantive claim supervision and direction, review a specific issue, and/or approve a reserve or payment transaction.

# Large Loss Review

*Large Loss Reports* (LLRs) are prepared by an adjuster based on the complexity and severity (e.g. injuries and damages) of the claim and the reserve and/or incurred claim activity level. The incurred claim activity reporting level for large losses will vary by company and may be in the $100,000 to $300,000 range, depending on the claim office authority level. Large loss reports are prepared on newly reported claims with new reserves and on existing claims which require a reserve adjustment or need to be reopened. Sometimes large loss reports may be needed for settlement authority requests.

Large loss reporting is critical to the claim operation and a shared responsibility between the adjuster and claim manager, with the claim manager being ultimately responsible. The reports must be timely and completed properly as the reports are distributed to the Vice President of

Claims, Vice President of Underwriting and other company executives. If the reserve entry or adjustment, or report, is late and should have been completed sooner, it is the claim manager's responsibility to provide an explanatory note on the report or cover note (email).

The adjuster completes the required large loss reporting and uploads the report to the electronic claim file for review and approval by the claim manager. The claim manager reviews the large loss report and adjuster recommendations; and provides substantive supervision and direction when warranted. The large loss report is then transmitted to the next claim management level for review, if applicable, or distributed to the designated large loss report recipients.

Large loss reports are prepared using different formats including email entry forms, electronic forms generated from the claim system, or as an uploaded document (e.g. Word®, Excel® or pdf).

The large loss report will include at minimum the information included in **Exhibit 4-C** below.

| Large Loss Report Content: Exhibit 4-C | | | |
|---|---|---|---|
| Claim Number | Policy Number | Effective Dates | Agent/Broker |
| Date of Loss | Date Reported | Claim Manager | Adjuster |
| Line of Business | Class of Business | Claim Type/Exposure | Claim Status |
| Insured Name | Claimant Name | State of Loss | Litigation – Y/N |
| Facts of Loss | Third Parties | Defense Counsel | Suit Venue/Jurisdiction |
| Coverage Analysis | Liability Analysis | Damage Evaluation | Recovery/Contribution |
| Items Completed | Items Outstanding | Recommendations | Settlement Discussions |
| Outstanding Reserves | Paid Loss | Paid Expense | New Reserves |

Large loss reports are important to other departments particularly the underwriting department. Underwriters use the large loss report to reevaluate the risk, determine if there were any unknown or unexpected hazards which may have contributed to the loss, and whether the risk should have been written by the underwriter. The underwriter may be required to prepare an additional underwriting risk report upon receipt of a large loss report. Executive management uses large loss reports to gauge severity and its impact on the loss ratio – the reports may be used as the basis to validate any fluctuations in the loss ratio caused by large losses.

Since the large loss reports are reporting high financial-impact losses, it is important to remember that company executives are reading the content of the reports – including the adjuster and manager's names. The reports should be accurate, have no typos and be timely. Submitting poor quality large loss reports is a reflection on the claim manager and their ability to communicate effectively.

Large loss reporting is a management control not only for the claim manager but also for claim executives, as well as other executives in the organization. As a claim manager, you should emphasize with your staff that large loss reporting is a critical claim function which should be timely, accurate and professionally prepared. A claim manager should always have knowledge of pending large losses within the department – when meeting with the Vice President of Claims or executive management, the claim manager may be questioned on the details of these losses.

# Claim Committee Review

Claim committees (sometimes referred to as "round-tables") are used to discuss claims in a small group comprised of claim and non-claim staff. The group may include the handling adjuster, the claim manager, and other claim department personnel. Non-claim staff such as underwriters or other departmental managers may be invited for observation and input. On high value claims, the home office staff, or the Vice President of Claims may also participate in the committee meeting.

The handling adjuster prepares a claim committee summary report (or uses the completed large loss report) and presents the claim evaluation to the claim committee. The purpose of the claim committee is to gain insight into liability/compensability and damage issues as a group to assist in establishing case values for purpose of reserves and authorizing settlement.

It is important to establish the claim committee's purpose and guidelines. The purpose of the claim committee is <u>not</u> to take a vote on the recommended reserve or settlement amount based on an "average" value recommended by all participants in the meeting. The purpose of the committee meeting is to discuss and review the claim in terms of its facts, liability/compensability, damages, and recommendations as a group so that the claim manager can gain input and make a final decision on the next steps.

The claim manager takes into consideration the group's comments and recommendations but has the ultimate responsibility to make sure the claim is evaluated properly (reserve and settlement recommendations).

By participating in the claim committee meeting the other adjusters and non-claim personnel gain valuable insight into the claim handling and evaluation process.

The use of claim committee reviews is a good management control in that it highlights the details of existing large losses or high exposure claims within the department, providing the claim manager with information on highly visible claims. It also allows the claim manager to decide whether the current handling adjuster has the knowledge and expertise to handle the claim, and any necessary follow-up by the claim manager.

# Management Reports & Analytics Tools

The use of claim management reports and analytics tools should be fundamental to any claim operation and utilized as an important management control for the claim manager. The types of management reports and analytics tools used by management will depend on the size of the claim operation, and the systems architecture, its functionality, and the availability of a data warehouse with reporting tools.

It is important to note that claim management reports and analytics reports may only point to a potential problem or issue, which may only be found within the claim files.

Management reports and analytics tools may come in a variety of types and formats, and may include but not limited to:

- Hard copy or *pdf* reports provided at various intervals (e.g. monthly or quarterly) by the IT department using legacy systems. These reports are published and distributed at the closing of specific financial periods and may not provide real time information as there will be a time lag.

- Real-time reports from a *data warehouse* or other data source allowing for comprehensive data analysis. These reports may be preformatted and provided to the claim manager automatically at various intervals, or *ad hoc* and available in an Excel® format allowing for the use of *pivot tables* and other analysis tools.

- *Dashboard Reports* and *Scorecards* provide a summary of key performance indicators (KPIs) used by the claim operation. The data for these key metrics are derived from the claim system and/or data warehouse. Metrics may include high-level claim productivity data (e.g. new claims, transferred claims, open claims, reopen claims, closed claims and closing ratio); average case lifespan by line of business and exposure; loss and expense incurred totals by exposure and claim type; average transactions such as average reserves and average payments (loss and expense); incurred losses by dollar value range; total ALAE expense categories such as *adjuster*, *appraiser*, *legal* and *expert*; large losses; catastrophe claims, etc. The dashboard may include a hyperlink to view (drill-down) the claim detail behind the KPI analysis, with the ability to filter or sort the data to show different views by adjuster, unit, department and company.

- Claim system reports which provide data directly from the claim system. The claim system will provide basic reports which are included in the claim module. These reports provide information included in various fields within the claim system, including operational data and financial transactions. The benefit of using these reports is that they are easily accessible, reported in "real-time", and provide important claim information. An example of a claim system report may include a *suit log report* tracking incoming and outgoing lawsuit activity.

Management reports are based on financial or operational data. *Financial* reports are management reports which include the reporting or analysis of claim transactions, ratios or metrics. These reports are used by the claim manager to monitor claim transactional activity and financial ratios which have an impact on the company. Financial reports also include P & L operational budget reports providing monthly variance reporting.

*Operational* reports are management reports which include the reporting or analysis of claim operational data used by claim management to monitor claim activity. For example, workload management and productivity reports – a tool to manage adjuster workloads and analyze productivity. Cycle time reports are also operational reports and may include an analysis of cycle times involving the date of the accident report to the first contact, the date of appraisal assignment to inspection, as well as average lost time days in workers' compensation claims.

**Chapter 9 – Claim Management Reports** provides a broad overview of typical claim management reports available in a claim operation.

# Claim Logs

Prior to the use of modern architecture claim systems and reporting platforms, the use of various logs was an important management control in the claim operation. These logs were retained in various formats including handwritten notes, Excel®-based reports and Word® documents.

With the advancement of new claim systems and reporting, these logs have either been eliminated and replaced by management reports or included as a screen or report in the claim system.

Examples of logs which may be used in the claim operation include:

- *Suit Log* which monitors new lawsuit activity including the date the suit was received, and the date referred to defense counsel.
- *Complaint Log* which records incoming service complaints including Department of Insurance complaints, the date the complaint was filed, the resolution date and resolution details.
- Some companies may also have a *Coverage Disclaimer Log* which records claim details involving coverage position letters issued on claims.
- *Salvage Logs* which record automobile salvage referred to a salvage facility and expected salvage proceeds with expense.
- *Third Party Deductible* log which tracks liability deductible billing and recoverables.

Many logs previously used in claim operations have been eliminated or replaced with system generated reports.

# Claims Quality Review Process

The *Claims Quality Review Process* establishes organizational expectations for the level of claim quality required in a claim operation. It provides the necessary tools to manage and control the most critical aspect of a claim operation – technical claim handling.

This process is directly handled by the claim manager to review a select number of claim files per month, per claim employee, to identify and evaluate claim handling trends – positive and negative – and to enhance the effectiveness of the claim operation. The process also provides the employee with monthly constructive feedback enhancing communication between the adjuster and claim manager on technical performance issues – identifying strengths and weaknesses by claim employee, unit, office and organization.

**Chapter 6 – Claims Quality Review Process** provides a broad overview of the claims quality review process, including a discussion on the various claims quality review *best practice* categories and recommended formats.

# Productivity & Workload Management Reports

Productivity and workload management reports provide critical information on adjuster workloads and production. These reports are utilized by the claim manager to evaluate workloads, adjuster productivity and staffing requirements.

As a claim manager, productivity and workload management reports are used as a daily management control to monitor adjuster assignments and productivity. Depending on the claim system utilized, productivity and workload management reports can be a very effective tool in managing the claim operation.

Proper management of adjuster workloads is critical to a claim operation and the quality of the work product produced by each adjuster. Adjusters with high pending workloads and excessive new assignments, will ultimately produce a poor-quality work product, including poor-quality investigations, inadequate case reserves, claim overpayments, customer service complaints and contribute to employee turnover.

It is important to establish workload standards for the claim operation including open pending claims, new claim assignments and closing ratios. This information will be critical in preparing a staffing analysis report.

**Chapter 7 – Staffing and Resource Management**, discusses appropriate staffing and workloads to achieve an optimum level of quality results and customer service.

# Profit & Loss Budget Report

The profit and loss or *P&L Report* is used to monitor financial budgetary performance (ULAE expense). The report will include all claim expense budget lines such as salary, benefits, travel and entertainment, automobile, education, licensing, etc. – comparing the actual expenses against budgeted expenses on a monthly and year-to-date basis, displaying variance reporting as a dollar value and as a percentage achieved.

At minimum, the claim manager should receive a copy of the operational budget variance report monthly for their area of responsibility. This report is an important management control for ULAE expenses. As a claim manager it is your responsibility to review the P&L variance report monthly to identify areas which require your attention. You may also be required to report to your manager with comments on category variances.

Operational budgets, including variance reporting, was discussed in detail in **Chapter 2 – Financial Operations**.

## Use of System Business Rules

The use of system-based *business rules* has increased substantially with the use of modern architecture claim systems.

Business rules are automated activities created to improve efficiency which may be used as a financial or operational control. A business rule may trigger some type of specific action, or the need for action by an adjuster or manager. Examples of *business rules* may include:

- All claim payments above the adjuster's authority level will be referred to the claim manager's work queue for approval.
- All losses over $250,000 will trigger an email to a designated list of recipients as a reminder to complete a large loss report or reinsurance advice.
- When certain claim attributes are included in the claim record such as potential fraud indicators or "red flags" the claim will be automatically referred to the SIU manager via email.
- If the incurred claim activity exceeds a certain dollar threshold, a claim manager diary will be automatically added.
- The claim system will automatically assign new losses and balance workloads based on predetermined criteria using business rules.

Manual tasks or tasks which involve several systems, may be improved by using system business rules to enhance efficiency and productivity. Business rules are programmable at the user and system level. The critical importance of business rules is that you eliminate any manual intervention and the potential to cause an error or mistake.

## Use of Microsoft® Applications

We mention the use of Microsoft® Applications (e.g. Outlook®, Excel®, OneNote®, SharePoint®, etc.) since most companies utilize these software applications during the normal course of business.

We sometimes take these applications for granted, but they all have functionality which can be used as a management control or provide support for the management controls we use.

As a claim manager, these applications may be helpful in monitoring and controlling the claim operation by using these applications in conjunction with other systems or tools.

Excel® is a very powerful tool to analyze data using *pivot tables* and other reporting tools. If you only have minimal knowledge of this application, ask the human resource department if there is any Excel® training available. It will be worth your time to increase your skill level and will prepare you for the next level of management in the organization.

# Chapter Comments

Management controls are any processes, systems or tasks used to manage, control, or monitor business operations, including financial transactions.

As a claim manager, you cannot and should not look at every claim file; however, the use of management controls allows the claim manager to focus on critical claim areas which require their attention or have the potential to develop into a problem or issue.

As a claim manager, the use of *management controls* is a key responsibility to ensure consistent quality results, and compliance with company guidelines, standards and procedures. Management controls can be *formal* and used daily, weekly, or monthly; or *informal* used on an ad-hoc basis in a special project or upon request.

The claim manager must use management controls effectively – these controls may include the new assignment process, claim authority, settlement approval, transaction approval (payments and reserves), management dual diary, periodic file reviews, review of coverage and claim denials, large loss reviews, use of workload management reports, P&L and other management reports, and various claim logs.

A primary management control used to effectively to manage claim technical quality is the *claims quality review process* reviewing a select number of claim files per adjuster per month. This process will be discussed in **Chapter 6 – Claims Quality Review Process**.

# CHAPTER 5
# MANAGING TECHNICAL
# CLAIM HANDLING

## Claim Manager's Role in Technical Claim Handling

One of the primary responsibilities of a claim manager is to manage the quality of technical claim handling by adjusters within the claim unit, or department.

Technical claim handling refers to all activities related to the handling of specific claims. These activities generally include the following *best practice* categories: contacts, coverage, investigation, recovery and contribution, documentation, claim analysis (liability or compensability) and evaluation, claim financial-management, litigation management, medical and disability management, workers' compensation case management, file reporting and documentation, claim disposition, diary management and claim control, compliance and other claim related activities.

With the advancement of modern architecture claim systems, most activities involving technical claim handling are documented within the electronic claim file, either as a structured field entry, within the electronic file notes, using an electronic form, claim screen, or as an uploaded attachment.

This chapter will focus on technical claim handling issues including the claim manager's role and responsibility in the technical claim handling process. The impact of poor-quality claim handling has the potential to critically impact a company's financial results; therefore, the claim manager needs to allocate enough of their time to monitor and control the technical claim handling process. We will review various technical claim handling categories, their impact on claim results, and how effective management can achieve positive outcomes.

As a claim manager, you do not need to be an expert in all technical claim handling; however, you do need to understand how adjuster performance can impact claim results. Claim managers who insist on being an expert in all claim situations may stifle adjuster performance and create a negative work environment. Being an effective claim manager does not mean being a "super" claim technician. An effective claim manager achieves quality claim outcomes by motivating employees, providing quality oversight and direction and using effective management controls.

To achieve consistency in the work product by the adjuster, the claim manager should manage to the company's established claim guidelines (best practices), standards and procedures. Following this approach will result in better claim outcomes and eliminate any confusion on requirements or subjective claim review evaluations by the claim manager. Repetitive non-compliance with company requirements should be addressed as a performance issue and not repeatedly documented in the claim file notes.

Listed below are various claim technical categories which apply to property and casualty claims. We will review each category in terms of its application in claim handling, its impact on the overall claim result, and how effective claim management can achieve the desired claim outcomes. Each claim category will ultimately impact the claim outcome; however, it may not always be obvious due to the inability to quantify the actual claim impact.

# Claim Technical Categories

The following claim technical categories are consistent with most **best practice** categories used by the insurance industry.

## Coverage

Prior to making any contacts with parties to the loss, the adjuster will verify and review coverage to confirm the loss is covered under the policy and determine whether any coverage issues or limitations are involved (e.g. coverage analysis).

In most claims, *Coverage Verification* is automated with the integration of the policy administration system and the claim system. The coverage verification process involves verifying basic insurance policy information as part of the claim process including the named insured, policy number, effective dates, limits, sub-limits, endorsements, deductibles, lienholders, loss payees, vehicles, property, locations, etc. Although the policy system will verify coverage there may be circumstances wherein coverage needs to be further verified or clarified to consider paying the loss. Coverage verification is routine and not very complex.

*Coverage Analysis* is a critical aspect of the claim handling process and the responsibility of both the handling adjuster and the claim manager, which requires education, training and experience to become proficient. Coverage analysis involves the review of applicable coverage forms and endorsements to determine if there are any coverage issues – which can be simple coverage issues (e.g. late notice of claim), or complex coverage issues (e.g. policy exclusion[s], loss not meeting the applicable policy definition, concurrent or excess coverage, etc.).

Since some policy forms and endorsements may have policy language deemed ambiguous by the courts, it is important that the claims staff also understand the local jurisdiction to determine if any *case law* will affect or modify the coverage analysis.

The adjuster should explore all available opportunities for coverage, carefully reviewing the declaration page, schedules, coverage forms and endorsements. The adjuster must evaluate coverage in a fair and equitable manner. If the adjuster's coverage evaluation is geared toward a determination as to how a claim can be denied, then the adjuster may not be treating the policyholder fairly and may also be engaging in unethical behavior, or possibly violating Fair Claim Acts.

Coverage analysis goes beyond coverage verification and relates to coverage provided under policy forms and endorsements, including insuring agreements, exclusions, conditions and definitions. After the analysis of coverage issues, a decision will be reached as to whether a coverage position letter should be issued, or a non-waiver agreement secured. The issuance of a coverage position documents should be appropriate, timely and consistent with established claims procedures (e.g. disclaimer letter, reservation of rights letter, non-waiver agreement, etc.)

When coverage analysis is not handled properly, it can have a material impact on the claim outcome. As a claim manager, you should be involved in all claims wherein a coverage issue exists, including reviewing and approving coverage position letters or taking non-waiver agreements.

Relevant coverage analysis documentation is posted to the electronic claim file as notes and attachments, which may include investigation and research for review and analysis of the coverage issue, copies of the declaration page(s), policy schedules, policy forms and endorsements, research and opinion by coverage counsel (if applicable), and documented notes detailing the coverage issue and decisions.

In some states, there are statutes or regulations regarding how coverage position letters are prepared and issued. For example, most states require the issuance of a coverage position letter within a certain time after the claim has been reported to the insurance company, and some states require the policyholder to sign a second copy of the coverage position letter (e.g. reservation of rights letter) and return it to the insurance company.

It is recommended that all coverage position letters be sent *certified mail – return receipt requested* with a copy of the receipt posted to the claim file attachments. Any material delays in the issuance of a coverage position letter (e.g. reservation of rights letter or coverage denial) can result in a "waiver and estoppel" (Murdock, Claim Operations: A Practical Guide) situation.

With the advancement of electronic claim files, the identification and follow-up on coverage issues may be in the electronic file notes and as an oversight may not be reviewed by the claim manager. Claims involving coverage issues should have the claim manager's diary on a very short cycle.

Improper handling of claims involving coverage issues are sometimes irreversible resulting in the payment of a claim wherein coverage may have been excluded or limited. By becoming promptly involved at the outset of the development of coverage issues, the claim manager can provide guidance and direction to the adjuster and avoid potential coverage problems.

An excellent method to improve an adjuster's knowledge level in handling coverage issues is to request that the adjuster research the coverage issue by reviewing the applicable policy forms and endorsements, preparing a proposed coverage position letter, and then referring the letter to the claim manager for review and discussion with the adjuster. This type of training increases the adjusters comfort level in identifying and analyzing coverage issues, as well as drafting proper coverage position letters.

Coverage analysis is critical to the claim handling process and should be incorporated into various training topics. There are many areas within the insurance policy which can impact coverage. Understanding insurance policies and being able to interpret policy language is an important job function for every adjuster. As a claim manager, you should encourage adjusters to take industry courses, and attend seminars, to improve their knowledge level of policy coverage and its application to claims.

## Contacts

*Contact* is the first claim activity upon receipt of the *First Notice of Loss* (FNOL) or *First Report of Injury* (FROI). When handling Worker's Compensation claims, contact is usually referred to as *three-point contact* involving the claimant, employer and primary treating physician.

The timeliness of contact (from the claim report date) has always been a metric used in most claim operations for several reasons including the need to secure the claim details as soon as possible after the loss to control the claim and loss costs, as well as its impact on customer service. Most claim operations require twenty-four-hour contact (i.e. one business day) with the claimant, and twenty-four to forty-eight-hour contact (i.e. one to two business days) with the insured/employer, the primary treating physician in workers' compensation claims, third parties and any known witnesses. There are some companies which require same-day contact with all parties to the loss.

Documented contact attempts establish compliance with *contact* standards as long there is a continued effort to make contact within a reasonable time-period from the initial contact attempt(s). Leaving telephone messages and sending emails are considered contact attempts to establish initial contact timeliness. Meaningful or substantive contact with the claimant and insured should include securing claim details, a recorded statement (if required), and requesting relevant claim information and documentation.

Contact requirements in workers' compensation claims also requires timely contact with the primary treating physician within twenty-four to forty-eight hours (i.e. one to two business days) from the claim report date to secure details on the claimant's injuries, diagnosis, prognosis, treatment and disability period. Receipt of a medical report, within the required contact period providing the same information should satisfy the initial physician contact requirement.

There are adjusters who will place little emphasis on contact times, thinking that a delay of a few days will not have much impact on the claim. As a claim manager, you should understand the impact of timely contact with parties to the loss including the following:

- Timely contact with parties to the loss provides an opportunity to secure the necessary claim details shortly after the loss or incident occurred. This means the information is *fresh* in the mind of the witness (e.g. claimant, insured, witness) which will yield more accurate information.

- With some claims such as property losses, the adjuster should be inspecting the loss as soon as possible to preserve the loss scene for a *cause and origin* inspection, mitigate further damages (e.g. water damages causing mold), as well as investigate potential subrogation.

- Property or cargo claims may have salvage involving frozen or perishable goods which requires a prompt inspection or timely handling.

- Certain types of claims require prompt contact to reduce the financial-impact of other elements of the loss. For example, when handling automobile physical damage or property damage claims, there may be a claim for rental reimbursement[15] or loss of use. Rental reimbursement and loss of use begins immediately after the accident when the vehicle is not drivable. If the claimant or insured is not contacted timely, there will be additional rental or loss of use days from the date of the accident to the date when the vehicle is inspected, and an appraisal report is rendered. Although two or three days of additional rental or loss of use may seem minor, multiplying the impact across all similar claims, can be significant.

- When handling worker's compensation claims, the timeliness of contact is critical in controlling indemnity and medical costs. The first several days of the claim are important to ascertain the necessary course of medical treatment, and the need for any ancillary services for disability and/or medical management, such as nurse case management.

- Consumers, in both personal and commercial lines, want prompt and reliable claim service. A measurement of service in the insurance industry is how effectively claims were handled, including timely and prompt initial contact. Although it may not always be specifically measurable, poor claim handling will certainly have a negative impact on policyholder retention.

- When not contacting all relevant parties to the claim, our claim analysis and evaluation may be flawed due to a lack of relevant information.

The claim manager should educate adjusters on the reasons for timely and prompt contact with parties to the loss, to gain a better understanding of its potential financial impact on the claim and its effect on customer service.

There are claim managers who will not place much emphasis on contact times when conducting claim file reviews, despite the requirement. Consequently, this message indirectly results in the adjuster following the same thought process. If the handling adjuster understands the potential impact of late contact(s), perhaps there will be an increase in awareness and compliance.

---

[15] When the automobile appraisal report is completed there will be a determination as to the number of rental days authorized for the claim – which may be one day per four hours of repair labor, plus weekends and delays resulting from parts orders.

# Investigation

The claim investigation process is fundamental to all claims, including liability, automobile, property, inland marine, professional lines and workers' compensation claims. It is the broadest *best practice* category as it includes many components which are detailed below. An incomplete or delayed claim investigation can have a material impact on the coverage analysis, liability or compensability analysis, and the overall claim evaluation.

As a claim manager, you are responsible for the quality of the claim investigations in your unit or department. The are many components of the claim investigation process – some are listed below which represent the primary investigation areas.

## A. **Investigation Timeliness and Completeness:**

The *timeliness and completeness* of the claim investigation is critical to a favorable claim outcome. Timely and complete claim investigations should be based on claim procedural requirements and established claim guidelines and standards. This includes completing all elements of the claim investigation to properly evaluate the claim.

Late claim investigations result in the inability to track down witnesses or witness recollection of the accident/claim details may be affected due to the delay in contact. Scene investigations may be negatively impacted as the accident scene may have changed, or the specific cause of the accident may no longer be present (e.g. hazard eliminated, debris cleaned up or defect repaired). If damages need to be inspected, any delays in inspection may adversely impact the claim evaluation due to repairs being completed or a material change in the damages due to water, weather, etc.

Liability or compensability decisions are impacted by late claim investigations, and in some claims, such as workers' compensation claims, a delay in the claim investigation will impact the ability to properly deny or accept the workers' compensation claim, and timely file the required state forms.

Property claim investigations are incorporated into the property adjustment process and include insured interviews, statements, official reports, damage scope, photographs and diagrams, assignment of experts, subrogation determination and preparation of a damage estimate. Property claims which are not investigated timely or properly may have errors in the scope of damages resulting in an inaccurate estimate, potential missed opportunity for subrogation or result in additional damages due to the late inspection (e.g. development of mold in a water damage claim).

B. **Investigation Quality:**

Monitoring the quality of the claim investigation is the claim manager's responsibility. The quality level of the claim investigation and results will have a financial-impact on the claim, either favorably or unfavorably.

The claim investigation must meet all claim guidelines, standards and procedures. Claim investigations take time and adjusters may take short-cuts due to workloads or do not feel the additional investigation is necessary or warranted. As the claim manager, you set the standards for what is an acceptable or an unacceptable work product, which should align with claim guidelines, standards and procedures.

Do not accept a mediocre claim work product. It will negatively impact the company's financial results and is a reflection on you as the claim manager. You do not want your adjusters to over-investigate claims, but you do want your staff to conduct timely, proper and complete claim investigations.

Adjuster workloads will impact the quality of the claim investigations and compliance with claim guidelines, standards and procedures. Adjusters who have excessive workloads are also more likely to have a lower quality work product, including deficient case reserves and claim overpayments. It is the claim manager's responsibility to monitor adjuster workloads to be sure workloads are appropriate and set at level wherein adjusters can meet or exceed company claim guidelines, standards and procedures.

C. **Investigation Documentation:**

The claim investigation process includes proper documentation of relevant claim details in the electronic file notes or attachments (categorized and labeled), which should be complete, relevant, succinct and in the proper format per the claim guidelines and standards.

Examples of claim investigation documentation include:

- Scene Photographs and Diagrams
- Insured Records
- Official Reports
- Expert Reports
- Copies of Codes and Statutes
- Signed Contracts
- Signed Statements
- Recorded Statements
- Authorizations (medical & wage)
- Medical & Hospital Records

- IME Reports
- Wage Documentation
- Litigation Documents (Pleadings, Correspondence, Etc.)
- Damage Estimates
- Damage Appraisals
- ISO ClaimSearch® Results
- Activity Checks and Surveillance Reports

Claim documentation is evidentiary and used in the claim evaluation – it should be legible and properly organized in the claim record. Poorly documented and disorganized claim records make it difficult to review and evaluate the claim and may result in missing critical information which was not properly documented.

### D. **Claimant Attorney Engagement:**

Adjusters may not have difficulty in discussing claims with an unrepresented claimant; however, if the claimant has retained an attorney, the adjuster may experience more difficulty or not be as effective. This may be due to the claimant attorney's demeanor or attitude toward adjusters, the adjuster being intimidated, or the adjuster's lack of experience in working with attorneys.

Adjusters need to feel comfortable in engaging the claimant attorney in discussion. It is a necessary component of the claim investigation when the claimant is represented – and it is the only method to secure relevant claim information, without having to go through litigation or formal discovery.

Effective claimant attorney engagement means timely and substantive contact with the claimant attorney to discuss relevant details of the claim, secure necessary claimant information and documentation, and establish a rapport for future discussions (e.g. future claim disposition).

Generally, the following should be part of the claimant attorney discussion which we refer to as *Attorney Allegations*.

- Attorney and law firm name, business address, telephone, fax number and e-mail address (if not already received by letter)
- Claimant name, address, age, date of birth, social security number (Medicare) and marital status
- Date, time and place of accident
- Description of accident and the attorney's *theory of liability*
- Claimant occupation, employer name and address, wage rate and disability period
- Injuries, diagnosis, treatment and prognosis

- Physician names, addresses and specialty
- Hospital name and address with inpatient or service dates
- Itemized special damages including medical, hospital, diagnostic, wages and property damage
- Confirmation of any *liens* (Medicare, medical, child support, etc.)
- Third-party involvement/other parties on notice (with insurer and attorney names)
- Witness names, addresses and telephone numbers
- Responding police agency and/or ambulance company
- Claimant vehicle make, model, and year; claimant vehicle damage and any available estimates
- Photographs of the accident scene and/or vehicles
- Workers' compensation and/or PIP insurer and claim reference numbers
- Litigation: yes/no (If yes, consider securing an extension of time to answer without waiving any defenses)
- Names and contact information for any experts retained

The claim manager should monitor the effectiveness of claimant attorney engagement during file reviews and the claims quality review process. Training and development, including role playing exercises, can be helpful in improving adjuster performance. Working with attorneys during the claim process is a routine activity and it is important that all adjusters become proficient and comfortable in the process.

E. **Taking Statements:**

Statements should be taken from all parties to the claim including the insured, claimant, witnesses, third party, or anyone else who has relevant information which may have a potential impact on the claim evaluation and outcome. Quality statements provide critical information used in the claim evaluation process and are fundamental to any claim investigation.

The quality of statements taken should be evaluated by comparing statement content to procedural requirements, claim standards and relevant statement guides. This may include a review of the statement summary posted to the claim file and/or listening to the actual recorded statement (or reviewing the signed statement) to determine the level of quality.

The objective in taking a statement is to confirm and record liability (or compensability) and damage (e.g. injuries) facts through an interview process. The factual responses are used by the adjuster and claim management to evaluate the claim or rule out a person being a witness by taking a "negative statement". Negative statements prevent a witness from giving testimony which may be materially different from the initial interview and can be used later to challenge a witness if the witness changes their version of the accident.

Statements may also be used when there is a coverage issue in a claim to determine whether coverage is applicable or excluded. For example, a statement may be taken from the insured in a property claim wherein the water damage loss was caused by frozen pipes and the building was vacant and unoccupied.

Statements are the foundation of any claim investigation and an important investigative tool. Adjusters are trained to take statements early on in their career but may need periodic supplemental training to improve the quality of statements.

The content and quality of the statement impacts important decisions made during the claim process such as confirmation of the accident facts and details (how, when and where), liability or compensability decisions, injuries and prior medical history, potential responsible third parties and identification of witnesses. If a statement is not taken, or not thorough enough, it could have a material impact on the financial outcome of the claim. For example, not taking a statement could result in improper acceptance or denial of a workers' compensation claim by not interviewing a critical witness, or by relying exclusively on the claimant statement and not taking a statement from the employer to verify details.

Statements should never be taken from a person who is represented by an attorney (claimant, employer or witness) without the attorney's written permission. Some attorneys will allow a statement of their client in the attorney's presence, and if a transcribed copy of the statement is provided to the attorney after the interview.

An adjuster should never take a statement from a person who is hospitalized, taking prescribed or illicit drugs, or intoxicated, which can adversely affect their judgment. This is not only unethical but may also be in violation of various *Fair Claim Act* statutes.

We take statements using a structured format in anticipation that the statement may be admitted into evidence in a legal proceeding at a future date. There are several factors which can affect the ability to have a statement admitted into evidence. For example, statements taken without a person's permission, and/or use of trickery or deceit may not be admissible. When there are "gaps" or other recording malfunctions during the interview, it may also be difficult to have a statement admitted into evidence. Typically, for a statement to be admissible in a legal proceeding, the person who gave the statement must attend the legal proceeding to verify the authenticity of the statement.

The most critical aspect of a statement is to be sure the statement is accurate and truthful. If the adjuster "leads" the witness in responding to questions during the interview, the statement may not be fully accurate or has the potential to be biased. It is important to ask the witness to respond in their "own words" and give the witness enough time to respond to each interview question without interrupting them. Asking open-ended questions which require more than a "yes or no" response will provide more details and allow for future questions to be framed based on the responses.

The quality of statements can be adversely affected by:

- Poor preparation in advance of taking the statement
- Not knowing the accident details before taking the statement
- Not following the proper statement format or guide
- Leading the witness during statement questioning
- Interruptions while taking the statement
- The witness is in a rush or has limited time for the interview
- Not listening to the witness's responses
- Not formulating additional questions based on witness responses
- The witness' poor recollection of facts
- A long time has passed between the date of the interview and the accident date
- The witness is not being truthful
- Language barriers or heavy accents causing communication issues

Many experienced adjusters do not use a formal recorded statement guide; however, it is recommended that a statement guide be used by all adjusters on all claims. While using the statement guide and listening closely to the person being interviewed, the adjuster can focus on asking additional questions that probe deeper into the facts of the claim. If a recorded statement is taken in person, a diagram by the person being interviewed may assist in conveying the accident details.

It's important for adjusters to be able to visualize how the accident or incident occurred. If the adjuster is unable to visualize the accident scene and details, he or she may be unable to frame the proper questions. The line of questioning should be orderly and consistent with the recorded statement guide.

After the statement is transcribed, it should read as a question-and-answer document, providing the reader with a complete story of the accident. If the adjuster haphazardly asks questions in no relevant order, and jumps around during the interview process, the statement will end up being very confusing and potentially not useful. Adjusters can supplement the statement guide with additional questions necessary to properly evaluate the claim.

There is a direct correlation between the preparation necessary to take the statement and the resulting quality of the statement. Again, it is important that adjusters not rush when taking statements and listen very closely to the responses given by the person being interviewed.

As an industry, statements have always been fundamental to the claim investigation, but in recent years some companies have placed less emphasis on statements. Statements are critical to the claim evaluation and there should be established guidelines and procedures on statement taking.

As a claim manager, you should establish expectations on statement requirements as part of the claim investigation process. This includes when statements are to be taken and from which parties to the loss. When conducting claim reviews, the claim manager should listen to recorded statements to evaluate the effectiveness of the statement. Periodic statement taking training provides relevant training for new adjusters and a refresher for experienced adjusters.

## F. **Field Investigation:**

Claim investigations can be conducted by telephone or in the field; however, some aspects of the claim investigation must be conducted in the field such as scene investigations.

Many companies use desk adjusters to handle most of the claim investigation and adjustment activities; and either have internal field adjusters, investigators and appraisers handle the field work, or outsource these tasks to independent vendors.

Field investigations may include a variety of tasks such as scene photos and diagrams, inspection, property damage scope, estimate or appraisal of dwellings, buildings, machinery, equipment or vehicles, and a canvass to identify any potential witnesses at the accident scene. It can also include claimant activity checks and surveillance investigation, SIU investigation, or picking up an official report (e.g. police or aided report, fire report, OSHA report, etc.) to expedite the process.

Claim managers should recognize when a field investigation is necessary and warranted. Some adjusters may not want to have a field investigation conducted due to the expense or cost, particularly if the work is outsourced. Unfortunately, this may not be a prudent decision if the field investigation is necessary to properly evaluate the claim. For example, by not inspecting the damages and securing a damage appraisal, the adjuster may over-pay the third party or first party claim, or by not contacting a witness (which you are unable to contact by telephone) the claim evaluation may be flawed, or by not reviewing the police report (which may have been delayed by mail), the liability analysis in terms of comparative negligence may have been improper.

Proper field investigation guidelines and standards communicated to the adjusting staff will improve the quality of claim investigations. It is recommended that field investigation guidelines be specific using examples when a field assignment is required. This will achieve consistency in claim handling and improve the quality level.

## G. **Third Party Investigation:**

Third party investigation refers to the identification and investigation of actual or potential third parties who caused or contributed to the accident – inclusive of contact with third parties and their insurance carriers. Insurance carrier information should be secured including the relevant carrier name and address, claim number and representative name, policy number, applicable coverage and policy limits.

The third-party investigation may include statements, records and documentation, contracts (e.g. lease agreement or construction contracts), product and machinery information, etc.

The identification and investigation of potential third parties has a direct impact on the claim outcome. Third party contribution mitigates the loss and reduces the loss ratio, whether it is a workers' compensation lien, third party contribution, or automobile and property subrogation.

Always encourage adjusters to investigate third party potential – it may not always be obvious to the adjuster and under your guidance and direction as a claim manager, you may be able to assist the adjuster in this aspect of the investigation. This component of the claim investigation is a good adjuster training topic.

H. **ISO ClaimSearch®:**

ISO ClaimSearch® (Verisk Analytics, Inc. | Verisk Analytics®) is an industry tool used for first and third-party claims. It is used on automobile, casualty (including workers' compensation) and property claim handling to identify prior claim history.

It is recommended that the following claims be entered in *ISO ClaimSearch*®:

- All third party bodily injury liability claims including automobile and general liability
- All personal injury, D&O and E&O claims
- All lost time workers' compensation claims
- All PIP (Personal Injury Protection) and Medical Payments claims
- All 1st and 3rd party automobile claims involving physical damage, property damage, total losses, salvage and vehicle thefts
- All 1st party property claims including inland marine, fidelity losses, fire and theft

ISO ClaimSearch® should be entered initially and then every six months thereafter. The adjuster should follow-up on ISO ClaimSearch® returns or "hits" which indicate prior claims and/or injuries, by contacting the insurance carrier for relevant claim details.

Some claim managers may not place enough emphasis on the need for the entry of ISO ClaimSearch® during the investigation or adjustment process. It is an essential component of the claim investigation and should be included in the claim manager's file review and claims quality review process.

The use of ISO ClaimSearch® is often impacted by the methodology used to facilitate the ISO entry. For example, companies which have fully integrated ISO ClaimSearch® into the claim system functionality may have the entries automatically completed when the claim is set up, with the results appearing in the document attachments, not requiring any manual work. As claim attributes change, the ISO ClaimSearch® is updated automatically.

In contrast, other companies must go to the ISO ClaimSearch® web portal to enter individual claims, convert the results to a pdf format, and upload the pdf document to the claim system as an attachment – this is very time consuming for both the adjuster and document management staff.

If your company has not integrated the ISO ClaimSearch® process into the claim system, we recommend "lobbying" management for the change. A *cost-benefit analysis* will clearly illustrate the savings in expense, with the reduction in manual labor for the manual entry, indexing claims, pdf conversion, and attachment to the electronic claim record.

ISO ClaimSearch® is an important investigative tool – impress upon your adjusters the need for timely entry and follow-up on results.

# Recovery & Contribution

Recovery and contribution mitigate loss costs and should be a key focus for the claim manager during periodic claim reviews and claims quality reviews. Isolating recovery claim handling in a specialized claim unit is recommended – it is more focused and produces better results, than having the adjuster who handled the underlying claim also handle the recovery claim. Specialized recovery units have specific subrogation knowledge and experience, a good understanding of state laws and legal doctrines, Inter-Company Arbitration and the litigation process.

As a claim manager, you should consider implementing subrogation and salvage goals (dollar values and/or percentage of paid loss) and pay close attention to the results. Claims with improper or inadequate claims investigations, improper liability analysis (e.g. comparative negligence), or inaccurate damage assessments[16], will have a negative impact on your recovery results.

Recovery dollars drop to the bottom line and mitigate loss results. It doesn't take much to a have a material impact on the overall loss results, with a few hundred dollars (salvage or subrogation) on each claim.

## Subrogation Investigation

As indicated in the third-party investigation category, the *Subrogation Investigation* focuses on identification of third parties who caused or contributed to the accident – conducting a timely investigation to support the third-party claim, including securing statements from relevant parties and necessary documentation and information.

---

[16] e.g. Physical damage claims submitted to *Inter-Company Arbitration* wherein the adjuster never assigned an appraiser to inspect the damages (paying the claim off the submitted repair estimate) – with the Arbitration award reducing the damages to an amount equivalent to an appraisal assigned by the adverse carrier or respondent.

The timely and documented subrogation investigation focuses on identifying and supporting potential subrogation recovery for payment on first party claims (automobile and property). The subrogation investigation includes all relevant documentation and investigation necessary to perfect the subrogation claim against the adverse party or carrier; through direct negotiations, arbitration or litigation.

Unfortunately, subrogation is not always a key focus for the handling adjuster. Adjusters should be proactive in pursuit of subrogation opportunities. The underlying claim investigation should focus on subrogation; however, some companies may have the dedicated subrogation specialist conduct any necessary follow-up investigation to support the subrogation claim and prepare the claim for submission to *inter-company arbitration* if necessary.

An important aspect of subrogation is the process of applying comparative negligence – be consistent in the claim evaluation for both the subrogation claim and any pending bodily injury liability claim. If you are accepting less than 100% on the physical damage subrogation claim from the adverse carrier you may be asked to contribute to a pending bodily injury claim with the same apportionment (even if it is a small percentage). For example, if the BI claimant was a passenger in the claimant vehicle, and you settled the physical damage subrogation claim at 90%, you may be asked to contribute as a co-defendant (e.g. 90% claimant operator and 10% insured).

## Salvage Handling

Salvage handling pertains to first and third-party automobile and first party property claims. It is important for the adjuster to handle salvage timely including moving the total loss vehicle from the body shop to a salvage facility to reduce storage costs, as well as timely handling of first party property salvage involving perishable goods, or cargo which may be spoiled due to the accident.

Salvage returns reduce loss costs. The determination of the salvage value should be left to a professional appraiser, salvor or auction facility. Leaving salvage with the vehicle owner on total loss automobile claims may be easier, but the returns may be less, and the vehicle may end up being used on the road and be unsafe for driving.

Salvage handling can be monitored using salvage management reports, including reports provided by salvage facilities. If the claim operation has internal staff appraisers and uses estimating software, the claim manager may have the ability to review salvage metrics by using the estimating software reporting functionality.

## WC Lien Filing & Management

When handling workers' compensation claims, it is important that any applicable lien be filed with the responsible party, their carrier and any other relevant parties to the claim. Managing the lien process and ultimate recovery or offset, is the adjuster and claim manager's responsibility.

ISO ClaimSearch® is an excellent tool to identify pending liability claims by an injured party collecting workers' compensation benefits. The ISO return will provide the relevant third-party name and insurance carrier information.

Before a workers' compensation lien is filed, encourage your adjusters to research and understand the insurance statutes and regulations. For example, in automobile accidents, some states (e.g. New York) may only allow the workers' compensation carrier to assert a lien against the responsible party after paying the equivalent of the no fault insurance statutory minimum limits (e.g. $50,000), unless one of the vehicles either weighs 6,500 lbs. or used to transport people or property.

## Recovery Third Party Notice

The adverse party should be placed on notice timely (in writing) of your subrogation rights. It is also important to protect the statute of limitations and/or filing a formal *Notice of Claim*, when warranted (e.g. requirement for a claim against a public entity or municipality).

If Inter-Company Arbitration is involved, the statute of limitations applies, which means arbitration should be filed within the applicable statute of limitations.

The third-party notice is sent either by the underlying adjuster or the subrogation adjuster – and should be a key area for the claim manager during file reviews, including monitoring the statute of limitations.

## Use of Experts

The adjuster should consider the need for an expert to support the subrogation claim. It is important that the adjuster control the assignment of the appropriate expert including written confirmation of the fee structure up front and timely reporting by the expert.

As a claim manager, you may want to limit the authority to assign experts – either by expert category (e.g. C&O expert) or by expense dollar authority. Implementing ALAE expense authority levels is an excellent management control to control expenses.

The use of experts is critical to perfect our subrogation claim but experts need to be assigned early in the claim process so that evidence is preserved. This is particularly relevant in first party property claims which have subrogation potential.

Encourage your adjusters to assign an expert as soon as they recognize the potential for subrogation, and make sure the proper experts are being used. There are cause & origin

(C&O) experts, engineers (electrical, mechanical, chemical, civil, etc.), forensic accountants, builders, etc. and assignment of the proper expert will improve your recovery potential.

# Liability Claims

## Liability Analysis

The analysis of liability on all parties to a claim includes the apportionment of liability on each party and the application of appropriate legal theories and doctrines, defenses, comparative negligence, statutes and case law.

The most critical aspect of a liability claim analysis is the application of comparative negligence, a negligence rule used in many states to allocate the degree of fault on the plaintiff and the defendant.

Comparative negligence allows for the plaintiff's damages to be reduced by a percentage representing the degree of contributing fault on behalf of the plaintiff. If the plaintiff's negligence is found to be greater than the defendant's negligence, the plaintiff will be barred from recovery (see *Modified Comparative Negligence*).

A. **Modified Comparative Negligence:**

*Modified Comparative Negligence* means damages will be reduced by the percentage of fault attributable to each party. Most states have adopted the *Modified Comparative Rule* which has two variations: *50 Percent Bar Rule* and the *51 Percent Bar Rule* – meaning if you are 50% or 51% negligent you will be barred from recovery (Wickert).

- Ten states follow the 50 Percent Bar Rule, meaning the plaintiff cannot recover if he/she is 50% or more at fault, but if he/she is 49% or less at fault, he/she can recover, although recovery is reduced by their degree of fault. The states which follow the *50 Percent Bar Rule* include Arkansas, Colorado, Georgia, Idaho, Kansas, Maine, Nebraska, North Dakota, Tennessee, and Utah. (Wickert).

- Twenty three states follow the 51 Percent Bar Rule under which the plaintiff cannot recover if he/she is 51% or more at fault. However, the plaintiff can recover if he/she is 50% or less at fault, but recovery would be reduced by their degree of fault. The states which follow the *51 Percent Bar Rule* include Connecticut, Delaware, Hawaii, Illinois, Indiana, Iowa, Massachusetts, Michigan, Minnesota, Montana, Nevada, New Hampshire, New Jersey, Ohio, Oklahoma, Oregon, Pennsylvania, South Carolina, Texas, Vermont, West Virginia, Wisconsin, and Wyoming (Wickert).

B. **Pure Comparative Negligence**:

*Pure Comparative Negligence* which applies in thirteen states means a party can collect damages from the negligent defendant, but recovery is reduced by the plaintiff's own negligence, even if the plaintiff is 99% at fault. There are no bars from recovery for being partially negligent (Wickert). The states which follow the *Pure Comparative Negligence* rule include Alaska, Arizona, California, Florida, Kentucky, Louisiana, Mississippi, Missouri, New Mexico, New York, Rhode Island, South Dakota (Slight/Gross negligence standard) and Washington.

C. **Contributory Negligence:**

*Contributory Negligence* means that the plaintiff will be barred from recovery in a lawsuit if the plaintiff's own negligence contributed to the damage, even if that percentage of negligence was deemed to be 1%. Contributory negligence has been superseded in many states by other methods of apportioning liability. Currently, only five states, follow the pure contributory negligence rule; Alabama, Washington DC, Maryland, North Carolina and Virginia.

In evaluating negligence on each party to the claim, we must apply the four elements of negligence: *duty owed*, *duty breached*, *proximate cause* and *damages*. Sometimes adjusters lose sight of why we investigate claims and how to properly evaluate negligence or liability. There is a structured process and for the liability evaluation to be accurate, we must investigate claims and then apply legal theories, doctrines and statutes.

The claim manager should require a detailed liability analysis on all liability claims for purpose of reserving and evaluating claims for settlement. It is important to address comparative negligence in every liability claim by commenting in the electronic notes or claim reporting how it is being applied. The electronic notes should reflect a liability analysis incorporating the percentage of negligence applied to each party even it is "zero", as well as the legal basis for the liability assessment.

The liability evaluation should not change unless the facts of the accident change with the development of additional information or documentation. The same liability evaluation should apply when you are evaluating the claim for a settlement disposition and establishing claim case reserves.

Since the legal system does not provide a guide as to what specific percentage of liability applies to each accident or claim circumstance, the application of comparative negligence is a subjective decision. There are no published standards or "rules" on precise percentages applied to specific types of accident descriptions. Therefore, the adjuster needs to use common sense in applying comparative negligence in a claim, but also apply legal theories, doctrines and statutes.

Generally, the "burden of proof" will ultimately be on the claimant or plaintiff to prove that the insured is responsible or liable in an accident; however, this will only occur if the claimant files litigation against the insured and the jury makes the final determination. Otherwise, the percentage determination or allocation is made by the parties to the claim, such as the insurance companies and any attorney(s) involved.

As an industry, some insurance companies may use a specific percentage of liability based on the accident description. For example, if the insured made a left turn in front of the claimant at an uncontrolled intersection, the adjuster may apply 20% to 25% liability apportionment on the claimant for improper lookout or excessive speed. Or, if the insured made a full stop at a stop sign, and then proceeded into the intersection seeing no oncoming vehicles and colliding with the claimant, the adjuster may apply up to 25% liability apportionment on the claimant. These percentages are not based on any law, guide or manual – they are simply based on industry practices.

There are no minimum percentages applied in comparative negligence, therefore, theoretically, the claimant could be 2% or 3% negligent. However, since there are no established allocation standards for types or description of accidents, as a practical matter we may not apply such a small percentage of comparative negligence evaluation in property damage liability claims (we may in bodily injury liability claims).

To properly apply comparative negligence, it is critical that the claim investigation be thorough and complete, including statements from all parties to the loss (insured, claimant, passengers and witnesses), scene photographs and diagrams (when appropriate), automobile photographs, copies of official reports, copies of applicable laws and statutes, copies of state motor vehicle reports, and other supporting documentation. We utilize the claim investigation as the basis to apply and support the specific percentage of comparative negligence on each party.

The liability evaluation or analysis may be a primary cause of "claim leakage" in a claim operation handling liability claims (automobile and general liability claims). The primary reason for *claim leakage* is related to the difference of opinion in the percentage of liability apportioned to the insured and whether the claimant may be barred from recovery based on modified or contributory negligence. The liability evaluation cannot be that precise that an adjuster or attorney can differentiate between a negligence percentage of 65% vs. 70%; however, the impact can be material on the claim evaluation.

For example, if the *gross* claim value of a bodily injury liability claim (without any offset for comparative negligence or contribution) is indicated at $100,000, then a 65% liability apportionment on the insured will yield a *net* claim value of $65,000. However, if the same claim with a gross value of $100,000, with a 70% liability apportionment on the insured will yield a *net* claim value of $70,000. This difference of opinion represents $5,000 or 5% of the gross claim value. Another 5% difference (e.g. 75%) will yield a $10,000 difference.

The key to properly applying comparative negligence is to have all the relevant facts and a completed claim investigation so the liability analysis is supported by evidence and not conjecture. Be fair in your evaluation and take into consideration all information, including information provided by the adverse party. Since it is difficult to be so precise in the negligence percentages applied, a compromise may sometimes be in order.

As a claim manager, you need to be sure the claim staff understands the comparative negligence statutes in the various claim handling jurisdictions and is applying the proper percentage of negligence on parties to the loss – sometimes easier said than done!

Training in the application of comparative negligence is critical to the claim operation and can have a material impact on the loss ratio if not applied properly. Work closely with your adjusters to understand their strengths and weaknesses in analyzing liability and provide guidance and direction where needed. When claims are referred for reserve approval or settlement authority it is an appropriate time for the claim manager to provide input and direction on the comparative negligence evaluation.

## Damage Evaluation

The damage evaluation discussion pertains to third party liability and first party claims – bodily injury, property damage, physical damage and first party property. Workers' compensation analysis and evaluation will be discussed later in this chapter.

Evaluating the damage exposure in property damage, physical damage and first party property claims is more objective than injury evaluations. There will be a damage or repair estimate submitted and a decision will be made as to whether an appraisal is necessary. The appraisal will be handled by a field adjuster or appraiser (internal or external) who will provide an indication of the total itemized damages for purpose of reserving or settlement (e.g. estimate), including a total loss evaluation (if applicable) and an indication of salvage value. There may also be an indirect loss such as vehicle rental or loss of use, loss of rents, or business income and extra expense in a commercial property claim.

However, injury claims are much more difficult to evaluate. Although there may be available computer programs to assist in the evaluation of claims, there is no one source that provides the evaluation of an injury claim by injury category or type. The same injury may be valued very differently by a claimant, an adjuster, defense counsel, the claimant attorney, or a jury.

Evaluating damages is critical to the claim evaluation process both in terms of case reserves and settlement dispositions. Damages are classified into several categories.

A. **<u>Compensatory Damages</u>:**

Compensatory damages are categorized as *general damages* (subjective) and *special damages* (objective).

- <u>General Damages</u>: Damages based on physical and emotional pain and suffering, loss of companionship, loss of consortium, disfigurement, loss of enjoyment of life, permanency, and mental or physical impairment.

- <u>Special Damages</u>: Damages include medical, diagnostic and hospital-related expenses, wage loss, property damage, and other out-of-pocket expenses.

B. **<u>Punitive Damages</u>:**

- Sometimes called *exemplary* damages, refer to damages which serve to punish a defendant for its conduct. Punitive damages are awarded when the defendant committed acts which are considered grossly negligent, intentional, or egregious.

- Punitive damage awards can far exceed general damage awards and in some states, are not insurable.

The adjuster should document the claim record with a detailed claim evaluation including all damage elements, to arrive at the *gross* value of the bodily injury liability claim such as compensatory damages and itemized special damages.

The most difficult damages to project are *general damages*. Special damages are easily calculated if you have been provided with medical, hospital, diagnostic and wage documentation. General damages are subjective and difficult to evaluate. For example, how much money do you attribute to pain and suffering and permanency? What is a fractured hip with open reduction and internal fixation worth? What is the value of the death of a 5-year old boy who was killed as a pedestrian in a truck accident?

A jury is comprised of laypeople and if the jury sympathizes with the plaintiff it may award the plaintiff a large damage verdict not contemplated by the adjuster in the evaluation. It's important to understand the difference between *settlement value* and *jury verdict value*. Settlement value is the amount an adjuster or claim manager expects to ultimately pay on a claim; and a jury verdict value is the projected verdict if the litigated claim is tried to conclusion. We are unable predict a jury verdict; and although defense counsel may provide an opinion on the potential jury verdict exposure it is only an opinion.

Adjusters tend to settle claims at values based on industry "custom and practice" (e.g. claims settled in the past with similar injuries and circumstances) or evaluate the claim based on a multiple of the special damages, (e.g. five times the specials) which is not an appropriate methodology, nor recommended.

Custom and practice may be helpful to generally arrive at a claim value, but only if the gross claim value is being calculated, then offset by any comparative negligence. If you consistently see soft tissue injury claims reserved at $7,500 you may want to verify that comparative negligence has been considered and applied to the gross claim value.

The gross value of an injury claim can be affected (upward or downward) based on many factors including:

- Venue or jurisdiction where suit will be filed
- Age of claimant – A younger claimant (e.g. age 35) with a severe permanent injury (or death) may have a significant wage loss. An elderly claimant is more susceptible to disease and illness which can develop from the original injury resulting in complications or even death post-accident
- Occupation of the claimant (e.g. office worker vs. construction laborer)
- Claimant wage loss amount
- Claimant disability period
- Permanency and/or disability rating
- Scarring
- Claimant's pain and suffering
- Trauma from accident (e.g. dog bite to child)
- Number of hospitalization days
- Special damages (medical and wage) including future damages
- Jury sympathy
- Type of defendant (e.g. gun manufacturer, trucking company, etc.)
- Type of damages (e.g. compensatory damages vs. punitive damages)

As a claim manager, be cognizant of the impact of these factors and provide guidance and direction to your staff during the claim evaluation and analysis phases of the claim.

## Five Step Liability Claim Evaluation Process

Evaluating liability claims is a structured process. Although there is no exact science in arriving at a bodily injury liability evaluation, there are steps that one can follow in the process to develop a more accurate evaluation.

The following five steps will provide for a more accurate evaluation of bodily injury liability claims:

## Step 1 - Coverage:

Evaluation of coverage is essential in all liability claims. The applicable policy coverage forms must be reviewed and analyzed for definitions, exclusions, limitations or exceptions.

After coverage has been reviewed, determine whether any coverage issues would affect the *net* value of the claim. If a coverage issue does exist, the adjuster should determine whether the evaluation will be offset due to the coverage issue. For example, the full value of the claim may be offset by 50% if there is concurrent coverage with another insurance carrier for the same loss.

In another example coverage may be denied after receipt of a coverage opinion from defense counsel – in the meantime the adjuster evaluates the success rate of the coverage disclaimer at 75%, therefore reducing the reserve recommendation by 75%.

## Step 2 – Liability Analysis:

Review the facts of the loss and claim investigation to make a liability determination and whether any items of investigation are outstanding which could affect the liability evaluation.

In this step, the adjuster should make a liability determination by assigning a narrative liability assessment description (e.g. clear, probable, questionable, doubtful, or none) and a percentage of liability on each party to the loss (e.g. insured, claimant, third party, codefendant, etc.). For illustrative purposes, these narrative assessments are described as follows:

- Clear Liability: Liability has been evaluated at 100% on the insured, meaning there is no negligence on the part of the claimant or other party(s). These claims should be directed toward a settlement disposition without the need for extended investigation or trial.

- Probable Liability: Involves a situation wherein the claimant may bear a small percentage of liability (5% - 20%) with the insured being the primary negligent party. These claims should be directed toward a settlement disposition on a compromised basis applying comparative negligence.

- Questionable Liability: Refers to a claim wherein the claimant and insured may both be liable. The percentage range of liability on the insured may range from 25% to 75%. The claim may result in a compromised settlement or denial if the claimant is deemed to be over 50% or 51% negligent in a modified comparative negligence jurisdiction, or in a contributory negligence jurisdiction.

  The questionable liability evaluation category is the broadest category in terms of the liability ranges, and many adjuster evaluations routinely fall within this category. When adjusters utilize this category during a claim evaluation it is important to specify the percentage of liability attributed to both the claimant and the insured. At times, adjusters may over-use this category, not wanting to commit to either the *doubtful* or *probable* liability category. The adjuster should carefully analyze the investigation and decide on liability, as it directly impacts the claim evaluation, including the case reserve.

- Doubtful Liability: Refers to a liability evaluation wherein both the claimant and insured may be liable; however, the claimant is the primary negligent party. The percentage range of liability on the insured may be 5% to 20%. These claims may be denied in a modified comparative or contributory negligence jurisdiction. In a pure comparative negligence jurisdiction, the claimant may still be able to recover some of their damages.

- No Liability or Zero Liability: Refers to a liability evaluation wherein the insured is not liable for the loss. The claimant would be barred from recovery in pure comparative, modified comparative and contributory negligence jurisdictions. These claims should be denied and may go to trial.

The liability assessment on each party should be clearly outlined and supported by applying various legal defenses, legal theories and doctrines (e.g. comparative negligence) and statutes. An accurate assessment in this category is critical as it drives the total *net* value of the claim used for reserve and settlement evaluation purposes.

### Step 3 – Damage Evaluation:

Review all items of *special damages* and *general damages* to develop a projected *gross* damage exposure range. By itemizing the damages, a monetary amount can be assigned to each component of the damage evaluation, arriving at a more accurate reserve. This step involves the following phases:

1) Review all medical, diagnostic and hospital records to determine the injuries, treatment (current and future), diagnosis, prognosis, permanency rating and disability period.
2) Determine if there are any preexisting injuries or illnesses which will affect the damage evaluation.
3) Calculate the special damages by medical category (e.g. physician, hospital, diagnostic, physical therapy, chiropractic, Rx, etc.). Project the future medical costs if applicable.
4) Calculate the wage loss by applying the wage rate to the disability period to arrive at the total wage claim. Project the future wage loss if applicable.
5) Determine if other damages (e.g. property damage and loss of use) are being claimed outlining the details and value.
6) Project the *general damage* exposure which includes pain and suffering, permanency, disfigurement, emotional impact, loss of companionship, loss of enjoyment of life, and mental or physical impairment. This is the most critical component of the damage evaluation and the most difficult to assess due to its subjectivity. It is important to evaluate each category of the general damage exposure separately by applying a monetary value (e.g. pain & suffering, permanency, etc.).

## Step 4 – Develop the Gross & Net Claim Value:

Calculate the total *special damages* by individual category (including projected future damages). Then calculate the projected *general damages* by individual category.

Add the total special and general damages to arrive at a total *gross* claim value. After the *gross* claim value has been calculated, apply the percentage liability assessment from **Step 2** to arrive at a *net* claim value.

## Step 5 - Recommendations:

Recommend a claim reserve or settlement value based on the calculations in **Step 4** above. When the claim evaluation includes a value range, consider establishing the claim reserve at the upper range. If settlement is being considered, use a low and high range for settlement negotiations purposes, and establish a target settlement amount.

Remember, the claim reserve should be a guide to the claim value – achieving a settlement disposition equivalent to the case reserve does not necessarily mean it was a good settlement. The objective is to bring the claim to an equitable conclusion. Not every claim is going to settle in the range calculated. Since the general damage component of compensatory damages is subjective, it would be impossible for an adjuster to be exact with every bodily injury claim evaluation. Some claims may settle for more and others for less.

When establishing bodily injury case reserves the adjuster may seek input from other claims personnel, their manager and defense counsel, as well as research jury verdicts for similar claims in the same jurisdiction. It's important to remember that, if a claim does not settle prior to or during trial, it goes to the jury for value determination. The jury is comprised of laypeople with no experience in claim evaluations. Many factors can contribute to an adverse jury verdict, such as witness demeanors, jury sympathy, venue, the presiding judge and the economy.

*Pattern reserving* occurs when an adjuster uses the same evaluation for a similar injury without considering liability issues or specific damage issues (e.g. all low back sprains are reserved at $7,500). For example, the adjuster may reserve a claim without taking into consideration the claim investigation results, medical documentation (including prior medical history and co-morbidities), or the unique characteristics of the claim, which may result in reserve redundancy or reserve deficiency.

Since the bodily injury reserve methodology is subjective, it is important to remain flexible in the valuation process. Not all claims have the same details; therefore, they may not fit into past injury valuation ranges.

Custom and practice may dictate the value of injury claims, which can vary by state, jurisdiction, and venue. As a claim manager, it is important to be consistent in the reserve methodology and philosophy. The adjuster and claim manager may not agree on the evaluation but it's important to discuss why the evaluation differs – is the difference in opinion the result of the liability analysis or the damage analysis. Both can vary, but the key is to separate the two components (liability and damages) to compare the analysis properly.

It is important to establish ranges for both reserve and settlement purposes. This will allow for more flexibility in negotiating the claim disposition and allow the claim manager to evaluate the adjuster's negotiations skill.

Insist on a detailed claim evaluation by your claim staff. It will produce more consistent and higher quality claim results, as well as improve the claim staff's evaluation skills.

# Workers' Compensation Claims

## Compensability Analysis & Evaluation

Workers' compensation claim handling is specialized and requires experience in the various jurisdictions, understanding coverage, statutes and benefits.

Workers' compensation has two primary elements of exposure – *compensation* (indemnity) and *medical* benefits. These benefits are paid according to the applicable statute, and the claim analysis and evaluation is based on the workers' compensation act, statutes and case law.

The basis for our workers' compensation compensability analysis is derived from the following information and documentation:

- A review of coverage to verify the jurisdiction is covered under the policy and rule out any exclusions or limitations.
- The results of the claim investigation, including statements, confirming compensability and evaluating course and scope of employment issues, as well as potential subrogation.
- The applicability of various legal concepts and statutes to the claim – confirming that compensability is not affected by any applicable statute or case law (e.g. substantial deviation, intentional injuries, recreational or social activities, horseplay, etc.).
- Establishing timely notice to the employer within the statute of limitations.
- Confirming whether the claim meets the elements for the injury to be compensable such as "arising out of employment" and "in the course of employment".
- A review of the medical and hospital records to confirm causation of the accident to the injuries sustained, treatment and disability period.
- A determination of the compensation benefits to be paid including indemnity wage benefits and permanency or impairment awards.

When evaluating a workers' compensation claim we look at the projected benefits we expect to pay on the claim, including *compensation* and *medical* related costs. This information is used to calculate projected reserves and for the evaluation of settlement dispositions.

*Compensation* costs are projected based on the compensation rate, expected period of disability and any potential permanency or impairment award. Projecting the compensation costs on a newly reported claim may be difficult as all medical, hospital and diagnostic information may not be available to evaluate the projected disability period and permanency. This may require the use of various online tools and resources to project these costs for reserve purposes.

The best method to project compensation costs is to determine the disability period for specific injuries and then estimate the total projected compensation costs (e.g. number of disability weeks multiplied by the compensation rate) by category (e.g. TTD, TPD, etc.), including any projected permanency or impairment award[17].

Experienced adjusters know the range of disability for certain types of routine injuries and use this knowledge in the evaluation process. The adjuster may also seek input for a nurse case manager and the claimant's attending physician, as well as reference material maintained by the claim department (including online subscriptions).

There are *variables* in the compensation cost evaluation, which will affect the disability period and total projected indemnity payments. For example, variables may include the following:

- Type of injuries
- Injury complications
- Claimant age
- Occupation (e.g. manual labor vs. sedentary)
- Type of injury and job requirements
- Pre-existing conditions (injuries or illnesses)
- Comorbidities (e.g. diabetes, hypertension, cancer, etc.)
- Claimant attitude
- Employer willingness to offer modified duty
- Permanency or impairment rating

The detailed compensability analysis supports the claim decision to accept or deny the claim. Accurate indemnity calculations (wages, awards and settlements) are important to control indemnity costs (and reserves).

---

[17] A permanent disability rating, sometimes known as a *permanency* or *impairment rating*, is an assessment of the severity of the permanent impairment.

*Medical* cost projections are itemized by specific category as illustrated below. The projections include the medical type, the treatment and cost projection. Medical cost projections generally include the following:

- Physician
- Hospital (ER and Inpatient)
- Diagnostics/Radiology
- Surgery
- Anesthesia
- Physical Therapy
- Chiropractic
- Prescriptions
- Durable Medical Equipment (DME)
- Ambulance/Transportation
- Travel & Mileage Expense
- IME Costs
- Funeral Costs
- Other Costs

There are also *variables* in the medical cost evaluation, which will affect the type and duration of medical treatment. For example, variables may include the following:

- Type of injury(s)
- Injury complications
- Claimant age
- Claimant occupation
- Pre-existing conditions (injuries)
- Comorbidities (e.g. diabetes, hypertension, cancer, etc.)

The analysis of workers' compensation claims is the responsibility of the adjuster and the claim manager. There are many variables in the workers' compensation evaluation which will affect the claim outcome.

The key to proper workers' compensation claim handling is to manage the disability and medical aspects of the claim to facilitate the claimant's return to work, which begins with an effective claim investigation and medical management. The adjuster utilizes the various tools available such as nurse case management, utilization review, vocational rehabilitation, medical bill review, activity checks, surveillance and use of IMEs.

Workers' compensation claim handling is very specialized and requires specific claim and jurisdictional knowledge. The more jurisdictions handled by an adjuster will increase the potential for errors or mistakes. It is critical that workers' compensation claims which have complexity and severity be assigned to experienced adjusters.

As a claim manager, it is important to control indemnity and medical costs. This is accomplished by implementing effective management controls and conducting routine claim quality file reviews. Some adjusters do not consistently manage workers' compensation claims properly, focusing more on facilitating the payment of benefits and not medically managing the claim. This is often impacted by experience and adjuster workloads. Effective medical and disability management will positively impact loss costs by facilitating the claimant's return to work.

Due to the long-term nature of workers' compensation claims it is important for the claim manager to monitor reserve adequacy and compliance with the company's reserve philosophy – to be sure the adjusters are not using a "step-ladder" approach to reserving. If adjusters are simply replenishing indemnity reserves with continued disability or replenishing medical reserves with continued medical treatment, and not reserving for permanency when warranted, you may have a problem with adjusters taking a short-term approach to workers' compensation reserving.

Workers' compensation claims should be reserved to exposure by projecting indemnity and medical benefits for the duration of the claim (including permanency). Thereafter, a reserve adjustment should only be necessary when there is a change in exposure (e.g. surgery, injury complications, etc.).

Use management controls to monitor how adjusters are managing case reserves. Review a sampling of claims and consider periodic reserve reviews by randomly selecting files from each adjuster to evaluate handling performance.

## Workers' Compensation Case Management

*Workers' Compensation Case Management* involves managing workers' compensation claims effectively by using various techniques, tools and services, which assist in medical and disability management.

Workers' compensation claims can be very costly and require focused attention on medical management (controlling medical costs) and disability management (controlling indemnity costs). Our objective is to facilitate timely indemnity and medical benefits to the claimant in accordance with the workers' compensation statutes and control costs.

Below are various aspects of workers' compensation case management techniques, tools and services, which assist in controlling costs and achieving favorable claim results:

- Requests for medical documentation and records to support the diagnosis, prognosis, treatment regime and disability period (e.g. medical records, hospital records, radiology reports and diagnostic reports).
- Request for *narrative medical reports* from the attending physician(s).
- Facilitating the claimant reaching *maximum medical improvement* or MMI status by working closely with the attending physician and nurse case manager.
- Working closely with the attending physician and the employer on disability management and return to work, including the availability of modified duty or light work.
- *Medical Bill Review* to re-price medical and hospital bills.
- *Utilization Review* by nurses who review medical or diagnostic treatment to determine if it is medically necessary and casual related to the accident.
- *Nurse Case Managers* who are trained nurses assisting the adjuster in the handling of medical claims which have complexity and severity, and act as a liaison between the treating physician and claimant.
- *Vocational Rehabilitation* by licensed rehabilitation counselors assisting the claimant in returning to work.
- *Independent Medical Examinations* (IMEs) of the claimant to provide an independent opinion of the claimant's injuries, diagnosis, prognosis, treatment, disability status, casual relation, permanency and impairment.
- *Activity Checks* and *Surveillance* of the claimant to determine current activities.

Workers' compensation case management techniques, tools and services assist adjusters in managing claims; however, sometimes these techniques, tools or services may be over-utilized (or under-utilized) either due to adjuster inexperience or not effectively controlling the vendor or internal service provider. Services such as utilization review, nurse case management, vocational rehabilitation[18], IMEs, activity checks, and surveillance all impact claim costs (loss and expense). Over-utilization will increase ALAE costs and under-utilization may increase loss costs.

Achieving the balance between over-utilization and under-utilization is not an easy task. How much should the adjuster invest in these techniques, tools and services for the claimant to reach MMI and return to work?

The claim manager should establish expectations on effective workers' compensation case management. This can be accomplished with training and implementation of claim guidelines and standards with examples and illustrations. Adjusters should be educated on the benefits of the case management techniques, tools and services, and when utilization will achieve the desired results.

---

[18] *Vocational Rehabilitation* is set up as a separate reserve exposure under VR or VOC.

Be proactive in managing workers' compensation claims – use management controls to monitor claim handling and the effectiveness of workers' compensation case management. Train and develop the staff to not only conduct proper claim investigations but also effective medical and disability management. Set the expectation that workers' compensation claim handling is not just the process of paying compensation and medical benefits.

# Litigation Management

Effective control of the litigation claim process is the responsibility of the handling adjuster and the claim manager – in compliance with litigation management guidelines.

There are various elements of the litigation management process which are established to control overall litigation costs (ALAE). As a claim manager, recognizing the critical importance of an effective litigation management program will not only improve overall claim outcomes, but maintain control of litigation expenses.

Effective litigation management starts with using only approved attorneys and law firms on the *Approved Defense Counsel* list, based on the type of litigation claim and the expertise of defense counsel.

The quality and timeliness of the initial *Suit Referral* (email or letter) sets the stage for activities to be completed by the adjuster and defense counsel. The suit referral includes relevant information and documentation such as suit service details, court and venue, style and caption, answer due date, any extensions, investigation completed, liability and damage analysis, defense counsel appearance and handling instructions, request for legal budget, adjuster follow-up items and attachments to include copies of relevant claim file documentation, pleadings and attorney litigation management guidelines.

Fostering a team environment with the adjuster and defense counsel will enhance litigation handling with timely, collaborative and documented communication between the adjuster and the handling attorney concerning litigation updates and progress, status reports, case strategy and the claim evaluation.

Litigation expense control is critical in managing ALAE costs and can be controlled more effectively with the use of *litigation budgets*, to manage and project legal costs, and hold defense counsel accountable for the accuracy of the submitted budget.

Legal bill review vendors provide legal bill review services for the insurance industry. As legal bills are received, they are routed to the legal bill review vendor who adjusts the legal bills based on industry legal practices and internal business rules. Legal bill review services can control excessive billing, and some companies have electronically integrated this process into the legal bill payment process, eliminating the need for the adjuster to review and approve the legal bill. The reviewed and paid legal bill is then automatically uploaded to the document management system. Legal bill review providers are typically paid as a percentage of the savings based on the amount of the submitted legal bill vs. the approved and paid amount.

Litigation management includes defense counsel providing an evaluation of the claim including settlement value and jury verdict potential, at various stages in the litigation process. This is an important function as it provides another viewpoint of the claim value for settlement and reserve purposes. Defense counsel's evaluation is just one component of evaluation process – it is not recommended that the adjuster or claim manager exclusively rely on defense counsel for the claim evaluation.

Litigation is costly and impacts ALAE costs. As the claim manager, you should be actively involved in litigation claims handled by your adjusting staff (unless you have a dedicated litigation claim unit with experienced litigation claim specialists). These are the costliest claims in terms of loss and expense, and your input is important for a successful outcome. Your input also includes identifying which claims should be directed toward a settlement disposition and guidance on when settlement negotiations should be initiated.

Litigating claims with lengthy discovery and depositions is a waste of internal resources and expense if you plan to ultimately settle the claim, or if you have determined that the insured is liable. Identify claims early on which can be settled (even by compromise) – this will control the adjuster workloads and reduce expense. We don't want to over-pay claims, but unfortunately claims never get better with time! Sometimes a compromise is in order.

# First Party Property Claim Handling

First party property and inland marine claims also have unique handling requirements, which require monitoring by the claim manager.

The *first party property* claim handling process may include the following components:

A. **Coverage Analysis** – Analysis of coverage to evaluate whether the loss is covered under the policy. The includes reviewing applicable policy schedules, coverage forms and endorsements, definitions, exclusions, limitations, exceptions, policy limits and sub-limits, and deductibles.

B. **Scope of Damages** – The damage *scope* involves an adjuster conducting an initial field inspection of the loss to determine:

   - The projected dollar amount of the loss (building, contents and time element)
   - Take measurements and photographs
   - Determine the building replacement cost value and *Insurance to Value* (ITV) calculation to determine whether co-insurance applies
   - Pick up the fire report (e.g. serious loss)

- Identify the cause of loss (e.g. cause of fire)
- Identify any subrogation potential
- Determine the need for an expert (e.g. cause and origin expert)
- Review public records (e.g. property search) if applicable
- Determine the need to hire a contractor or building consultant to assist with the damage assessment

C. **Damage Repair Estimate** – Requesting a repair estimate from the insured to determine the extent of the damages being claimed. If the damages are extensive, the insured may retain a builder or contractor who will work with the adjuster to agree on the cost of repairs.

D. **Property Appraisal (Estimate)** – An appraisal (or estimate) is prepared by the property adjuster who will work with the insured's contractor to get an agreed price on repairs. The appraisal is prepared using computerized property estimating software and may be prepared by a staff adjuster or an independent adjuster.

E. **Use of a Builder or Contractor** – If the damages are extensive, the adjuster may retain a contractor or building consultant to assist in preparing a damage estimate.

F. **Use of Experts** – Experts should be retained if there is potential for subrogation or the cause of the loss cannot be determined (e.g. undetermined cause of a fire may require retaining a cause & origin expert [C&O] or engineer).

G. **Personal Property Inventory** – The adjuster will provide the insured with inventory claim forms to prepare a personal property (contents) list of damaged or stolen property. The inventory forms are categorized by room or location, and include the date purchased, original cost and replacement cost amount.

H. **Controlling Time Element Loss** – *Time element* losses are: (1) additional living expenses when the insured is unable to remain at the premises due to the damages and/or repairs being completed – the insured may stay at a hotel or even have a trailer placed on the insured premises as temporary living quarters; (2) loss of rents when the property is unable to be rented due to the damages; and (3) loss of income or business interruption in commercial property losses.

I. **Statements** – Statements should be taken from the insured(s) and witnesses on large property losses, losses which have the potential for subrogation, claims involving coverage issues, property thefts and suspicious claims (e.g. fire loss).

J. **Subrogation** – All property claims require an investigation to either rule out subrogation, or firm up the subrogation claim with additional investigation, documentation and use of experts. Preservation of evidence when subrogation is involved is very important.

K. **Official Reports** – Fire and police reports provide relevant investigative information including the cause of the loss, witnesses, and information on potential responsible parties.

L. **ISO ClaimSearch®** – ISO ClaimSearch® should be filed on all property claims which provides detailed information on prior property losses as part of the claim investigation process. The entry needs to be done at the ISO ClaimSearch® web portal, unless the process is integrated with the claim system.

M. **Property Search** – Property searches are done on property losses to confirm ownership and the existence of mortgagees and property liens.

N. **Background Check and Financial Report** – If the investigation indicates the loss is suspicious, the adjuster may request a background check and financial or credit report on the insured(s), which may be handled by the *Special Investigative Unit* (SIU).

O. **Advances** – When a claim involves additional living expenses or funds are needed to begin repairs, the insured may request an advance on the claim. An advance should never be approved unless the cause of loss has been confirmed, and you are able to rule out the insured's involvement in the loss.

P. **Proof of Loss & Loan Receipt** – After a property loss has been concluded, a *Proof of Loss* supporting the claim should be provided to the insured(s) for signature. A *Loan Receipt* or *Subrogation Receipt* should also be requested if there is a potential for subrogation.

Q. **Replacement Cost Holdback** – When a policy provides replacement cost coverage, the insured may not receive full payment based on replacement cost until the repairs have been completed or the property has been replaced. A *Replacement Cost Hold-Back* document may be provided to the insured which allows the insured to make an additional claim for the difference between the actual cash value (ACV) and replacement cost value (RCV) after confirmation has been submitted that repairs have been completed or the property has been replaced.

R. **SIU** – Claims are referred to the *Special Investigative Unit* (SIU) if the investigation indicates the claim is suspicious.

When a company has staff property adjusters, they may use electronic property estimating software which is deployed to the staff adjusters using laptops or mobile devices. Some property estimating software vendors include *Xactware Solutions, Inc.* (Xactimate®), *Simultaneous Solutions Inc.* (Simsol®) and *Hawkins Research, Inc.* (PowerClaim®). Property estimating programs provide property appraisal solutions for insurance companies which include appraisal estimating software, and comprehensive reporting to effectively manage loss costs.

Property is a line of business which can have significant fluctuations in claim activity due to catastrophe losses such as hurricanes, tornados, earthquakes, flood, and hailstorms. Catastrophe (CAT) losses not only have a huge financial-impact on a company's loss ratio, but also on its staff resources. When a CAT loss occurs, a company could receive thousands of claims in a brief period seriously impacting staff resources, which affects the ability to manage CAT losses, as well as non-Cat losses.

As a claim manager, you need to plan for catastrophe loss handling both in terms of adjusting resources and CAT loss management and reporting. CAT loss handling needs to be organized and requires comprehensive reporting to identify loss activity in specific territories to determine frequency and severity, the amount of staff resources needed, and providing ongoing reporting to senior management.

Some companies may handle CAT losses using their own adjusting staff or outsource to independent adjusters, or a combination of both. The downside of outsourcing to independent adjusters, is that they are already handling losses for other companies and you may not get preferential service. An effective method to handle CAT losses is to contract with a *Third-Party Administrator* (TPA) specializing in CAT loss handling. The TPA contract should stipulate the number of experienced adjusting resources available in the event of a CAT loss. The TPA staff can handle all CAT losses or supplement the company's own staff adjuster resources.

Property losses can be costly and require specialized claim handling skills, particularly in coverage analysis and estimating property damage. The claim manager who has responsibility for managing a property claim unit should have specialized property claim skills. The manager does not need to be an expert but should have a comfort level in reviewing the accuracy of property estimates and be familiar with the property estimating software and any available reporting tools.

Property claim handling has the potential to cause claim *leakage* in the estimating process, from both internal staff resources and independent adjusters. It is important to periodically conduct a leakage review on property estimates, either through an internal property *reinspection program* or by retaining a third-party vendor to conduct a leakage review. You may be surprised as to the extent of the leakage found, even with your best adjusters.

## Automobile APD & PD Claims

As a claim manager, you should focus on key areas of the *Automobile Physical Damage* (APD) and *Property Damage* (PD) claim process to monitor claim quality and customer service.

APD and PD claims require specific claim handling tasks, which are monitored by the claim manager. These tasks are the foundation to maintain consistent quality results relative to the inspection, review and appraisal of damages.

Below are various aspects of the APD/PD claim process which affect quality and service. These areas are often incorporated into a claims quality review process and/or monitored using cycle time and metrics reports.

A. **Repair Estimate Review** – Review of the repair estimate provided by the vehicle owner to determine if it is fair and reasonable and whether a vehicle appraisal or desk review is necessary.

B. **Alternative Appraisal Methods Considered** – In lieu of an automobile appraisal the adjuster may refer the estimate to a third-party vendor to provide a *desk estimate review*, especially for claims under $5,000. If the company has *direct repair facilities* the vehicle owner may be referred to an approved shop for repairs.

C. **Timely Appraisal Assignment** – Timely assignment of the appraisal in accordance with claim handling guidelines and standards is important to maintain quality customer service and control *rental reimbursement* or *loss of use* costs.

D. **Timely Appraisal Completion** – Timely completion of the appraisal in accordance with claim handling guidelines and standards (also to maintain quality customer service and control *rental reimbursement* or *loss of use* costs).

E. **Quality of Appraisal** – The quality of the appraisal report in terms of its damage estimate accuracy – including use of proper labor (rate and hours) and parts.

F. **Timely Supplemental Assignment** – Timely assignment of the supplemental appraisal in accordance with claim handling procedures and standards.

G. **Quality of Supplemental Appraisal** – The quality of the supplemental appraisal report in terms of its damage estimate accuracy – including use of proper labor (rate and hours) and parts.

H. **Timely Total Loss Evaluation** – Timely declaration of the total loss and completion of the total loss evaluation report by the adjuster in accordance with claim handling procedures and standards. This includes communication with the vehicle owner confirming the vehicle is a total loss and must be moved to a salvage facility.

I. **Quality of Total Loss Evaluation** – The quality of the total loss report in terms of using the appropriate methodology and tools – inclusive of an underlying written appraisal, all itemized total loss calculations, including state sales tax and the proper conditioning report.

J. **Salvage Handling & Disposal** – Proper and timely handling, and disposal of salvage to reduce storage and handling costs and continued rental or loss of use. This includes timely referral of the salvage vehicle to the salvage facility.

K. **Control of Rental / Loss of Use** – Proper and timely control of automobile rental and loss of use claims including the daily rental rate and number of rental days.

Automobile appraising requires specific skills which are learned at automobile estimating schools, or by experience in working at an automobile repair facility or body shop. Companies with larger APD and PD claim volume may have their own staff appraisers; however, the smaller companies may outsource appraisals to independent appraisers.

When a company has staff appraisers, they may use electronic automobile estimating software which is deployed to the staff appraisers using laptops or mobile devices. Some automobile estimating software vendors include *Mitchell International, Inc.* and *CCC Information Services, Inc.* These services have become sophisticated in providing automobile appraisal solutions for insurance companies which include appraisal estimating software, as well as, metrics, cycle time and other reporting capabilities to effectively manage APD and PD loss costs.

Companies which outsource appraisal services may require all their appraisers to use a specific software program for consistency and allow for an aggregation of data for internal reporting. In lieu of a full automobile appraisal, some companies use *desk estimate reviews* or *estimate audit services*. These vendors review repair estimates and photographs, and then prepare an appraisal without physically inspecting the automobile. Some desk review audit service companies include *Hybrid Claims Group* and *American Computer Estimating, Inc.* (ACE)

To control loss costs, and reduce appraisal expenses, some companies have implemented a *Direct Repair Program* (DRP). DRP is a network of automobile repair shops approved by an insurance company for use by their policyholders or claimants. The DRP facility is vetted and pre-qualified by the insurer meeting specific experience, quality and customer service criteria, and subject to periodic re-inspections by the insurer. After providing a detailed repair estimate, the DRP facility will make the repairs.

Rental reimbursement and loss of use claims should be managed closely to avoid overpayments on rental claims. Some insurers may contract with automobile rental companies for reduced daily rates and ease of doing business. This may include a web-based portal for assignments and management of rental claims.

Automobile physical damage (APD) and property damage (PD) claim handling can have a material adverse impact on the company's financial results if not handled properly. When you have a large volume of these types of claims, it only takes a few hundred dollars per claim to deteriorate results.

APD and PD claims can be managed effectively with the use of metrics and cycle time reports. For example, monitoring the appraisal assignment date to completion date, or the number of days it took to move the total loss vehicle to the salvage facility to reduce storage costs, or the number of rental days compared to repair labor hours.

Implementing a comprehensive *Automobile Appraisal Reinspection Program* will have a positive impact on the claim organization, by establishing a baseline for an acceptable work product and consistency in writing automobile appraisals. It is a tool to compare actual performance to claim standards and estimating best practices (i.e. preparing fair and accurate automobile appraisals utilizing proper parts and labor rates) and a documented methodology to evaluate the quality of automobile appraisals with comprehensive reporting tools. It also provides the organization with trending capabilities which can be communicated to the appraisers – identifying strengths and weaknesses and areas which may be causing potential claim *leakage*.

The quality level of automobile appraisals has a direct impact on the Company's financial results (e.g. loss ratio and LAE), customer service, policyholder retention and assures compliance with Fair Claim Acts.

As a claim manager you should understand the importance of managing these "small claims" effectively. APD and PD claims can be costly, and *leakage* can be subtle. If the appraiser writes an additional $300 on an APD or PD appraisal, and the adjuster loses control of the rental claim paying an additional $100, we have a $400 overpayment. Take that same claim scenario and multiply it across 3,000 claims, and you have $1.2M in leakage.

Be cognizant of average paid loss trends in APD and PD claims, and monitor the quality of automobile appraisals, the quality and timeliness of total loss claim handling, and handling rental claims properly to control overall costs. Training is important in APD and PD claims to avoid mistakes and overpayments. Use your estimating software reporting tools to understand APD and PD claim trends.

## Claim Financial-Management

A key aspect of the claim manager's responsibility is the management and control of claim financial transactions, including reserves and payments. Effective management of claim financial transactions in the technical claim handling process is critical to control loss and expense costs which impact the company.

*Reserve management* includes the proper and timely management of case reserves at the exposure level in accordance with claim guidelines and standards, inclusive of new reserves and reserve adjustments.

When we establish case reserves we utilize a *reserve worksheet* (manual or electronic) which will provide a breakdown of the relevant claim details and recommended reserves as illustrated in **Exhibit 2-O** (liability), **Exhibit 2-P** (property) and **Exhibit 2-Q** (workers' compensation) in

**Chapter 2 – Financial Operations**. With reserve adjustments, the reserve worksheets are updated with projected future costs to establish new projected reserves.

The *reserve evaluation* is documented in the electronic file note, reserve worksheet, or electronic reserve evaluation screen, which supports the current reserves or proposed reserve adjustment, in accordance with the claim reserve guidelines and procedures. The reserve evaluation should include all applicable exposures (e.g. bodily injury, property damage, PIP, ALAE, etc.) and be supported by relevant claim details developed during the claim investigation and adjustment process.

The level of the adjuster's claim authority will determine whether the new reserve or the reserve adjustment will require the claim manager's approval. The claim manager will approve the reserve through a system work queue, which involves the adjuster referring the claim to the claim manager for review and approval. Prior to the referral, there may be communication between the adjuster and claim manager on an appropriate reserve if the reserve exceeds the adjuster's claim authority level, or even discussed in a *claim committee*.

The claim manager should use the reserve approval request to provide substantive feedback on the claim evaluation and analysis (e.g. application of comparative negligence). If the claim manager disagrees with the adjuster's recommendation, the claim manager should make the necessary reserve change, but explain the basis for the change in the electronic file notes. This serves two purposes; it provides education and training to the adjuster and properly documents the claim record with the revised claim evaluation.

It is important that new reserves and reserve adjustments are entered timely. All new reserves should be entered within the required time frame (e.g. 15th day or 30th day from the report date). If there is a change in exposure (including liability or damages), the claim reserve should be adjusted within thirty days of recognition of the change in exposure. This procedure should be closely monitored by the claim manager as the late adjustment of reserves (particularly large reserve increases in prior accident or underwriting years) may impact the company's financial results.

*Step ladder* reserving involves incremental reserve increases over time to accommodate payments, instead of reserving the claim initially to the full exposure. This type of reserving methodology is not recommended as it delays the posting of timely and proper case reserves and has the potential to cause *reserve deficiency*.

If the claim value exceeds the adjuster's claim authority, the settlement approval process will begin with the adjuster requesting approval to initiate settlement discussions with the unrepresented claimant or their attorney. The adjuster will document the claim record with a settlement evaluation detailing liability and damages, including the *gross* value (without offset for comparative negligence or contribution) and *net* value of the claim (settlement ranges should be encouraged). The evaluation should be consistent with the results of the claim investigation.

The claim manager should review the settlement evaluation and request for authority. If the claim manager agrees with the adjuster's evaluation, settlement authority should be extended in a settlement range. If the claim manager disagrees with the adjuster's evaluation, the claim manager should provide an alternative settlement evaluation, but explain the basis for the change in the electronic file notes. As indicated above, this provides education and training for the adjuster and properly documents the claim record with the revised settlement evaluation.

The payment approval process involves the claim manager approving a claim payable or check over the adjuster's claim authority. Most claim systems have functionality which will refer payments over the adjuster's authority to the claim manager for approval in a work queue. If the payable is for a settlement over the adjuster's claim authority, presumably the claim record will be documented with the claim manager's approval of a settlement range. The approval process is a *management control* and provides the claim manager with an opportunity to review the claim outcome (and negotiations) after claim authority has been extended.

The claim manager is responsible for expense control in their unit or department. This includes allocated loss adjustment expenses or ALAE, for payments relating to a specific claim (e.g. attorney, expert, etc.), and unallocated loss adjustment expenses or ULAE which includes fees for internal and external adjusters/appraisers, the expenses related to the evaluation of coverage, and the overhead cost of the claim operations. Expense control also pertains to effective and efficient use of internal field claim staff resources (e.g. not using field resources for tasks which can been handled by telephone, email or mail). See **Chapter 2 – Financial Operations**.

The management and control of ALAE is at the claim file level and should be monitored and controlled by the claim manager with file reviews and the quality review process. The largest component of ALAE are litigation related costs. To control ALAE expenses effectively, it is recommended that ALAE authority levels be established for each adjuster. Authority should include ALAE reserve and payment authority, with unit and departmental ALAE goals by category such as attorney, legal, expert and other expense.

ULAE expense is not claim file specific – but does involve some file specific expenses for internal and external adjusters/appraisers, and the expenses related to the evaluation of coverage. The largest component of the ULAE expense is for the claim department salaries and benefits (over 50% of the expense) and other related costs. The claim manager is responsible to control these expenses through budget and resource management. Resource management will be discussed further in **Chapter 7 – Staffing & Resource Management**.

## Disposition and Resolution

The disposition and resolution of claims should be a primary focus for all adjusters. We use the investigation, information, documentation and records developed during the claim process to support the claim analysis and evaluation. Thereafter, once the claim analysis and evaluation has been completed, the claim becomes positioned for disposition and resolution.

It should be noted that depending on the company *settlement philosophy*, preparing a claim for disposition and resolution may begin before the investigation is fully completed if it is determined that the insured has liability (in a casualty claim). **Chapter 3 – Managing Effectively** provides a sample claim settlement philosophy.

The claim disposition and resolution category have several subcategories or components including:

A. **Efforts to Conclude Claim** – The adjuster's effort to direct the claim toward closing or positioned for a settlement disposition.

B. **Settlement Negotiations** – Timely and effective settlement negotiations with the insured, claimant, carrier or claimant attorney. Settlement negotiations should be documented in the electronic file notes inclusive of negotiation tactics and points (e.g. strengths and weaknesses of the insured's defense), settlement ranges, target settlement offer, as well as the details of all settlement demands and offers.

C. **Utilization of Settlement Options** – Utilization of various settlement options to achieve an equitable settlement including arbitration, mediation, lump sum settlements, commutations, or structured settlements.

This process includes compliance with Medicare concerning *Medicare Set-Aside Arrangements*[19] as part of the settlement process (workers' compensation and liability claims). For example, if you are considering settlement of a workers' compensation claim, you need to ascertain if Medicare is or will be involved at a future date, to determine if their interests need to be protected.

D. **Claim Disposition Results** – The prompt and appropriate disposition of claims with an acceptable or better result.

E. **Proper Closing Documentation** – Appropriate closing documentation in the claim file including settlement agreement, release, discontinuance, proof of loss and other documents.

---

[19] **Medicare Set-Aside Arrangements** (MSAs). A Workers' Compensation Medicare Set-Aside Arrangement (WCMSA) is a financial agreement that allocates a portion of a workers' compensation settlement to pay for future medical services related to the workers' compensation injury, illness, or disease. After there is a settlement in a workers' compensation claim, the amount of the settlement that is "set-aside" for medical care must be put into a special account called a Medicare Set-Aside Account or MSA Account. These funds must be depleted before Medicare will pay for treatment related to the workers' compensation injury, illness, or disease. All parties in a workers' compensation claim have significant responsibilities under the Medicare Secondary Payer (MSP) laws to protect Medicare's interests when resolving cases that include future medical expenses. The recommended method to protect Medicare's interests is a WCMSA (U.S. Centers for Medicare & Medicaid Services).

F.   **Proper Payment Processing & Payee** – Issuance of a proper claim payment (amount and payee) based on the settlement criteria and agreement, and other requirements as lienholders, loss payees, spouse, etc.

As a claim manager, it is important to review claim dispositions by adjuster including dispositions within the adjuster's claim authority and authority you have extended above the adjuster's authority. The disposition of a claim represents the total payment for that exposure – the reserve is now closed, and the incurred loss activity will be equivalent to the paid amount unless it is offset by recovery. The claim manager now has an opportunity to review the adjuster's work product from inception to closure.

After the claim disposition, the claim manager has an opportunity to review the adjuster's coverage analysis, the quality of the claim investigation and adjustment process, file documentation, the *gross* claim evaluation (e.g. injury or damage value), the liability analysis (e.g. application of comparative negligence), the adjuster's negotiations skill and effectiveness, consideration of appropriate settlement options, and potential claim leakage.

# Diary Management & Claim Control

Diary management and claim control drives the "tempo" of the claim file development. Claims with diaries which are late, missed, or too long between diary review periods, contribute heavily to the timeliness and quality of the claim investigation, analysis and evaluation of the claim, poor customer service, and unfavorable claim outcomes or results.

The diary management and claim control category has several subcategories or components including:

A.   **Current & Appropriate Adjuster Diary** – Timely and substantive diary of the claim in accordance with claim procedures, guidelines and claim standards. Diary intervals should be appropriate for the type of claim, with more serious and complex claims having shorter diary cycles.

B.   **Documented Plan of Action (POA)** – A detailed **Plan of Action** (or *Action Plan*) in the file notes or as an attachment providing file direction inclusive of coverage, facts of accident or incident, liability or compensability issues, evaluation of the injuries, disability, and damages, investigation completed and outstanding, recovery, litigation status, settlement evaluation (settlement discussions), reserves and future items to be completed. The plan of action should be substantive allowing the reader to fully understand the claim details, evaluation and overall file direction.

C.   **Pro-Active Control of Claim** – Documented control of the claim process and claim file development. This includes pro-active control of the claim investigation, evaluation, disposition and financial control of loss and expense (reserves and payments).

D. **File Tempo** – Timely development of the claim to complete all outstanding activities, inclusive of directing the claim toward an appropriate disposition or resolution. Claim files with poor file *tempo* lack the attention needed and result in late activities, or unnecessarily extend the duration of the claim.

Diary management and claim control is easier to monitor when the claim manager is already following the claim on dual diary. However, claims handled by the adjuster within their authority level requires a different approach. The most effective way to monitor diary management and claim control is by reviewing claim files, but a claim manager may not always have the time to conduct a high volume of file reviews to identify deficiencies in this *best practice* category.

An effective monitoring approach is to use management controls and reports to review adjuster performance. Most modern architecture claim systems have integrated dashboards which illustrate claim diaries and highlight adjuster diaries which are not current. This allows the claim manger to selectively review claims which may not be current. Business rules can also be developed which notify the claim manager by email when an adjuster diary date is well beyond the acceptable overdue range (e.g. 10 - 15 days). Another approach is to use a reporting tool to identify claims, by adjuster, with overdue diary dates – and then review the relevant claim files listed in the report.

# Compliance

Claim compliance is a broad category and may also include adjuster licensing, continuing education and other regulatory requirements. In this book, we will focus on the following compliance categories:

A. **Claim Guideline Compliance** – Compliance with internal claim guidelines, standards and procedures.

B. **Procedural Compliance & Claim Coding** – Compliance with all internal claim procedural and processing requirements, as well as accurate coding of claim transactions (by the adjuster).

C. **Claim Authority Compliance** – Compliance with the designated claim authority relative to reserving, settlement and payment of claims. This applies to both loss and expense transactions (by adjuster).

D. **Compliance with State Workers' Compensation Acts** – Compliance with the State Workers' Compensation Act and statutes inclusive of jurisdictional filings, timely and proper issuance of workers' Compensation benefits, claim forms, letters and other requirements.

E. **<u>Fair Claim Act / State Regulation Compliance</u>** – Compliance with State *Fair Claim Acts* and Insurance Regulations inclusive of required fair claim handling with parties to the loss, timely and proper issuance of letters, forms and correspondence required by the insurance department or state regulations.

F. **<u>CMS Medicare Compliance</u>** – Compliance with CMS Medicare rules and regulations including proper and timely identification of Medicare eligible parties, reporting to Medicare, and facilitation and preparation of MSA's.

The adjusting staff should be familiar with and understand all internal claim guidelines, standards and procedures.

Compliance with designated claim authority is a primary management control and claim security is managed by the claim system through the IT department or internal audit (using the system administrative module). However, the claim system security may not control exceeding authority based on the *gross* value of the claim. For example, if the adjuster has $50,000 in claim authority, the authority level is based on the *net* reserve or payment authority level controlled by the claim system. If a claim has a gross value of $100,000, with a 50% liability assessment, the claim will be within the adjuster's authority level in the claim system (e.g. $50,000).

If the claim manager wants to control claim authority at the *gross* damage level, other management controls will need to be used by the claim manager to monitor and control these losses. This can be accomplished with management reports and system business rules to identify the *gross* evaluation of claims in structured system fields. The procedures and process should also be incorporated into the claim guidelines and procedures.

As a claim manager, you should understand state and federal claim handling requirements and make sure your adjusting staff is in compliance. Non-compliance with state claim handling requirements can lead to regulatory fines and a potential *bad faith claim* against the insurance company based on unfair claim practices. These claims are very costly and can be avoided with proper controls and training.

Compliance requires monitoring through claim file reviews and an effective claims quality review process, but also requires adjuster training and development, particularly in claim jurisdictions which have comprehensive insurance regulations with stringent requirements (e.g. California, New York, etc.).

## <u>Reporting & Documentation</u>

Reporting and documentation are a critical component of the claim handling process and serve as a method to document the claim file with relevant notes, reports, information and documents, providing relevant details and summaries of important claim information.

The reporting and documentation category may include the following subcategories or components:

A. **Proper & Timely File Reporting** – Compliance with claim reporting requirements in accordance with claim guidelines, standards and procedures, inclusive of internal and external reporting. This includes all required reporting at various intervals in the claim process by email, system screen, document upload or electronic note entry.

B. **Clear & Concise File Notes** – Clear and concise electronic file notes which are substantive with a minimum of typographical errors. Notes should not include editorial comments nor information, which could <u>not</u> be read publicly, unless the note is specifically designated as confidential. Electronic notes should not be typed in all capital letters.

C. **Proper File Management** – Proper management of claim file contents including organization and labeling of attachments, reports and notes. The claim records should be well organized and managed, so the reader can understand the investigation and adjustment results, claim evaluation and future file direction.

D. **File Documentation & Attachments** – File attachments posted to the electronic claim file including all appropriate documentation developed during the claim investigation and adjustment process such as emails, letters and correspondence, medical & hospital bills and reports, damage estimates and appraisals, photographs, statements, etc.

The use of electronic claim files has streamlined the claim handling process; however, many claim systems require structured fields to be completed inclusive of various claim elements and attributes, to facilitate analytics programs and reporting. This is in addition to the claim reporting referenced above.

The key to effective reporting and documentation is for it to be timely, clear, concise and substantive. This category is important as reporting and documentation provides the foundation to summarize the investigation and adjustment process, the claim evaluation, and ultimate disposition. It also provides the basis for case reserving and request for claim authority.

Avoid redundant file reporting and consolidate or eliminate reports when appropriate. Reporting should be useful and not a compilation of information already reported elsewhere in the claim file, or of limited value. Modern architecture claim systems have structured fields within various screens providing claim summaries and evaluations. Adjusters should use these tools instead of preparing summary reports in Word® or some other application.

# Supervision

When a claim manager is responsible for subordinates who are in a supervisory capacity, there needs to be a framework in place to evaluate claim supervision.

The supervision category may include the following broad subcategories or components:

A. **Initial Supervisory Direction** – The timeliness and quality of initial up-front supervision to the adjuster providing input and file direction. Not all claims require up-front initial supervision, and the supervisor should be selective based on the adjuster's knowledge and experience.

B. **Follow-Up Supervisory Direction** – The timeliness and quality of follow-up supervision to the adjuster providing input and file direction, with emphasis on adjuster compliance with prior supervisory direction.

C. **Substantive & Specific Supervision** – The quality of supervision should be substantive, specific and relevant to the claim. This includes providing the necessary level of supervision required based on the complexity and severity of the claim, as well as the adjuster's knowledge, experience and claim authority.

D. **Effective Delegation** – Delegating activities to the adjuster which are above their claim authority such as settlement or reserve authority. This includes *charging back* claims to the adjuster for handling by extending additional claim authority above the adjuster's claim authority level.

E. **Supervisory Diary Management** – Timely and appropriate supervisory diaries. The supervisory diary should comply with established claim guidelines and procedures. The diary intervals will vary based on the claim exposure and adjuster's role and experience.

The supervision category includes all the *best practice* categories as the claim manager is responsible for the adjuster's work product and claim outcome. When reviewing a claim file from a supervisory perspective the manager is looking for specific strengths and weaknesses in management.

In addition to the above broad subcategories, the manager will want to review the following:

- Does the claim work product meet company guidelines, standards and procedures?
- Is the claim manager delegating effectively?
- Is the claim manager proactive in resolving technical claim issues by coaching and mentoring the adjuster?
- Do the adjusters comply with the claim manager's instructions and direction?

- Are there performance issues developing in the claim work product which need to be addressed by the claim supervisor or manager? Has the claim supervisor or manager taken any action on the performance issue?

# Supervisory Best Practices

We evaluate the technical claim staff based on adherence to claim *best practices* which include various technical claim handling best practice categories (e.g. coverage, contacts, investigation, evaluation, etc.). It is also important to have *Supervisory Best Practices*, which outline claim supervisor and manager requirements when providing oversight of technical claim handling.

A supervisory best practice *framework* may include the following.

## Supervisory Management Controls

Typically, supervisory *best practices* incorporate the technical claim handling best practice categories, but also include guidelines on how to supervise or management effectively. As a claim supervisor or manager, utilization of *management controls* is a key responsibility to ensure consistent quality results, and compliance with company best practice guidelines, standards and procedures. When supervising technical claim files, it is important to focus on claim trends, which is where there will be the most financial-impact.

Management controls for the claim supervisor or manager revolve around technical claim handling and best practice compliance. The claim supervisor's routine oversight of technical claim file activities includes:

- Claim assignment instructions (upfront supervision when warranted)
- Technical claim supervision within the electronic file notes providing file direction and oversight
- Claim file discussions with the adjuster documented in the electronic file notes
- Supervisory *diary* reviews including designated auto-diary reviews at specific intervals
- Managing reserves and reserve approval for new reserves and reserve adjustments
- Payment approval (e.g. payable approval above adjuster's authority)
- Extending claim authority (e.g. settlement authority)
- Adjuster *Action Plan* review and approval
- Compensability denial review and approval (WC)
- Coverage issue review and approval of coverage position letters
- Claims quality review process
- Routine file reviews
- Use of large loss & claim committee reviews (e.g. claims at $150,000 and over)

## Diary Management & Supervisory Review:

*Diary Management* is the primary control for the adjuster and claim supervisor to handle claim activities timely and in accordance with the required *Best Practices*. Compliance with diary management avoids missing critical dates, which can impact the claim development, compliance and filing requirements, and claim outcomes.

Diary management is an effective oversight tool used by claim supervisor. The claim supervisor maintains a supervisor diary on an adjuster's claim file to monitor its progress and provide substantive supervision and direction. It also provides a second review of the claim to be sure it is being handled timely, properly and in accordance with company *Best Practices*.

Claim supervisory diary should be <u>required</u> on the following claims:

- Claims which <u>exceed</u> the adjuster's claim authority (based on an individual outstanding reserve exposure)
- Claims pending in litigation
- Claims involving coverage issues
- Claims involving compensability denials (WC)
- Claims with Insurance Department or Regulatory Complaints
- Claims involving Fraud issues, Arson Fire or SIU involvement
- Claims involving Extracontractual and/or Excess of Policy Limits exposure
- Claims with allegations of Fair Claim Act violations and/or Bad Faith claim handling
- Claims which name the Company or its affiliates as a defendant in a lawsuit and/or administrative hearing
- Claims involving a Class Action lawsuit
- All claims with the following types of <u>injuries</u>:
    o Fatality
    o Spinal cord injury resulting in paraplegia or quadriplegia
    o Amputation (significant)
    o Full thickness burns and/or burn injuries requiring admittance to a hospital burn unit
    o Electrocution with resultant burns
    o Traumatic brain injuries (TBI)
    o Severe head injury resulting in unconsciousness/hospital admission
    o Heart attack / Cardiac dysfunction
    o Non-union bone fractures
    o Internal injuries
    o Injury requiring life-flight services
    o AIDS exposure
    o Mental disorders where total incapacity is being claimed
    o Permanent total disability claims with on-going medical care

- o Occupational disease (e.g. asbestos, lead, pesticide, infectious, cancer, PTSD, etc.)
- o Any other type of injury which will result in long-term medical treatment and/or disability

The claim supervisor has the option to add a *supervisory diary* on any claim within their area of responsibility. The expectation is that the claim supervisor will not need a supervisory diary on most claims which are within the adjusters claim authority; however, the claim supervisor remains responsible for all claims within their unit, and area of responsibility. The claim supervisor should encourage adjusters to work autonomously within their designated claim authority, with the supervisor using management controls including diary management to monitor claim activities.

The time span between supervisor diary dates will depend on the type of claim and its overall exposure. The claim supervisor diary review dates should be based on the file development stage, type of claim, complexity and severity, type of exposure, file activity and the adjuster assigned to handle the claim. At minimum, the supervisor diary intervals should be in the 30 – 60-day range.

The claim supervisor may only need to provide minimal supervision on a claim, allowing the adjuster to handle the claim with limited supervision due to the adjuster's experience and qualifications; however, the claim supervisor remains responsible for the claim. The claim supervisor may also extend claim authority to the adjuster and allow the adjuster to handle the claim on their own up to a designated monetary authority level, authorized (in writing) by the claim supervisor.

To achieve quality claim outcomes and provide consistency in diary management and supervisory oversight, the following key supervisory diary dates are recommended.

- **Initial 15-Day Review:** This diary review requires the supervisor to review and provide direction on key aspects of claim handling including coverage, investigation, liability or compensability, damages, first party property claim handling (scope, inspection, cause & origin and damage estimate), subrogation, reserves and review of the adjuster's initial *Plan of Action* (POA).

- **45-Day File Review:** This diary review is used as a follow-up to the *15-Day Review* to confirm the *Plan of Action* (POA) is being followed properly and the claim file development is on track. The claim supervisor should provide relevant and substantive feedback on any outstanding claim investigation (including subrogation), liability or compensability, damages, first party property claim handling, reserves, medical and disability management (including RTW), claimant attorney engagement, compliance, litigation management and file administration.

- **90-Day File Review:** This diary review is used as a follow-up to the *45-Day File Review* to confirm the *Plan of Action* (POA) is being followed properly and the claim file development is on track. The claim supervisor should provide relevant and substantive feedback on any outstanding claim investigation (including subrogation), liability and damages, first party property claim handling, reserves, medical and disability management (including RTW), claimant attorney engagement, compliance, litigation management, settlement opportunities, and file administration.

- **180-Day File Review(s):** This diary review begins at the first 180 days after the claim is set-up and occurs <u>every</u> 180 days thereafter. The *180-Day Review* is a management control and requires a thorough review of the claim file development by the claim supervisor. The claim supervisor should provide relevant and substantive feedback on reserves, outstanding investigation, liability and damages, first party property claim handling, medical and disability management (including RTW), claimant attorney engagement, litigation management, settlement opportunities, and file administration. The adjuster should be required to prepare a *Plan of Action* (POA) prior to this review date for supervisory review and comment.

The claim supervisor should use these diary review dates to provide effective supervision. If the claim file development is on track and you are confident in the adjuster's ability to handle the claim to a final resolution, consider extending claim authority (in writing) above the adjuster's claim authority level and not actively follow the claim.

Remember, the claim staff requires both positive and negative feedback, but consistent negative feedback will result in a negative work environment.

## Claim Authority:

Claim authority is a critical management control as it provides the basis for authority for financial transactions and/or claim dispositions. Claim authority for a specific claim transaction may go through several levels of approval depending on the dollar size of the transaction.

Having levels of claim authority within an organization provides control of loss and expense transactions which impact the Company's financial results. Each claim role or position has a designated claim authority; however, the claim supervisor may reduce or adjust the claim authority level based on an individual adjuster's claim experience and/or knowledge. Claim authority should be earned and may not always be consistent with the claim role authority level.

There are four types of claim authority:

1. **Reserve Authority** – monetary authority to establish new reserves and reserve adjustments at the claim exposure level without supervisory approval.

2. **<u>Payable Approval Authority</u>** – monetary authority to approve claim payables at the claim exposure level without supervisory approval.

3. **<u>Settlement Authority</u>** – monetary authority to extend a settlement offer (first or third-party claim), or commit the company to a settlement offer, without supervisory approval.

4. **<u>Expense Authority</u>** – monetary authority to incur or pay an individual claim expense (ALAE) on a claim file without supervisory approval.

Claim authority is the maximum monetary amount that a claims employee may use in the establishment of a claim reserve, negotiation of a settlement, payment of a claim, or payable approval, without seeking the approval from a claim supervisor or manager.

Within this authority framework, the adjuster handles and manages claims within their designated claim authority with minimal active supervision by the claim supervisor or manager. The claim supervisor is responsible to supervise all claims over the adjuster's claim authority and claims within the adjuster's authority which may require supervision depending on the line of business, type of claim, injury(s) and damages, specific circumstances such as coverage issues, complex liability or compensability issues, claim denials, or litigation claims. This structure also allows the claim supervisor to extend claim authority to the adjuster above the adjuster's authority (e.g. settlement authority).

The *reserve worksheet* (or reserve evaluation screen) should be completed in detail with all new and adjusted case reserves – for claims within and above the adjuster's claim authority level. The claim supervisor should approve all reserve transactions which <u>exceed</u> the adjuster's claim authority level.

## **<u>Supervisory File Reporting & Documentation</u>:**

*File Reporting* is critical to the claim handling process. It provides a summary of the claim, activities completed and outlines what needs to be done to bring the claim to a conclusion, or to the next stage, or phase. File reporting includes status reports, large loss reports and action plans.

File reporting benefits the adjuster in not having to re-review the claim file at a diary review date and for the claim supervisor or manager to understand and evaluate the overall file handling by the adjuster and the file direction.

The adjuster reports to the file and documents file developments. The claim supervisor reviews the adjuster's work product and provides constructive feedback and direction. The adjuster should document the *Plan of Action* (POA) and provide file direction, and the claim supervisor provides relevant comments and direction based on the adjuster's plan and file development. The claim supervisor may add or supplement the adjuster's plan or provide additional insight and/or file direction.

The claim file must be documented with supervisor's comments and instructions. This can be accomplished with a supervisory file note or email pasted to the file notes. If the claim supervisor met with the adjuster to discuss a claim, the relevant and salient points of the discussion must be documented in the claim file notes either by the adjuster or supervisor.

It is appropriate to provide guidance and direction in the claim file notes, even commenting on mishandling, mistakes or tardiness when necessary; however, it is not appropriate to criticize handling using the claim notes as a communicative tool to document poor-performance. This is particularly true when the same poor-performance issues are in multiple claim files.

Take the performance issue out of the claim file and work with the Human Resource department to develop an employee performance plan to address any claim handling deficiencies. Poor-performance can be a temporary isolated incident or continuous. Obviously, continuous poor-performance is more serious and requires more attention.

## Compliance:

The claim supervisor is required to monitor and manage compliance with claim *best practices*, fair claim acts, department of insurance regulations (including no fault or PIP regulations, licensing, etc.), and workers' compensation statutes, acts and commissions. Non-compliance may result in fines, penalties, audits and/or other state or regulatory inquiries.

Managing compliance is an integral part of the claim supervisory process – it requires diligence by the claim supervisor in providing input and direction to the adjusters to avoid compliance issues and recognizing when compliance issues occur to mitigate any potential damages.

## Quality Assurance (QA) Process:

The primary objective of a QA process is to identify and evaluate claim handling *trends* – positive and negative – and to enhance the effectiveness of the claim operation. See **Chapter 6 – Claims Quality Review Process** for details.

# Chapter Comments

In this chapter, we reviewed various claim handling *best practice* categories in property & casualty (including workers' compensation) claims. In each category, we reviewed the individual components to emphasize specific claim handling requirements and provided relevant comments on applicable supervision.

The quality of claim handling directly impacts the claim outcome or result and impacts the overall *loss rat*io. For example, if the claim investigation is inadequate or incomplete, the liability analysis may not be accurate, potentially resulting in a claim overpayment. Or, if a repair estimate is submitted and the adjuster accepted the estimate without having the damages appraised, the damages may have been overstated resulting in a potential claim overpayment.

As a claim manager, you need to establish expectations for quality claim handling. This is accomplished by having clear, concise and consistent claim handling guidelines, standards and procedures. These provide the foundation for *best practice* requirements and serve as a benchmark to evaluate claim handling by the claim staff.

Provide substantive claim supervision, but do not over-supervise – delegate to your staff when appropriate. You should not have a supervisor diary on every claim file. You will dilute your effectiveness as a claim supervisor. Allow your staff to work autonomously within their claim authority level and only diary those claims within the adjuster's authority level which require your attention.

Motivate the staff to get the job done by leading effectively – do not micromanage. Use management controls and the *claims quality review process* to monitor compliance with best practices, and track claim handling trends (positive and negative).

# CHAPTER 6
# CLAIMS QUALITY REVIEW PROCESS

## Claims Quality Review Process

To manage the technical claim handling process effectively, and achieve high quality claim results, it is important to implement and maintain an effective *Claims Quality Review Process* sometimes referred to as a *Quality Assurance Process*.

A claims quality review program, properly implemented and managed, establishes organizational expectations for the level of claim quality required in a claim operation. It provides the necessary tools to manage and control the most critical aspect of a claim operation – technical claim handling.

The quality level of technical claim handling achieved in a claim operation has a direct impact on the company's financial results (e.g. loss ratio and LAE). The overall quality of the claim investigation, evaluation and other critical adjusting activities impact the ability to reserve claims properly and achieve quality claim dispositions. Quality claim handling also has a positive impact on customer service, policyholder retention and assures compliance with Fair Claim Acts.

A comprehensive claims quality review program has a positive impact on the claim organization in many ways, for example, it:

- Establishes the *baseline* for an acceptable work product and consistency in claim handling.
- Provides a tool to compare actual performance to established claim guidelines, standards and *best practices*.
- Provides a documented methodology to evaluate claim performance using a structured process and comprehensive reporting tools.
- Allows the organization to trend the quality of claim handling in specific areas at a *major category* level (e.g. Investigation) and *sub-category* level (e.g. statements, witness identification, scene photos, etc.).
- Provides constructive feedback to the claim staff monthly enhancing communication between the adjuster and manager on technical performance issues – identifying strengths and weaknesses by claim employee, unit, office and organization.
- Identifies and tracks reserve redundancy and deficiency by claim employee, unit, office and organization.
- Identifies and tracks claim dollar *leakage* by pinpointing the specific leakage cause and its financial-impact.

- Provides management with a sophisticated tool to evaluate organizational performance and institute action plans and training to correct any deficiencies, on a timely basis.

# Auditing Tools & Methodologies

Claims quality review processes have been in existence for many years in the insurance industry. The key to a successful quality review program is to focus on the review components which are most impactful to the claim operation (e.g. based on claim *best practices*) – then trend the results to identify operational strengths and weaknesses. Conducting quality file reviews and not using the data to improve performance and the quality of claim handling in the organization is a waste of time and management resources.

In the last 8 - 10 years, claim auditing tools have become more sophisticated with integrated reporting functionality. Not too long ago (and for some companies it still exists) a claim operation would use paper forms to record and quantify the results of a claim review. Although the manual review process was effective it had limited application as it was difficult to trend data over periods of time at a granular level when using a manual process.

Claim files had to be manually selected by the supervisor often resulting in adverse selection – with a claim file selected for review even though the supervisor knew the claim had quality problems based on a prior file review (e.g. for reserve or settlement approval). If the file sampling is not randomly selected, the results will be skewed and not accurately represent the condition of the claim files.

After the manual review forms were completed, the supervisor or manager then needed to manually complete a summary form to calculate the results by adjuster and unit. When the reviews were completed (typically monthly), the results would be communicated to the adjuster attaching the review forms to the hard copy claim file for reference. If the adjuster disagreed with the review findings, there would be further discussion. Although the process was manual and time consuming it provided feedback on adjuster performance.

The industry then moved to using Excel® as a method to capture results electronically and report on the results using Excel® reporting tools. Individually tabbed Excel® spreadsheets are used as a *review entry form*[20] to capture relevant data as the basis to calculate review scoring on each claim file comparing actual results to *best practices*. Additional spreadsheets are used to summarize the results in a scorecard format.

Scoring is then derived from the Excel® summary sheets by specific review categories (e.g. investigation) and subcategories (e.g. statements, scene photos and diagram, ISO ClaimSearch®,

---

[20] The Excel® review forms are created as an electronic entry form with fillable boxes and "drop-downs" for data entry. The forms include *best practice* categories and subcategories providing the reviewer with a methodology to score each individual claim file after review. The forms are "locked" in Excel® except for the entry data. Formulas are used to calculate results for compilation to develop summary scorecards on the results.

etc.) using a summary scorecard methodology. Although more effective than a manual review process, this methodology does have its challenges with multiple formulas and limited reporting capability, as well as limitations on the number of Excel® entry forms one could retain in a file without crashing the program. Some claim operations still use an Excel® based process, with *Pivot Tables*, *Slicers* (to filter data) and other reporting tools to analyze data developed from the review entry forms.

Many companies have moved their claims quality review process to a *database* format. Specific review categories and subcategories are developed based on claim *best practices*. An electronic review entry form is developed to capture all the data needed to conduct the claim file review, with the ability to score the claim file in various categories and subcategories (using drop-down menus). The electronic review forms are web-based and accessed from a web browser for entry and submission – with entry data populating the database for reporting purposes.

After the electronic form is completed and *submitted*, it populates the database. A database reporting tool is then used to access the database to develop reports – which can be routine reports accessed regularly or *ad hoc* customized reports. The database allows for granular reporting and advanced trending of data over long periods of time. The trending provides a tool for the claim supervisor and manager to focus on specific strengths and weaknesses in the organization at the adjuster, unit and department level. The same audit tools can be used when conducting home office or annual administrative claim reviews to compare the review results by the claim supervisor and manager against the audit team's results.

Developing databases and the use of database reporting tools is very common in many insurance organizations. Building an electronic quality review process using a database format is not that difficult with standard database applications on the market. Some companies have used Microsoft® SharePoint® to build the electronic review platform, exporting the data to a database reporting tool.

The key to an effective quality review tool is to capture relevant and useful claim data and have a reporting tool which can retrieve specific data from a database to provide comprehensive reporting and analytics. The reporting tool functions should be flexible to allow for customized reporting on data developed in the file review process.

There are claim auditing tools on the market which provide comprehensive claim audit functionality and reporting/analytics. Some tools can be purchased, while others are licensed based on a specific contract term. Examples of industry claim audit tools include *Aon Inpoint Claims Monitor®* by Aon plc and *Teamthink®* by Athenium, Inc.

## Claims Quality Review Objective

As indicated in other chapters, the primary objective of a *Claims Quality Review Program* is to identify and evaluate positive and negative claim handling trends to enhance the effectiveness of the claim operation. By analyzing claim trends, the claim manager is able to effectively address the overall strengths and weaknesses in the claim operation.

Consider the claim manager who reviews claim files throughout the month but does not quantify or trend the results. The claim manager records the file review results on manual review sheets which are filed away never to be reviewed again, other than perhaps on a summary level at a year-end performance review. The adjuster loses the benefit of constructive feedback throughout the year and the claim manager never really identifies key trends which are both positive and negative in their unit or department. The overall organizational results are not consolidated for analysis, nor is there a methodology to validate the claim manager's individual review results to determine if they are accurate and consistent with the overall claim organization. If the entire claim management team is using the same manual process, you can see the potential adverse impact on the claim operation.

For a claims quality review program to be effective it must include the following characteristics:

- Be in an electronic format with:
    - Utilization of a database program to capture and store results.
    - *Individual claim review forms* in a web-based format with the ability to capture structured and unstructured data (e.g. notes and comments) to populate the database.
    - Core claim system integration to allow for random file selection with pre-determined criteria and pre-population of key information on the claim review forms when entering (or linking) a claim reference number – this will reduce timely manual entry inclusive of information such as date of loss, date reported, insured, claimant, policy information, financial transactions, accident description, office, adjuster and manager name, etc.
    - Multi-user concurrent access to allow for group claim reviews such as home office reviews with the ability to quantify group results.
    - The ability to compare claim review results by individual managers to a group claim review, such as a home office claim review, to compare and validate the claim manager's review results throughout the year.
    - Comprehensive reporting and analytics tools allowing for reporting and trending at the adjuster, manager, office and company level.
    - The ability to allow inquiry access for the adjuster to view their own individual file review forms and trending reports to foster transparency in the review process.
- Provide detailed data to identify specific trends in claim handling at a granular level.
- Flexibility to add, modify or remove claim review categories and subcategories, and modify the review form format.
- Utilization of ratings which are quantifiable, consistent and understood by both the reviewer and reviewee, inclusive of objective descriptions of each *category* and *sub-category*. The reviewer can then evaluate each claim using consistent and uniform definitions for

established standards (e.g. what is considered *unsatisfactory*, *satisfactory* [meeting standards], and *exceeding standards*).

- Be constructive – providing constructive feedback to the employee on technical claim performance and offering suggestions for improvement through one-on-one discussion, education and training.
- Integrated with the employee *performance management* process and heavily weighted toward the overall employee performance rating – to emphasize the critical importance of meeting technical claim handling standards.

For a claims quality review program to achieve the desired results if must be embraced by the entire claim organization as a constructive tool to maintain the quality of technical claim handling. If claim management considers the claims quality claim review process as a tedious monthly task which has limited impact and merit, it will not be embraced by the claim staff. Employees want feedback on their work product – and an effective comprehensive claims quality review program allows for a fair and equitable methodology to review all employees using the same standards and metrics.

Quality file review results should be communicated to the adjuster – including monthly results and a prior 12-months of trending. Since effective quality review programs use trending to evaluate performance, and not just one fixed period (e.g. monthly), the communication of quality review results to the adjuster should include monthly and trended results. This provides the adjuster with feedback on whether their monthly results are an anomaly or trending over a prior 12-month period.

# Management & Operational Impact

The larger the span of control (e.g. number of employees supervised by one manager) the more difficult it is to manage technical claim handling effectively. Manager's with a large span of control may only pay close attention to large losses, touch claim files without any substantive input or specific supervision and provide minimal input and direction to the claim staff. Since there are limitations in how much you can accomplish in one day, managers will either spend less time supervising and directing claim file development or less time on people issues such as coaching, mentoring, training and development. Both can have an adverse impact on the company and results.

An inherent advantage of an effective claims quality review program is that a claim manager does not need to look at every claim file – trying to look at every claim file is ineffective and stifles adjuster development. Adjusters should handle claims within the designated claim authority extended by management. Claim authority should be based on a monetary threshold for reserving, settlement and payable entry, as well as certain non-monetary reporting criteria such as home office reporting files, claims pending in litigation, coverage issues, allegations of *bad faith* and consumer complaints. If the claim manager is concerned that the adjuster cannot work on their own within the designated claim authority level, there are two critical questions; is the claim authority too high and/or is the adjuster properly placed in that position.

A properly implemented claims quality review program provides the framework to allow the claim manager to delegate, but still have an effective management control in place to monitor adjuster technical claim handling performance. The adjusters are encouraged to operate within their claim authority and make decisions on their own. Their technical claim handling performance is evaluated based on the results of the monthly claim reviews, along with other routine claim reviews conducted by the claim manager.

# Claims Quality Review Framework

The *Claims Quality Review* framework will vary by organization. Some companies may want to review a smaller or larger sampling of claims than others and may have different review categories (i.e. *best practice* categories) and scoring methodologies. The line of business being reviewed may also affect the framework. For example, if the line of business is GAP[21] insurance or Guaranteed Asset Protection, the *best practice* categories may be limited compared to the workers' compensation line of business which will be more detailed.

Typically, a claim review framework will consist of a review of 3 to 4 claims per employee per month conducted by the claim supervisor or manager, a dedicated claim audit team, or a combination of both. The claim audit objective is to review the claim files against *best practices*, capture the data results in a database format, and identify trends (strengths and weaknesses) at a granular level for analysis and review – using the reporting results to enhance the quality of the claim operation and individual adjuster performance.

Some companies have dedicated resources to conduct claim reviews which can provide valuable insight into the quality of claim handling and *best practice* compliance. Although the use of a dedicated claim review or audit team can be effective and reduce the claim manager's workload in needing to conduct claim reviews, there may be friction or contention if the claim manager disagrees with the results or does not feel the claim auditors have credibility (e.g. experience, qualifications, practicality, etc.) in conducting fair and reasonable claim reviews. If the claim *best practices* and claim review process is well documented (particularly defining *satisfactory* performance) and calibrated regularly there should be minimal disagreement with the review results.

The claim files should be randomly selected and reviewed throughout the month with the results trended over a specific period (e.g. rolling 12 months). The claim reviews can be conducted using a web-based *electronic claim review form* for each claim file selected and reviewed, rating the quality of claim handling in various *best practice* major categories and subcategories.

---

[21] GAP insurance, or loan-lease payoff coverage, pays the difference between the actual cash value (ACV) of the vehicle and the current outstanding balance of the loan or lease.

Regional or home office claim management can use the same claim review process to validate the monthly claim supervisor or manager reviews, and/or to conduct an annual claim review for comparison purposes (i.e. validation and trending comparison).

The *best practice* categories and subcategories are incorporated into the claim audit tool and may vary by organization depending on the lines of business written and types of claim handled. Rating methodologies may also differ by using a numeric rating, a percentage score, or an alpha description (e.g. satisfactory). The key to an effective rating methodology is that it is objective, quantifiable and fair.

In an alpha description rating process, each subcategory is rated using a scoring methodology of *Exceeding* (E), *Good* (G), *Satisfactory* (S) or *Unsatisfactory* (U) standards by checking the applicable box (or drop-down selection). Each subcategory is *weighted* based on its overall impact compared to other subcategories and the overall total category scores. For example, subcategories in "Contacts" may have less of a weighted score than subcategories included in the "Investigation" category.

The narrative scoring of *Exceeding, Good, Satisfactory* or *Unsatisfactory* standards would be translated into a base numeric score to allow for specific numeric subcategory and category ratings and a total file numeric score rating. For example, *base numeric scores* may include: Exceeding = 4, Good = 3, Satisfactory = 2 and Unsatisfactory = 1. A *weighting factor* would be automatically applied to the base numeric score on a scale of 1 to 3, with 3 being the highest weighting.

The electronic claim review form calculates a total numeric score for each subcategory, category and a total for all categories which are the final weighted scores. The total technical claim review scores are then illustrated with and without the supervision rating. The electronic review includes a "N/A" (not applicable) selection – these claims would be omitted from any scoring calculation.

The numeric scores are translated into a percentage score at the subcategory and category level, as well as the *total file score*. The percentage achieved as a final score is illustrated below indicating the narrative rating description and its equivalent percentage achieved. The total file percentage achieved results will provide the file rating. Any file rating under 80% would be considered *unsatisfactory*.

**Exhibit 6-A** provides an overview of the scoring process using a *Rating Matrix*.

| CLAIM AUDIT RATING MATRIX – EXHIBIT 6-A | | |
|---|---|---|
| **Rating** | **Description** | **Explanation** |
| 100% | Excellent | Outstanding work product – beyond expectations with excellent results. |
| 90% | Good | Above average work product - exceeding expectations. |
| 80% | Satisfactory | Fully satisfactory and acceptable work product - meeting expectations. |
| 70% | Unsatisfactory | Unsatisfactory or unacceptable work product – not meeting expectations. |
| 0% | N/A | Not applicable to the review and excluded from any scoring calculation. |

For the review tool to yield objective results there needs to be a documented explanation of the specific rating categories. Outlined below are broad definitions of the four narrative scoring categories which assist in reducing rating subjectivity in the evaluation process. The narrative scoring or rating applies to each individual subcategory item, the total category ratings, and rolls up to the total claim file review rating. The four rating categories are broadly defined as follows:

- **Excellent Standard (100%):**

Outstanding work product – beyond expectations with excellent results. The claim adjuster (or manager) went substantially beyond what is normally expected in handling that aspect of the claim, understands the "big picture" and thinks beyond the documented details. Performance was well above expectations in completeness, timeliness and independence. There was a demonstration of mastery of skills and tasks involved, working independently in planning, anticipating problems and taking appropriate action. Work was completed on schedule with a high degree of accuracy with minimal supervision and follow-up on required tasks.

- **Good Standard (90%):**

Above average work product - exceeding expectations. The claim adjuster (or manager) went beyond what is normally expected in handling that aspect of the claim. Performance was above the average or satisfactory standard in completeness and timeliness. The was a demonstration of high performance in going beyond what is expected or required. Work was completed on schedule with a high degree of accuracy with minimal supervision and follow-up on required tasks.

- **Satisfactory Standard (80%):**

Fully satisfactory and acceptable work product - meeting expectations. The claim adjuster (or manager) met the basic requirements of what is normally expected in handling that aspect of the claim, as outlined in the *requirements details* in each subcategory. The handling of that aspect of the claim fully meets expectations and claim standards. Most ratings will be in this category which is considered *fully acceptable*.

- **<u>Unsatisfactory Standard (70%)</u>:**

Unsatisfactory or unacceptable work product – not meeting expectations. The claim adjuster (or manager) has <u>not</u> met the basic requirements of what is normally expected in handling that aspect of the claim, as outlined in the *requirements details* in each subcategory. The handling of that aspect of the claim does <u>not</u> meet expectations and claim standards.

An *unsatisfactory* rating also means the claim adjuster (or manager) did not demonstrate the knowledge or ability to handle the tasks with shortcomings in execution, achieving quality results, timeliness, and overall adherence to claim standards. Situations which involve repeated unresponsiveness to supervisory or manager requests to complete the task(s) are also considered unsatisfactory.

# <u>Electronic Review Format</u>

A claims quality review program should be developed using a *database* program to allow for robust reporting and analytics. The *electronic review form* is used as the front-end data entry mechanism to populate the database with the results of all reviewed claims, including structured and unstructured data (e.g. sub-category comments).

The electronic format should include:

- An automated file review selection process, wherein the claims are randomly selected for monthly claim reviews (based on predetermined criteria) by the claims system and appear in the claim manager's work queue (or worklist) as *QA File Review*. When the claim review is completed, and the "submit" button is executed on the electronic review form, the claim file will no longer be on the claim manager's work queue and the *QA File Review* will indicate "completed".
- Claim system integration to allow for pre-population of key information on the claim review forms when entering (or linking) a claim reference number – this will reduce timely manual entry inclusive of information such as *Claim Details* and *Financial Details*[22] as illustrated below in **Exhibit 6-B** and **Exhibit 6-C**:

| CLAIM DETAILS: EXHIBIT 6-B | | |
|---|---|---|
| Claim Number | Policy Number | Division/Company |
| Insured Name | Claimant Name | Claim Status (i.e. Open) |
| Date of Loss | Date Reported | Date Received |
| Loss State | Exposure Count | Litigation (Y/N) |
| Line of Business | Claim Type | Accident Description |
| Injury Description | Type of Audit | Claim Unit |
| Adjuster Name | Manager Name | Audit Completion Date |
| Audit Completed By: | | |

---

[22] Financial Details should include recommended *Reserve Adjustments*. This information will be helpful when tracking claim reserve redundancy and deficiency

| FINANCIAL DETAILS: EXHIBIT 6-C | | | | | |
|---|---|---|---|---|---|
| Claim Exposures | Outstanding Reserves | Paid Amount | Recovery $ | Incurred $ | Reserve Adjustments |
| Auto BI | $50,000 | $5,000 | $0 | $55,000 | $25,000 |
| Auto PD | $8,500 | $0 | $0 | $8,500 | $0 |
| Auto Phys Dam. | $1,500 | $11,500 | $11,000 | $2,000 | $0 |
| PIP | $6,500 | $2,500 | $0 | $9,000 | $0 |
| ALAE | $4,500 | $500 | $0 | $5,000 | $10,000 |
| **Totals:** | **$71,000** | **$19,500** | **$11,000** | **$79,500** | **$35,000** |

- The ability to export data into various reporting formats, including an *Excel*® format, to create reports, charts and tables.

# Electronic Review Forms

The *electronic review form* format should be flexible to allow for modifications and changes. The review forms should include categories and subcategories and allow for notes and comments next to each subcategory, as well as overall comments at the bottom of the electronic review form.

The top section of the review form should be pre-populated with basic *Claim Details* and *Financial Details* as illustrated above in **Exhibit 6-B** and **Exhibit 6-C**.

Electronic review forms and the audit process should be tailored to a specific line or class of business (e.g. liability, workers' compensation, property, APD/PD, etc.). This allows for granularity in reporting and trending. An effective format is to develop general review categories and then develop *supplements* for each different line or class of business (e.g. workers' compensation or APD/PD). The review forms should also be flexible to allow for capturing and tracking of claim and financial data such as leakage in specific areas of claim handling (e.g. comparative negligence evaluation, rental and loss of use, automobile and property appraisals, etc.).

The review form should include categories and subcategories which are illustrated in **Exhibit 6-D** below, providing an illustrative example of the *Contacts, Coverage,* and *Investigation* categories, as well as *Summary Comments*.

| SAMPLE SECTIONS OF ELECTRONIC REVIEW FORM: EXHIBIT 6-D | | |
|---|---|---|
| CONTACTS | | |
| Subcategory | Rating | Comments |
| Claimant Contact | 80% | *Comments* |
| Insured Contact | 90% | *Comments* |
| Witness Contact | 70% | *Comments* |

| COVERAGE | | |
|---|---|---|
| Coverage Verification | 80% | *Comments* |
| Coverage Analysis | 90% | *Comments* |
| Coverage Documents | N/A | *Comments* |

| INVESTIGATION | | |
|---|---|---|
| Timely & Complete | 80% | *Comments* |
| Investigation Quality | 90% | *Comments* |
| Documented Details | 100% | *Comments* |
| Attorney Engagement | 90% | *Comments* |
| Statements Taken | 80% | *Comments* |
| Quality of Statements | 90% | *Comments* |
| Scene Investigation | 80% | *Comments* |
| Witness ID/Interview | 80% | *Comments* |
| Activity Check/Surveillance | N/A | *Comments* |
| Official Reports | 80% | *Comments* |
| 3rd Party ID & Investigation | 100% | *Comments* |
| ISO ClaimSearch | 80% | *Comments* |
| Fraud/SIU | N/A | *Comments* |

| SUMMARY COMMENTS |
|---|
| |
| |
| |

The scoring of 100%, 90%, 80%, 70% or N/A is selected from a "drop-down" box. The *comments* should be limited to two lines. The *summary comments* section should allow for 4 – 6 lines.

The total file score is not illustrated on the electronic review form and should be accessed in the database using the reporting tool after the electronic form has been submitted. The reason for this is to avoid the distraction of viewing subcategory and total file scores during the review process, as we want the supervisor or claim manager to focus on claim trends, and not individual scores.

# Reporting & Analytics Tool(s)

The claims quality review results are analyzed and trended using a *Reporting & Analytics Tool* which accesses the database. Standard reporting should be provided to allow for ease of reporting and analysis, but also include the ability to tailor or customize reporting to a supervisor or manager's individual needs.

Access to the reporting & analytics tool should be limited to the supervisory and management staff and have functionality to carve out an employee performance electronic summary report to communicate the results to the technical claim staff.

The reporting tool should include various filters and date range options to allow for flexibility in trending analysis. If the data field exists in the database, it should be accessible for reporting purposes. Filters and sorting should include:

- Audit Type (claim manager or annual audit)
- Adjuster Name
- Manager Name
- Section/Unit
- Department
- Division
- Claim Number
- Claim Status (open, closed or reopen)
- State
- Date of Loss
- Date Reported
- Date Received
- Claimant Name
- Insured Name
- Policy Number
- Litigation (Y/N),
- Reserve Amounts (by exposure)
- Paid Amounts (by exposure)
- Recovery Amounts (by exposure)
- Recommended Reserve Adjustments (by exposure)
- Review Category
- Review Subcategory
- Line of Business
- Exposure Type
- Rating Levels
- Percentage Achieved

The total category percentage score is an average of all the subcategory scores for that category. The total file score is an average of the percentage achieved in all categories and will provide the total file rating. Any file rating under 80% should be considered unsatisfactory. Generally, we should see total scoring in the 80% to 90% range with 85% - 90% being a target score.

Claim review categories and subcategories are detailed in **Appendix I** with a brief description of each subcategory. Each subcategory provides a base description of *satisfactory* performance expectations in the *Requirements Details* section under the specific *Category* in the exhibit.

The review results should be summarized at the *category* and *subcategory* levels in a *scorecard* format, using review date ranges to select results for analysis. A *Summary Scorecard* provides the results of the electronic claim review forms on a summary level, with percentages achieved in each category and subcategory. A sample *Category Summary Scorecard* is illustrated below as **Exhibit 6-E**. The rating scores illustrated are derived from the subcategory scores for each category yielding an average of all subcategory scores, excluding any N/A scores.

| CATEGORY SUMMARY SCORECARD: EXHIBIT 6-E | |
|---|---|
| **Category** | **Rating %** |
| Contacts | 80% |
| Coverage | 83% |
| Investigation | 85% |
| Subrogation Recovery | 85% |
| Diary Management & Claim Control | 90% |
| Compliance | 85% |
| Reporting & Documentation | 85% |
| Analysis & Evaluation | 80% |
| WC Case Management | 90% |
| Financial Management | 80% |
| Litigation Management | 75% |
| Disposition & Resolution | 80% |
| Supervision | 70% |
| **Total File Rating without Supervision:** | **83%** |
| **Total File Rating with Supervision:** | **82%** |

A *Subcategory Summary Scorecard* should also be developed providing a breakdown of the subcategory scoring for each individual category, rolling up the total of all categories for a total file score. The subcategory scorecard should allow for reporting of all subcategories in one report or filter on individual subcategories. A sample *Subcategory Summary Scorecard* is illustrated below as **Exhibit 6-F**.

| SUBCATEGORY SCORECARD: EXHIBIT 6-F | |
|---|---|
| **Contacts** | **Rating %** |
| Claimant Contact | 80% |
| Insured Contact | 70% |
| Witness Contact | 90% |
| **Total Category – Contacts:** | **80%** |
| **Coverage** | **Rating %** |
| Coverage Verification | 80% |

| Coverage Analysis | 90% |
|---|---|
| Coverage Documents / Letters | 80% |
| **Total Category – Coverage:** | **83%** |
| **Investigation** | **Rating %** |
| Timely & Complete Investigation | 90% |
| Investigation Quality | 90% |
| Documented Details | 100% |
| Attorney Engagement | 90% |
| Statements Taken | 80% |
| Quality of Statements | 90% |
| Scene Investigation | 80% |
| Witness ID/Interview | 80% |
| Activity Check/Surveillance | 80% |
| Official Reports | 80% |
| 3rd Party ID & Investigation | 100% |
| ISO ClaimSearch | 80% |
| Fraud/SIU | 70% |
| **Total Category Rating – Investigation:** | **85%** |

The analysis and reporting may include other relevant information with the ability to sort and filter data. If there is a field to track on the form, the data can be pulled into a report for analysis. The information to track and analyze may include the following (but not limited to):

- **Claim Volume:**
  - Number of claim exposures reviewed
  - Number of claim files reviewed
  - Open claims
  - Reopen claims
  - Closed claims
  - Litigation claims
  - Exposure types (e.g. indemnity, medical, medical-only, vocational rehab, ALAE, etc.)

- **Financial Impact:**
  - Total reserves
  - Total paid
  - Total recoveries
  - Total incurred activity
  - Total recommended reserve adjustments
  - Claim Leakage

- **Claim Metrics:**
  - Average paid loss
  - Average paid expense
  - Average reserves
  - FNOL timeliness
  - Contacts
  - Date received to date of final payment
  - Date of vehicle inspection (appraisal) to payment
  - Number of vehicle rental days

The use of graphs and charts can illustrate trends over specific time periods, by section, by adjuster, etc. See sample charts below as **Exhibit 6-G**, **Exhibit 6-H** and **Exhibit 6-I**. These charts are used to illustrate claim results at the category or subcategory level, by office, unit, adjuster, etc. Using charts and exhibits to illustrate claim quality review results, either at the category or subcategory level, is a simple method to provide relevant feedback.

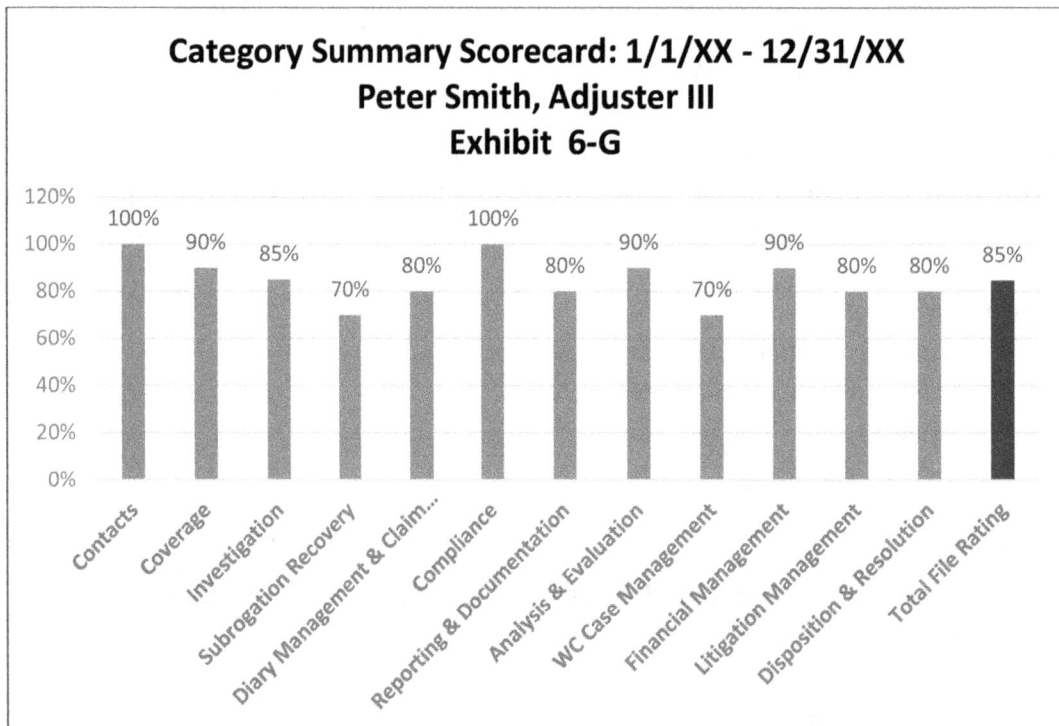

**Category Summary Scorecard: 1/1/XX - 12/31/XX**
**Peter Smith, Adjuster III**
**Exhibit 6-G**

## Subcategory Scorecard - Investigation
## June 20XX
## Exhibit 6-H

## Category Summary Scorecard
## XYZ Claim Operation: June 20XX
## Exhibit 6-I

# Chapter Comments

As indicated at the beginning of this chapter, a claims quality review program, properly implemented and managed, establishes organizational expectations for the level of claim quality required in a claim operation. It provides the necessary tools to manage and control the most critical aspect of a claim operation – technical claim handling.

The claim review process provides a methodology to review a sampling of claim files on a regular basis, without having to review, or dual diary, all claim files in the claim manager's unit.

In this chapter, we reviewed the overall claims quality review process including the objective, framework, management and operational impact, and various tools and methodologies. We discussed a sample electronic claims quality review process using basic *best practice* categories as a benchmark to compare against actual claim review results. The process illustrated a methodology to capture quality review results and then score the results at a granular level.

The industry has evolved with respect to claim review or claim audit tools and methodologies. Electronic review tools are now more prevalent and being deployed in many claim organizations. With the use of modern architecture claim systems and the availability of robust audit tools with integrated analytics and reporting packages, the process has developed into a routine and effective management control used by claim management.

Reporting and analytics is the future of a claim operation. Use of analytics in the claim review process has allowed claim operations to quickly identify strengths and weaknesses and then take appropriate action.

The claims quality review process should be constructive providing both positive and negative feedback to employees. By focusing on claim trends in *best practice* categories, we become laser focused on claim operational strengths and weaknesses. When we recognize strengths, we should provide positive feedback and when we recognize weaknesses, we should work with the employee to correct the deficiency(s) directly and/or through training and development.

**Appendix I – Claims Best Practices** provides basic requirements to achieve an acceptable rating in each *best practice* subcategory.

# APPENDIX I
## CLAIMS BEST PRACTICES

| Contacts | Requirements Details |
|---|---|
| **Contacts:**<br><br>• **Claimant (24 hours)**<br>• **Insured (24 hours)**<br>• **Witnesses (48 hours)**<br>• **Third Parties (48 hours)**<br>• **Physician Contact (WC 48 hours)** | • Timely contact (e.g. 24 or 48 hours) with the claimant, insured, witnesses and third parties within the required contact time frame from the claim report date.<br><br>• Documented contact attempts will meet *contact* requirement standards as long there is a continued effort to establish actual contact within a reasonable period from the initial contact attempt(s).<br><br>• Leaving telephone messages and sending emails are considered contact attempts to establish initial contact timeliness.<br><br>• Meaningful and substantive contact is required inclusive of securing claim details, a statement (if necessary) and relevant claim information.<br><br>• Timely contact with the primary *physician* within 48 hours from the claim report date to secure details on the claimant's injuries, diagnosis, prognosis, treatment and disability period (WC).<br><br>• Receipt of a medical report within the required period, providing the above information will satisfy the primary *physician* contact requirement. |

| Coverage | Requirements Details |
|---|---|
| **Coverage Verification** | • Basic coverage information verified as part of the claim process including named insured, policy number, effective dates, limits, deductibles, lienholders, etc.<br><br>• Although the policy system will verify coverage there may be circumstances wherein coverage needs to be further verified or clarified to consider paying the loss (e.g. additional insureds, endorsements, co-insurance, etc.). |
| **Coverage Analysis** | • Substantive analysis of coverage related issues.<br><br>• Coverage analysis can involve complex coverage issues (e.g. policy exclusionary language applying to the claim) or simple coverage issues (e.g. late notice of claim). |
| **Coverage Documentation** | • Relevant coverage analysis documentation posted to the electronic claim file.<br><br>• This includes investigation and research in the review and analysis of coverage issues, documented notes detailing the coverage issue and decisions, as well as coverage opinions from coverage counsel.<br><br>• Issuance of a coverage position document which is appropriate, timely and consistent with procedures (e.g. coverage disclaimer letter, reservation of rights letter or securing a *non-waiver agreement*). |

| Investigation | Requirements Details |
|---|---|
| **Timely & Complete Investigation** | • Timely and complete claim investigation based on claim guidelines, standards and procedures.<br>• This includes completing all elements of the claim investigation to properly evaluate the claim. |
| **Documented Claim Details** | • Documentation of relevant claim details in the electronic file notes, structured fields and screens, or attachments.<br>• The documented claim details must be complete, relevant, succinct and in the proper format per claim guidelines, standards and procedures. |
| **Statements Taken** | • Securing timely statements from relevant parties to the loss including the insured, claimant, passengers, witnesses and any other third parties relevant to the investigation. |
| **Quality of Statements** | • Quality of statements taken – comparing statement content to statement taking requirements and statement guide utilized.<br>• This may include a review of the statement information summary posted to the claim file and/or listening to the actual recorded statement (or reviewing the signed statement) to determine the level of quality. |
| **Claimant Attorney Engagement** | • Timely initial contact with the claimant attorney by telephone and in writing to secure relevant claim information.<br>• Securing *Attorney Allegations* from the claimant attorney to develop claim information, including the claimant attorney's theory of liability.<br>• Ongoing contact with the claimant attorney to determine the status of the claimant's injuries, treatment and disability.<br>• Securing copies of all special damages and directing the claim toward a resolution. |
| **Scene Investigation** | • Securing photos and diagram of the accident scene, property damage and vehicles.<br>• This is inclusive of conducting an onsite scene investigation when warranted (either by field staff or independent adjuster). |
| **Witness Identification & Interview** | • Identification of witnesses, conducting in-depth witness interviews, taking witness statements (if necessary) and documenting the claim file with relevant information.<br>• This also includes conducting a *witness canvass* at the accident scene to identify potential witnesses when warranted (either by field staff or independent adjuster). |
| **Official Reports** | • File documented with required police, fire, aided, ambulance, motor vehicle, OSHA, and other official reports.<br>• Securing copies of available police and fire photographs and accident reconstruction reports (if necessary and available). |

| Third Party Investigation | • Identification of actual or potential third parties who caused or contributed to the accident – this is inclusive of third parties, co-defendants and their insurance carriers.<br>• Insurance carrier information includes relevant company name and address, claim number and adjuster name, policy number, applicable coverage and policy limits.<br>• Conducting a timely investigation to support the third-party claim including securing statements from relevant parties and necessary records and documentation. |
|---|---|
| Claimant Activity Checks / Surveillance | • Conducting periodic claimant *activity checks* when warranted and in accordance with claim guidelines, standards and procedures.<br>• Assigning a surveillance investigator to identify any claimant activity which would be considered an exaggeration of the claim or fraudulent. |
| ISO ClaimSearch® | • Entering ISO ClaimSearch® for each bodily injury or WC lost time indemnity claim initially and every six months thereafter.<br>• Following up on ISO ClaimSearch® returns or "hits" which indicate prior claims and/or injuries, by contacting the insurance carrier for relevant claim details. |
| Other Searches | • Conducting background checks and/or criminal searches when necessary and appropriate, and in accordance with claim guidelines, standards and procedures. |
| Fraud / SIU | • Identification of potential fraud and timely referral of claim to the Special Investigative Unit (SIU) for handling. |

| Recovery | Requirements Details |
|---|---|
| Subrogation Investigation | • Timely and documented investigation to identify and support potential subrogation recovery of payments on first party claims.<br>• The subrogation investigation should include all relevant documentation and investigation necessary to perfect the subrogation claim against the adverse party or carrier; through direct negotiations, arbitration or litigation. |
| Experts | • Consideration of the need for experts to support the subrogation claim and assignment including control of the appropriate expert and expense.<br>• Controlling the scope of the expert engagement including written confirmation of the assignment and fee structure up front, as well as monitoring the quality and timeliness of reporting by the expert. |
| Third Party Notice / Arbitration | • Timely placing the third party on notice (in writing) of our subrogation rights with acknowledgement by the third-party carrier or sent via certified mail with return receipt requested.<br>• Filing of Inter-Company Arbitration. |

| | |
|---|---|
| | • Protecting the applicable statute of limitations. |
| **Lien Filing & Management (WC Only)** | • Timely filing of the appropriate workers' compensation lien with the responsible party, their carrier and any other relevant parties to the claim, with acknowledgement by the third-party carrier, or sent via certified mail with return receipt requested.<br>• Management of the lien process including monitoring the third-party claim to protect the lien.<br>• Negotiate settlement of the lien as part of the third-party settlement, either as a lien recovery or offset against future benefits. |

| Diary Management & Claim Control | Requirements Details |
|---|---|
| **Documented Plan of Action – POA (Liability and WC)** | • A detailed *Plan of Action* (POA) in the electronic file notes or attachment providing file direction inclusive of specific categories such as coverage, facts of accident, investigation completed and outstanding, liability or compensability analysis, damage evaluation, negotiations, injuries (diagnosis, prognosis and treatment), work & disability status, RTW plan, medical and disability management, litigation status, reserves, recovery and future direction.<br>• The action plan should be substantive allowing the reader to fully understand the claim details, evaluation and overall file direction. |
| **Pro-Active Control of Claim** | • Documented control of the claim process and claim file development.<br>• This includes pro-active control of the claim investigation, evaluation, disposition and financial control of loss and expense (reserves and payments). |
| **Current Adjuster Diary** | • Current diary at time of review.<br>• Timely and substantive diary in accordance with claim guidelines, standards and procedures.<br>• No gaps in claim handling which impact the timeliness of required claim activities. |
| **File Tempo** | • Timely development of the claim to complete all outstanding activities, inclusive of directing the claim toward an appropriate disposition. |

| Compliance | Requirements Details |
|---|---|
| **Fair Claim Act & State Regulations** | • Compliance with State Fair Claim Acts and Insurance Regulations inclusive of timely and proper issuance of letters, forms and correspondence required by the insurance department or state regulations.<br>• Timely and proper handling of regulatory complaints (e.g. department of insurance). |

| Compliance with State WC Acts | • Compliance with the State Workers' Compensation Act and statutes inclusive of jurisdictional filings, timely and proper issuance of WC benefits, claim forms, letters and other requirements. |
|---|---|
| Claim Guidelines & Procedures | • Compliance with internal claim guidelines, standards and procedures.<br>• Compliance with internal claim procedural and processing requirements.<br>• Accurate coding of claim transactions |
| Claim Authority Compliance | • Compliance with designated claim authority in reserving, settlement and payment of claims – loss and expense transactions.<br>• Claim authority is based on the *gross value* of the claim <u>excluding</u> any comparative negligence, contribution from other parties, or other available coverage. |
| CMS Medicare Compliance | • Compliance with the CMS Medicare rules and regulations including proper and timely identification of Medicare eligible recipients, proper completion of system fields, and facilitation and preparation of MSA's. |
| **Reporting & Documentation** | **Requirements Details** |
| File Reporting | • Compliance with required company claim reporting requirements in accordance with claim guidelines, standards and procedures, inclusive of internal and external reporting.<br>• This includes all required reporting at various intervals in the claim process by email, document upload or electronic note entry. |
| Electronic Notes - Clear & Concise | • Clear and concise electronic file notes which are substantive with a minimum of typographical errors.<br>• Notes should not include editorial comments nor information, which could not be read publicly, unless the note is specifically designated as *confidential*. |
| File Management (Administration) | • Proper management of claim file content including organization of attachments, reports and notes in sequential order.<br>• The claim records should be well organized and managed so that the reader can understand the investigation results, claim evaluation and future file direction. |
| File Documentation & Attachments | • File attachments posted to the electronic claim file including all appropriate documentation developed during the claim investigation such as emails, letters and correspondence, reports, estimates, appraisals, invoices, statements, special damages, etc.<br>• Proper category labeling of attachments to maintain efficiency and improve productivity. |

| Analysis & Evaluation | Requirements Details |
|---|---|
| **Liability Analysis** | • Analysis of liability on all parties to the claim including the percentage of liability on each party.<br>• Application of appropriate legal theories and doctrines, defenses, comparative negligence, statutes and case law to support the analysis. |
| **Compensability Analysis (WC Only)** | • Detailed compensability analysis supporting the claim decision to accept or deny the claim.<br>• Application of appropriate legal theories and doctrines, defenses, statutes and case law to support the analysis. |
| **Accurate Indemnity Calculations (WC)** | • Accurate indemnity calculations inclusive of the average weekly wage (AWW), compensation rate, awards and settlements.<br>• Proper classification and calculation of indemnity benefits and payments throughout the claim process (e.g. TTD, TPD, PPD, PTD, etc.). |
| **Documented Claim Evaluation** | • Detailed damage evaluation inclusive of all damage elements to arrive at the *gross value* of the claim such as itemized special damages and general damages in liability claims, and compensation and medical benefits in WC claims.<br>• Utilization of the approved claim evaluation format, as outlined in the claim guidelines, standards and procedures.<br>• Documented claim evaluation at appropriate intervals in the claim process such as reserving and claim disposition evaluations. |

| Financial Management | Requirements Details |
|---|---|
| **Reserve Management** | • Proper and timely management of case reserves at the exposure level in accordance with the claim reserve guidelines, standards and procedures inclusive of new reserves and reserve adjustments.<br>• Proper and documented detailed analysis and evaluation of reserves using the required reserve evaluation format.<br>• Documented review and analysis of claim reserves at regular intervals (e.g. 30 days, etc.) as required by the claim guidelines, standards and procedures |
| **Expense Control** | • Effective control of claim expenses – including allocated and unallocated loss adjustment expenses – both external vendors and internal resources.<br>• Expense control also pertains to cost-effective and efficient use of field claim staff and staff appraiser resources. |
| **Vendor Management & Control** | • Effective management and control (including expense control) of all approved vendors.<br>• Proper vendor assignment including documented assignment scope, agreed fee structure and target completion date. |

| Litigation Management | Requirements Details |
|---|---|
| **Use of Approved Defense Counsel** | • Use of approved defense counsel using only attorneys and law firms included on the company approved defense counsel list.<br>• Use of the appropriate defense attorney and law firm based on the type of claim in litigation and the expertise of defense counsel. |
| **Suit Referral Quality** | • Timely and quality suit referral email or letter including relevant information and documentation such as enclosures, suit service details, court and venue, style and caption, answer due date, any extensions of time to answer, investigation completed, liability and damage analysis, defense counsel handling instructions, request for legal budget, and adjuster follow-up items.<br>• Suit referral attachments to include copies of relevant claim file documentation, pleadings and company attorney litigation management guidelines. |
| **Defense Counsel Responsiveness** | • Evaluation of defense counsel's responsiveness to telephone, email and written communication and inquiries. |
| **Control of Defense Counsel** | • Effective control of defense counsel in management of the litigation claim and compliance with the company litigation management guidelines.<br>• Collaborative engagement with defense counsel to achieve a successful outcome.<br>• Development of an effective and mutually agreed litigation plan. |
| **Litigation Expense Control** | • Effective control of litigation expenses inclusive of attorney fees.<br>• Request and management of litigation budgets provided by defense counsel, aligned with the approved litigation plan activities. |

| Closing & Disposition | Requirements Details |
|---|---|
| **Efforts to Conclude Claim** | • Efforts to direct the claim toward a closing disposition, when warranted. |
| **Negotiations Effectiveness** | • Effective settlement negotiations with the insured, claimant, carrier and claimant attorney.<br>• Documented *target settlement amount* and settlement range.<br>• Settlement negotiations documented in the electronic file notes inclusive of negotiation tactics and points (strengths and weaknesses of the insured's defense), as well as the details of all settlement demands and offers. |
| **Use of Settlement Options** | • Utilization of various settlement options to achieve an equitable settlement including lump sum settlements, commutations, or structured settlements.<br>• Effective use of Medicare MSAs as part of the settlement process. |

| Disposition or Results | • Prompt and appropriate disposition of the claim with an acceptable or better result. |
|---|---|
| Closing Documentation | • Appropriate closing documentation in the claim file including settlement agreement, release, discontinuances, proof of loss, etc. |
| Proper Claim Payment | • Issuance of proper claim payment (amount and payee) based on the settlement criteria and agreement, and other requirements such as lienholders, loss payees, spouse name, etc. |

| Supervision | Requirements Details |
|---|---|
| Initial Direction | • Initial up-front supervision which provides quality input and file direction. |
| Follow-Up Direction | • Follow-up supervision which provides quality input and file direction. |
| Effective Delegation | • Delegating activities to the adjuster which are above their claim authority such as settlement authority. |
| Substantive & Specific Supervision | • Providing supervision which is substantive and specific to the claim activities. |
| Supervisory Diary Management | • Timely and appropriate supervisory diary with intervals commensurate with the claim type and the handling adjuster's experience level. |

| Automobile APD / PD Supplement | Requirements Details |
|---|---|
| Repair Estimate Reviewed | • Review of the repair estimate provided by the vehicle owner to determine if it is fair and reasonable and whether a vehicle appraisal is necessary. |
| Alternative Appraisal Methods | • Consideration of alternative methods to evaluate damages such as a desk appraisal review or use of a direct repair facility. |
| Timely Appraisal Assignment & Completion | • Timely assignment of the appraisal to the appraiser and timely completion of the appraisal by the appraiser in accordance with claim handling guidelines, standards and procedures. |
| Quality of Appraisal | • The quality of the appraisal report in terms of its damage estimate accuracy – including use of proper labor (rate and hours) and parts. |
| Timely Supplemental Assignment & Completion | • Timely assignment of the supplemental appraisal to the appraiser and timely completion of the supplemental appraisal by the appraiser in accordance with claim handling guidelines, standards and procedures. |
| Quality of Supplemental Appraisal | • The quality of the supplemental appraisal report in terms of its damage estimate accuracy – including use of proper labor (rate and hours) and parts. |
| Timely & Quality Total Loss Evaluation | • Timely declaration of the vehicle total loss and completion of the total loss evaluation report by the adjuster in |

| | |
|---|---|
| | accordance with claim handling guidelines, standards and procedures. <br>• The quality of the total loss report in terms of using the appropriate methodology and tools – inclusive of all itemized total loss calculations, state sales tax and the proper conditioning report. |
| **Salvage Handling & Disposal** | • Proper and timely handling and disposal of salvage to reduce storage and handling costs, and rental or loss of use. |
| **Control of Rental / Loss of Use** | • Proper and timely control of automobile rental and loss of use claims including the daily rental rate, number of rental days, and proper rental documentation. |

| Property Supplement | Requirements Details |
|---|---|
| **Coverage Analysis** | • Analysis of coverage to evaluate whether the loss is covered under the policy. <br>• This includes reviewing applicable policy schedules, coverage forms and endorsements, exclusions, limitations, exceptions, policy limits and sub-limits, and deductibles. |
| **Scope of Damages** | Comprehensive *Scope of Loss* including: <br>• The projected dollar amount of loss (building, contents and time element loss components). <br>• Measurements and photographs. <br>• Evaluation of the building replacement cost to determine the *insurance to value* (ITV) calculation and applicability of co-insurance provision. <br>• Secure the fire report (e.g. serious loss). <br>• Identify the cause of loss (e.g. cause of fire). <br>• Identify any subrogation potential. <br>• Determine the need for an expert (e.g. cause and origin expert, engineer, etc.). <br>• Review public records (e.g. property search) if applicable. <br>• If the damages are extensive, determine the need to retain a contractor or a building consultant to assist with the damage assessment. |
| **Damage Repair Estimate & Property Appraisal** | • Requesting a repair estimate (e.g. contractors estimate) from the insured to determine the extent of the damages being claimed. <br>• Assign an appraiser to inspect the damages and get an agreed price on repairs. |
| **Use of Experts** | • Experts should be retained if there is potential for subrogation or the cause of the loss cannot be determined (e.g. which may require retaining a cause & origin expert [C&O] or engineer). |
| **Personal Property Inventory** | • Providing the insured with inventory claim forms to prepare a personal property (contents) list of damaged or stolen property. |

| | |
|---|---|
| **Control of Time Element Loss** (Additional Living Expenses, Business Interruption or Loss of Income) | • Identification of *time element* exposures.<br>• Assessment of *time element* loss by reviewing records and documentation provided by the insured.<br>• Proper management and control of time element losses including using experts to assist in calculation of damages (e.g. accountant). |
| **Statements** | • Statements should be taken from the insured(s) and witnesses on large property losses, losses which have potential subrogation, claims involving coverage issues, property thefts and suspicious claims (e.g. fire loss).<br>• If there is a pending coverage issue, the statement should not be secured from the insured until a non-waiver agreement has been taken or a reservation of rights letter has been issued and received by the insured. |
| **Subrogation** | • All property claims require a timely investigation to either rule out subrogation, or firm up the subrogation claim with additional investigation, documentation and use of experts.<br>• Preservation of evidence when subrogation is involved is critical to a successful subrogation claim. |
| **Official Reports** | • Fire and police reports provide relevant investigative information including the cause of the loss, witnesses, and information on potential responsible parties. |
| **ISO ClaimSearch®** | • Filed on all property claims which provides detailed information on prior property losses as part of the claim investigation process.<br>• ISO entry at time of the initial report and reentry every six months thereafter.<br>• The entry can be done at the ISO ClaimSearch® web portal, or through an integrated process with the claim system.<br>• Following up on ISO ClaimSearch® returns or "hits" which indicate prior claims, by contacting the insurance carrier for relevant claim details. |
| **Property Search/ Background Check** | • Property searches are done to confirm ownership and the existence of mortgagees and property liens.<br>• If the investigation indicates the loss is suspicious, the adjuster may request a background check and financial or credit report on the insured through SIU. |
| **Advances** | • When a claim involves additional living expenses or funds are needed to begin repairs, the insured may request an advance on the claim.<br>• An advance should never be approved unless the cause of the loss is known, and you are able to rule out the insured's involvement in the loss. |
| **Proof of Loss & Loan Receipt** | • After a property loss has been concluded, a *Proof of Loss* supporting the claim should be provided to the insured(s) for signature. |

| | |
|---|---|
| | • A *Loan Receipt* or *Subrogation Receipt* should also be requested if there is a potential for subrogation. |
| **Replacement Cost Holdback** | • When a policy provides *replacement cost* coverage, the insured may only be paid on an actual cash value (ACV) basis until the repairs have been completed or the property has been replaced. |
| | • A *Replacement Cost Hold-Back* document should be provided to the insured which allows the insured to make an additional claim for the difference between the actual cash value (ACV) and replacement cost value (RCV), after confirmation has been submitted that repairs have been completed or the property has been replaced. |
| **Special Investigative Unit (SIU)** | • Claims should be referred to the Special Investigative Unit (SIU) if the investigation indicates the claim is suspicious. |
| **Catastrophe (CAT) Losses** | • Effective handling of catastrophe losses both in terms of claim results and customer service impact. |
| | • Cat Loss Management – adjusting resources and CAT reporting. |

| WC Case Management Supplement | Requirements Details |
|---|---|
| **Effective Medical Management** | • Effective medical management including ongoing communication with the attending physicians(s). |
| | • Requests for medical documentation and records to support the diagnosis, prognosis, treatment regime and disability period. |
| | • Directing the claim toward a Maximum Medical Improvement (MMI) status using all available tools including Nurse Case Management (NCM), Utilization Review (UR), use of attending physician Narrative Medical Reports and Independent Medical Examinations (IMEs). |
| **Effective Disability Management** | • Effective disability management using all available tools including Nurse Case Management (NCM), use of attending physician Narrative Medical Reports, Independent Medical Examinations (IMEs), Activity Checks and Surveillance, and internal resource material (e.g. online resources to determine disability periods). |
| | • Ongoing contact with the claimant's attending physician to review the treatment regime and disability status. |
| | • Effective RTW management by engaging in ongoing communication with the attending physician, NCM, and the employer to determine the availability of light work or modified duty. |
| | • Utilization of Vocational Rehabilitation (VR) services to assist the claimant in returning to a work status. |
| **Timely Issuance of WC Benefits** | • Timely issuance of compensation indemnity benefits to the claimant in accordance with the applicable WC Statutes. |

| | |
|---|---|
| | • Timely issuance of medical payments to providers in accordance with the applicable WC Statutes. |
| **Appropriate Medical Records (medical, hospital and diagnostic)** | • Documented file with all appropriate medical records including medical reports (and physician notes), hospital records (at minimum discharge summaries), and diagnostic reports (radiology, MRI, CT Scan, etc.) |
| **Medical & Hospital Bill Review** | • Timely review and referral of medical and hospital bills for *bill review* and payment processing in accordance with the bill review schedule, as well as claim guidelines, standards and procedures. |
| **Effective & Timely Use of IMEs** | • Effective & timely use of Independent Medical Examinations (IMEs) during the claim process to manage medical causation and disability issues. |
| **Effective Use & Control of *Nurse Case Management (NCM)*** | • Effective use and control of *Nurse Case Management* services.<br>• Timely discontinuance of NCM services when no longer necessary.<br>• Not using NCM services for activities which can be handled by the adjuster. |
| **Effective Use & Control of *Utilization Review / Peer Review*** | • Effective use and control of *Utilization Review / Peer Review* services.<br>• Timely discontinuance of UR services when no longer necessary. |
| **Effective Use & Control of *Vocational Rehabilitation* (VR)** | • Effective use and control of *Vocational Rehabilitation* (VR) services.<br>• Timely discontinuance of VR services when no longer necessary and/or not achieving the desired results. |

# CHAPTER 7
# STAFFING & RESOURCE MANAGEMENT

## Claim Organizational Structures & Roles

Claim organizational structures may vary; however, roles, hierarchy and staffing are typically similar among companies. For example, roles in most claim organizations include claim managers, claim supervisors, adjusters and claim support staff. The specific names for the roles may differ from one organization to another. A claim facility may refer to technical claim roles as a claim representative, claim service representative, adjuster, field adjuster, desk adjuster, claim specialist, litigation specialist, technical claim specialist, etc. Within each role there may be further variations based on experience and knowledge such as a claim representative or adjuster having three levels CR I, CR II and CR III.

The specific roles in the claim structure should have a job description which provides an overview of the role, and requirements in terms of experience, education, responsibilities, expectations and claim authority. These roles establish the foundation for staffing by distributing claim assignments based on job description, adjuster experience level and claim authority levels.

The adjuster role, proper claim assignment to each role and the number of staff resources are critical to effectively manage claim expenses (ULAE).

## Financial Impact of Staffing

As a claim manager, you are responsible to control Loss Adjustment Expenses (LAE) which includes Unallocated Loss Adjustment Expenses (ULAE) and Allocated Loss Adjustment Expenses (ALAE).

Both ULAE and ALAE have an impact on staffing, and it is important to recognize how both impact your LAE. ULAE is impacted by claim overhead (e.g. claim salaries, benefits, etc.), external vendor services (FNOL reporting services, claim estimating software, etc.) and some adjusting expense. ALAE expense is impacted by outsourced claim and legal services (legal, experts, adjusting, etc.). If you hire temporary help or use independent adjusters in lieu of adding to staff, your total LAE will be impacted by the expense.

Sometimes management may hedge against the cost of staff resources and the adverse impact on the loss ratio by not maintaining proper staffing levels. This is a mistake often made by claim managers or senior management – intentionally maintaining a lower staffing level to improve ULAE results, overlooking the fact that overloaded adjusters take shortcuts, make mistakes, generate leakage, and are unable to sustain the claim quality level to positively impact the loss ratio. It will also result in increased employee turnover with lack of continuity in claim handling.

As illustrated in **Exhibit 7-A**, the claim quality level will improve as the ULAE $ expenditure increases with additional staffing. Correspondingly, ULAE expense will decrease with reduced staffing, but the level of claim quality will deteriorate.

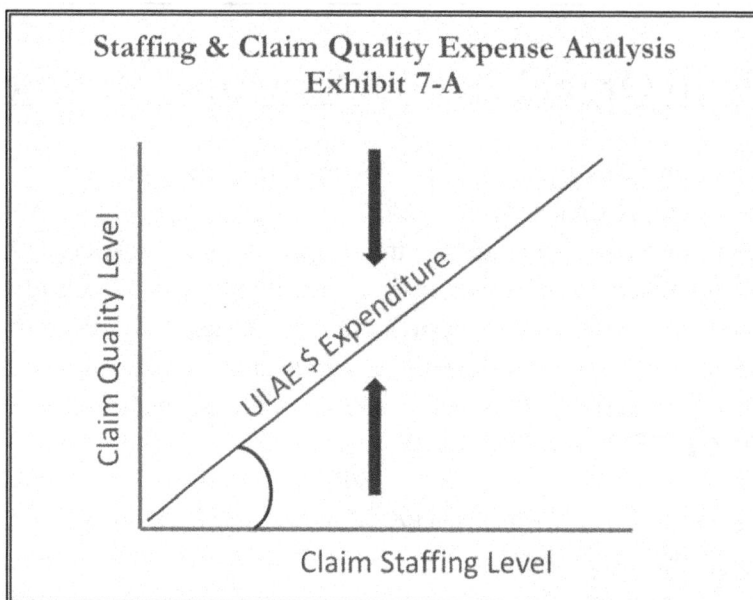

Staffing & Claim Quality Expense Analysis
Exhibit 7-A

With increased staffing you will eventually reach a point wherein you will continue to increase expense, but not necessarily improve claim quality. Workloads will be at an optimum level to achieve claim quality and any further increase would be expense waste. This is an important concept in that overstaffing contributes to expense waste and does not add value to quality claim outcomes.

What level of staffing achieves the balance of meeting budgetary constraints and quality claim handling? **Exhibit 7-B** below illustrates an example of the point of compromise between the impact of expense and achieving quality results based on outstanding claim volume or pending claims by adjuster.

Lower workloads obviously achieve higher quality results, favorable loss ratios, less adjuster stress, favorable employee retention and good customer service – but at a higher cost than your expense budget may be able to sustain. On the other hand, higher workloads have the opposite effect with poor-quality results,

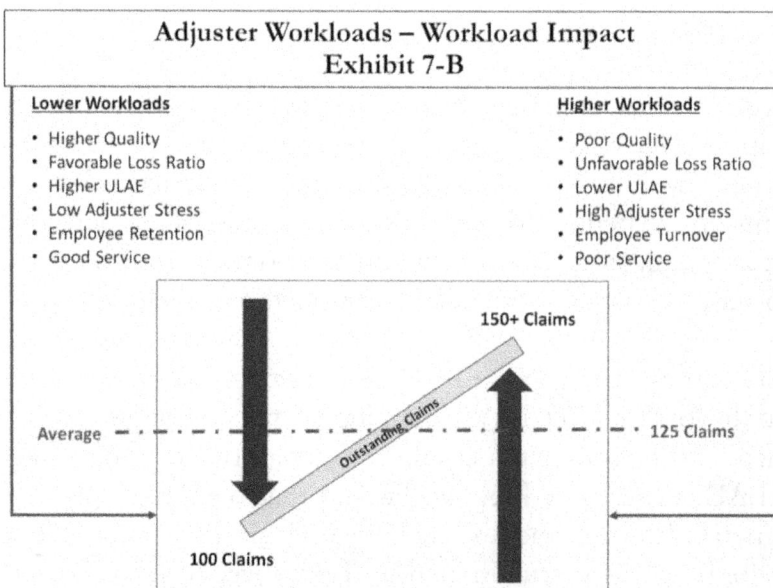

Adjuster Workloads – Workload Impact
Exhibit 7-B

**Lower Workloads**
- Higher Quality
- Favorable Loss Ratio
- Higher ULAE
- Low Adjuster Stress
- Employee Retention
- Good Service

**Higher Workloads**
- Poor Quality
- Unfavorable Loss Ratio
- Lower ULAE
- High Adjuster Stress
- Employee Turnover
- Poor Service

150+ Claims

Average — — — — — 125 Claims

Outstanding Claims

100 Claims

unfavorable loss ratio, high adjuster stress, high employee turnover and poor customer service – but at a lower cost favorably impacting the expense budget (ULAE).

How do we know what is an appropriate staffing level? This takes experience, but generally appropriate staffing levels are based on the newly reported claims received per month and the volume of open pending claims. Both impact staffing and to determine the appropriate level of staffing you must understand the types of claims being handled by the staff (e.g. line of business, class of business, complexity, severity, etc.), communicate with the staff on the ability to handle workloads, review claim files to evaluate quality, timeliness, and compliance with *best practice* standards, and understand industry average workloads for comparison purposes.

Keep in mind that using a standard workload based on your best performer is not necessarily a good idea – use a workload blend of all adjusters. You want workloads to be manageable (and achievable) but not too high or too low, use a workload which represents what the group can handle on average.

## Workload Management

As a claim manager you should recognize the impact of understaffing and overstaffing – as both have an impact on expenses and results. Understaffing adversely impacts quality results but has a positive impact on expense. Overstaffing has a positive impact on quality results but a negative impact on expense.

The days of handling 200 – 300 bodily injury claim files per adjuster are over (we hope!). Most claim organizations understand the impact of excessive workloads but need to achieve a balance between quality expectations and expense. Be proactive and realistic in your assessment of workloads. Implement workload standards so you can gauge capacity levels for each adjuster throughout the month. The claim manager should adjust workloads as needed to achieve the desired results.

It is critical that claim volume and staffing levels be monitored closely to determine whether additional staffing is necessary, or possibly a reduction in staff. As the claim volume increases due to increased premium volume, poor underwriting results with increased claim frequency, multiple long-term catastrophe storms or other causes, staffing needs to be evaluated. The claim manager should be proactive in adjusting staffing levels based on known facts. Work closely with your manager to make staff adjustments before there is a negative impact on quality results.

Do not overreact and request unnecessary staffing due to temporary increased claim volume (e.g. an unexpected catastrophe loss). Your staffing needs may only be short-term and not necessarily require additional staffing – but you may need temporary help. As a manager your job is to recognize staffing needs, and when to execute on the actual staff adjustments.

There are many factors or variables (see below) which affect workloads and results, and although you may have established workload standards, you may need to make adjustments based on the type of claim assigned and the impact of these variables on the workload.

# Various Impacts on Staffing & Workloads

There are many variables impacting staffing and workloads sometimes making it difficult to manage staff resources effectively. The claim manager should take into consideration all variables which may impact the adjuster's ability to produce a quality work product with an acceptable or better outcome.

As illustrated below workloads may need to be adjusted or deviated from your workload standard if the workload is impacted by one or more of the following issues.

## Feature or Exposure vs. File Count

Workloads can be misinterpreted by senior and executive management if claims (new and/or pending claim volume) are not counted properly.

Typically, in workers' compensation, claims are counted as one claim (open indemnity and medical feature or a medical-only claim). Property may be counted as one open claim, or some carriers may separate building, contents and time-element claims (e.g. extra expense, business interruption, etc.) as separate features or exposures.

Casualty and automobile claim counts may be problematic if they are counted as one claim due to the potential for multiple claim features or exposures. For example, a casualty claim may have multiple claimants, or an automobile claim may have multiple claimants with multiple claim features or exposures (e.g. bodily injury liability, property damage liability, physical damage, PIP, etc.). With multiple claimants and/or multiple claim features or exposures, workloads may be distorted and impacted due to the increased work tasks and required handling for each exposure – and the adjuster only receives credit for one claim.

Casualty and automobile claim workloads should be based on claim features or exposures, and not claim files.

## Type of Claim

The type of claim being assigned and handled will have a material impact on the number of new claims one can handle per month and effectively manage a pending claim volume. For example, a workers' compensation medical-only or automobile physical damage adjuster can handle a higher volume of new claim activity due to the limited claim activities involved and the average duration of the claims. Typically, these claims are short-term and fast-track, handled by the less experienced adjuster. New claim volume is high, but most claims close within 90 days from the report date. As a result, the new claim volume is higher, but the pending claim volume will be lower.

Conversely, claims which are more complex, or have severity, will entail more claim activities, and pend longer than the smaller less-complex claims. For example, a workers' compensation indemnity or bodily injury casualty adjuster can only handle an average volume of claim activity due to the work involved and the duration of the claims. Typically, these claims pend longer and require more work than a smaller claim being handled by the less experienced adjuster. New claim volume will be lower, and many claims pend over one year from the report date. As a result, the pending claim volume is higher limiting the number of new claims which can be handled per month.

## Line of Business

Examples of lines of business include automobile, casualty, property, workers' compensation and professional liability. Each line of business has its own claim handling requirements based on the types of accidents/incidents and exposures.

It should be noted that workloads and productivity are impacted whether the claim is personal lines or commercial lines. Some commercial lines claims are more time consuming than personal lines claims (e.g. complex general liability, commercial property, workers' compensation, etc.). Automobile claim handling will include physical damage, property damage (liability), personal injury protection and medical payments claims which can be handled by a less experienced adjuster and bodily injury or uninsured motorist (UM)/underinsured motorist (UIM) claims which can be handled by a more experienced adjuster.

Casualty will also have different claim assignment levels based on adjuster experience and knowledge such as general liability property damage and general liability bodily injury or personal injury.

Property will have multiple levels of claim handling based on knowledge of coverage and property claim technical skills. As complexity and severity increase a more experienced level adjuster needs to be assigned to handle the claim.

Lastly, professional liability is more complex and requires an experienced level adjuster who understands the coverage and policy forms, and how to conduct proper claim investigations. These claims can be time consuming, typically have coverage issues, and are often pending in litigation, resulting in the need for a lower workload (new and pending claims).

## Class of Business

Class of business refers to specific types of exposures within a line of business, which may also include sub-classes. For example, automobile may include private passenger automobiles, livery or public auto, buses, passenger vans, long haul trucking, automobile rental, trash haulers and tow trucks, all of which have different claim handling requirements and the potential for both low and high severity.

Property and casualty classes of business may include dwellings, farms, habitational (e.g. apartment buildings), offices, high-rise buildings, nursing homes, churches and religious institutions, retail stores, hotels, restaurants, warehouses and storage facilities, garages, convenience stores and gas stations, contractors, exterminators, logging operations, amusement parks, waste management, etc.

Certain types of casualty claims (e.g., PIP or no-Fault) and workers' compensation claims may be more labor intensive because of the volume of payment transactions, medical management (e.g., medical bill review, nurse case management, IMEs, etc.), and required form filings.

Professional liability classes may include architects and engineers, accountant E&O, agent and adjuster E&O, lawyers' professional liability and medical malpractice liability. These claims are labor intensive, may have complex coverage issues, and often pending in litigation.

Each class of business may represent a required claim handling skill to handle the claim properly and effectively. Assignments and workloads will vary depending on the complexity and severity involved. For example, a construction liability claim, or medical malpractice liability claim may require a more comprehensive investigation with multiple witness interviews and complex documentation for review and analysis, as well as complex coverage and/or contractual issues.

## Complexity & Severity

Claims with complexity and severity take more time to handle properly. These claims will also have more impact on the loss ratio, therefore, require more attention.

Examples of complexity and severity claims may include construction liability claims with significant injuries and complex contractual liability and coverage issues (e.g. indemnification and additional insured issues). These claims are time consuming and require more time to investigate, handle and evaluate. An adjuster handling complex construction liability claims may only be able to handle 10 – 15 new claims per month and a pending claim volume of 90 – 110 claims.

Fatality claims and claims with significant injuries require a more comprehensive and in-depth investigation. For example, a claimant with a catastrophic injury such as paraplegia or amputation has significant exposure and requires more investigation, evaluation and ongoing handling. If an adjuster is handling a larger volume of claims with complexity and severity, the new claim assignments and pending claim volume will need to be lower to achieve an acceptable level of quality claim handling. This will impact staffing with the need to have additional staff.

## Litigation Claims

Litigation claims are time consuming and require a higher and specialized skill level. These claims often include high complexity and severity and have a material impact on ALAE due to legal and defense costs.

Controlling legal and defense costs is critical to properly managing ALAE and can only be accomplished with a comprehensive litigation management program. This means working with defense counsel closely to control costs – including knowing when to engage in settlement discussions with the plaintiff attorney vs. directing a claim toward defense and trial.

The larger number of litigation claims handled by an adjuster, the less emphasis will be placed on effective litigation management and expense control. This will result in a significant increase in legal and defense costs (ALAE) which will far exceed the costs of adding additional staff.

Litigation adjusters can handle a new claim volume of 10 – 15 claims per month and 90 – 120 pending claims, depending on complexity and severity, as well as the jurisdictions involved.

## Multi-Jurisdictions

Handling multiple claim jurisdictions is time consuming and can have a material impact on productivity, upward of a negative 10% - 15%. Claims which are pending in litigation or have regulatory and compliance requirements will be impacted when handling multiple jurisdictions.

For example, the laws, statutes, court systems and litigation processes, will vary by state. If an adjuster is unfamiliar with a state or jurisdiction, the claim handling will be negatively impacted, potentially resulting in the need for additional staff.

In workers' compensation and PIP claims, the problem is even more compounded with strict state and regulatory requirements including meeting time and form filing compliance requirements, as well as managing benefits timely and properly.

It is difficult for an adjuster to manage multiple jurisdictions which will impact productivity and workloads. Limiting the adjuster to 3 – 4 jurisdictions may lessen the workload impact.

## Adjuster Experience & Knowledge

Adjuster experience and knowledge impact productivity and workloads. If an adjuster is unfamiliar or not trained in a specific line of business or class of business, there will be a negative impact on productivity and workload – the adjuster may not be able to handle a full workload even though the role or position requires the workload. This results in a productivity or workload gap – the same work volume exists, but you now need to reassign claims to another experienced adjuster (potentially increasing their workload).

It's important to fill roles or positions with experienced and qualified adjusters, especially if your staffing is based on a fixed number of full time equivalents or FTE's. If you are going to fill roles or positions with an inexperienced adjuster for mentoring and training purposes, you should contemplate a lower workload and adjust you staffing needs upward to fill the staffing gap.

As a cautionary note, inexperienced or unqualified adjusters handling claims beyond their expertise, may result in claim leakage. Whatever expense you thought you saved in salary costs will be eroded by a negative impact on loss and expense. Areas such as coverage analysis, investigation, liability and damage evaluation, reserve management and negotiations, will all have a potential impact on claim leakage.

## Adjuster Claim Handling

Sometimes a claim supervisor or manager may be puzzled why an adjuster is unable to handle a reasonable workload, when the other adjusters handling similar claims can handle the claim volume. Oftentimes, the reason may be simple and subtle, and attributed to the adjuster's own handling of the claim, their handling methodology, making effective use of their time, or lack of a specific skillset.

You need to determine if the adjuster is "over-working" the claim and making quality use of their day. Wanting to be recognized by their supervisor, the adjuster may do more than required, negatively impacting their productivity. Over-handling a claim is costly and unnecessary.

Listed below are examples of activities which may impact productivity due to adjuster claim handling:

- Too many personal calls throughout the day.
- Visiting coworkers throughout the day discussing business and non-business issues.
- Taking recorded statements, which are not warranted.
- Sending too many letters or emails which may be unnecessary.
- Spending too much time on the telephone with the agent, claimant, insured or attorney which may include personal or non-business discussion.
- Lengthy and redundant file notes which do not add value to the claim or ultimate outcome.
- Lengthy and redundant file reporting which does not add value to the claim and could be consolidated into one report.
- Desk adjuster visiting an accident scene which may be more cost-effective if handled by a staff field adjuster, an independent adjuster, or using other internet tools.
- Personally, visiting defense counsel's office to discuss litigation claims which could be handled by conference call.

- Attending hearings, mediations or depositions when unwarranted.
- Lack of a specific skillset which may impact the adjuster's day such as:
  - o Preparation of coverage position letters
  - o Technology skills
  - o Typing or keyboard skills

## Subrogation-Only Claims

Typically, subrogation claims have limited activity because the claim investigation has been completed and the loss has been concluded. The remaining work revolves around subrogation activities such as follow-up investigation, preservation of evidence, communicating with third parties, their carriers and subrogation counsel, submitting claims to inter-company arbitration, and protecting workers' compensation liens.

Since subrogation claims have limited activity, adjuster diaries can be on a longer schedule, limiting the number of pending files reviewed per month, and leaving time to handle incoming new subrogation claims. Hence, the subrogation adjuster can handle more claims than a line adjuster, for example outstanding claim workloads may be in the 200 – 250 range.

## Technology

Sometimes, technology can negatively impact productivity. Legacy technology which requires manual "work-arounds" and multiple system access can materially impact claim productivity. Modern architecture claim technology can also adversely impact productivity if not implemented properly or only partially.

Listed below are examples of activities or issues which may impact productivity due to technology related issues:

- Coverage verification process is not integrated with the claim system requiring manual coverage verification, or the need to access a separate policy administration system manually entering the policy information into the claim system.
- Lack of claim support. For example,
  - o Requiring the adjuster to set-up new claim files including system field and screen completion, coding, and sending acknowledgement letters, in lieu of having the support staff handle.
  - o Requiring the adjuster to issue form letters, enter data in ISO ClaimSearch®, and process minor expense payments.
- A poor document management system or process which includes the requirement for the adjuster to scan incoming mail (and email attachments) and attribute the mail to determine the claim file number and mail identification for attachment and filing purposes.

- Lack of system email integration requiring the adjuster to either paste the content of the email into an electronic file note or convert the email to a pdf file and upload as a file attachment.
- A form letter or free-form letter writing system, which is difficult to use, time consuming to issue letters and difficult to make letter modifications.
- A claim form generation module which has limited forms available and/or forms do not electronically pre-fill with system data when issued.
- System work-arounds developed by adjusters or management due to limited system capability, or the lack of IT support to develop a system enhancement. These work-arounds create more work and adversely impact productivity. An example would be the need to manually prepare large loss reports using a Word® document due to system constraints. The reports could be prepared electronically in the claim system and then exported to a predetermined group by email automatically, if the system enhancement was available.
- Lack of vendor application or system tool integration with Automobile and Property Estimating Programs, Medical Bill Review, Pharmacy Management, Medicare CMS, ISO ClaimSearch®, etc.
- Statement taking process is cumbersome and not integrated with the VOIP telephone system.
- Limited reporting capability impacting management controls.

Modern architecture claim technology implemented properly can have a positive and material impact on adjuster productivity by up to 15% to 20%. We will further discuss claim technology in **Chapter 8 – Technology & Claim Systems**.

## Compliance Requirements

Some states such as California and New York have strict claim handling compliance requirements which should be contemplated in your staffing analysis.

States which have comprehensive compliance requirements may include many letter and form filing requirements at various intervals in the claim process such as automobile APD/PD, Personal Injury Protection (PIP) and Workers' Compensation claims. These requirements impact productivity with more labor required per claim file on behalf of the adjuster and claim support.

Compliance is critical to avoid regulatory fines and reputational issues; therefore, proper staffing is required.

# Company Claim Handling Requirements

We require adjusters to handle claims in accordance with claim *best practices*, claim handling guidelines and claim procedural manuals.

If your claim handling requirements are too stringent or labor intensive, you may need to adjust your staffing requirements upward to achieve compliance. Conversely, if claim handling requirements are less stringent, or less labor intensive, you may need to adjust your staffing requirements downward.

Claim handling requirements impact staffing as they dictate the requirements for an adjuster to handle and manage claims. Typically, claim handling requirements incorporate *best practice* categories inclusive of coverage, contacts, investigation, liability/compensibility, damage evaluation, reserve management, subrogation, file management, vendor management, compliance and litigation management. Depending on the specific requirements in each category, adjusters may find it difficult to meet compliance standards if the requirements are too labor intensive given the adjuster workload.

Listed below are examples activities which may impact productivity due to claim handling requirements:

- Too many fields and screens required to be completed by the adjuster vs. claim support
- Repetitive *action plans* which do not add value to the file development
- Low claim authority levels requiring supervisor approval
- Burdensome and redundant file reporting requirements (e.g. action plans, status reports, investigative reports, captioned reports, large loss reports, claim committee reports, etc.)
- Taking unnecessary statements
- Requiring unnecessary claim contacts on all claims
- Requiring litigation management activities which are not positively impacting the claim outcome or expense
- Use of closing reports or letters
- Requiring the adjuster to attribute and label scanned documents
- Short and unnecessary diary cycles
- Adjuster handling the ISO ClaimSearch® process using the ISO web portal vs. claim support
- Doing too much work on low-value claims when unnecessary or not warranted (e.g. WC medical-only claims)

As a claim manager you want to achieve an optimum quality level, but you will have budgetary restrictions. If you have claim handling requirements which include tasks, activities or procedures which are no longer necessary, then eliminate them. You would be surprised how many claim operations continue to do things which have been done for many years and no longer necessary. As a claim manager it is your responsibility to make sure claim handling, including process and workflow, are efficient and effective, and not wasting valuable resources.

## Field Work vs. Desk Work

A *desk adjuster* (one who sits at a desk and handles claims) can handle a larger volume of claims than a *field adjuster* who is impacted by travel time and scheduling, limiting the volume of claims one can handle.

Field claim work is necessary on certain types of claims – such as the need for scene photographs and diagram, a statement taken in person, inspecting property damage and preparing a damage estimate, witness canvass, surveillance, or a claimant activity check.

Desk adjusting is a cost-effective way to handle many types of claims and allows for a higher workload than field adjusting, with a desk adjuster potentially able to handle twice as many claims. Since there are some claims which require field work, many insurance companies supplement the desk adjuster workload with task assignments handled by field adjusters or appraisers to reduce costs, which may include outsourcing to independent adjusters and appraisers.

When evaluating staffing you should specifically identify which adjusters are field adjusters vs. desk adjusters, emphasizing the impact on staffing and workloads.

## Using Claim Vendors

Many insurance companies use vendors to supplement their internal claim staff with independent adjusters and appraisers. Depending on the extent of the services performed by vendors, it may have a positive or negative impact on staffing requirements.

For example, if a company staffs its property claim unit with desk adjusters who utilize outsourced independent adjusters to handle most of the property adjusting activities then the desk adjuster may be able to handle a higher workload. If a casualty desk adjuster uses an independent adjuster to handle the claim investigation, including contacts, statements, scene photographs and diagram, etc., the desk adjuster may be able to handle a higher workload.

Conversely, if the desk adjuster handles most claim activities this should be taken into consideration when evaluating workloads and staffing.

## Claim Authority Levels

Claim authority levels will impact workloads for both the adjuster and supervisor or manager.

If claim authorities are set too low, it will require more communication between the adjuster and the claim supervisor, or manager, when the claim (reserve, payment or settlement) exceeds the adjuster's authority. These approval activities may include the need for additional evaluation forms, and further discussion between the adjuster and the claim supervisor, or manager. This reduces the amount of time an adjuster can spend on other claims, impacting adjuster workloads and productivity.

Claim authority should be set at a reasonable level to allow the adjuster to work autonomously, but within their level of expertise. Low claim authority levels have a negative impact on productivity and expense and should be avoided.

## Special Claim Handling

Special claim handling will typically involve large premium policyholders who require special claim services. For example, the following are considered special claim handling activities:

- Designated adjusters for the account.
- Notification to the policyholder's *risk manager* on all new claims which exceed a certain reserve dollar threshold (either a new reserve or adjustment).
- Settlement approval requirement for claims which exceed a certain dollar threshold.
- Quarterly summary reports on claim activity inclusive of financial information.
- Providing summaries on individual claims.
- Attendance at risk management meetings to discuss specific claims.
- Providing comprehensive claim management reports.
- Special claim coding.

Special claim handling services have a high impact on adjuster productivity due to the volume of additional services required. Since special claim handling has a material impact on workloads, staffing must be adjusted upward to meet these requirements.

It is important to work closely with the underwriting and marketing staff when special claim handling is being negotiated and agreed to. There are additional claim costs which need to be contemplated in the transaction due to increased staffing costs (ULAE).

## Adjuster Performance

Poor adjuster performance not only affects quality, customer service and claim outcomes, but also negatively affects other members of the claim unit. If a poor performing adjuster cannot keep up with the workload, or not handle the work properly, the tendency is to overload co-employees with additional work, which causes morale and potentially poor claim quality issues with increased workloads.

Managing poor performance on a timely basis is critical. Penalizing the other claim staff with increased workloads to compensate for a poor performing adjuster will ultimately result in other claim quality issues and potential staff turnover.

We always want to be fair to employees who may need additional coaching or assistance. But unresolved poor performance should be managed timely and properly to avoid workload issues. Staffing should never be adjusted upward to compensate for a poor performing adjuster.

## Employee Turnover Impact

Employee turnover critically impacts a claim unit, particularly when the balance of the workload has been redistributed to other remaining staff members. Unfortunately, employee turnover creates more turnover and it can result in a claim manager's worst nightmare if not resolved timely and properly.

The claim manager's challenge is to first identify the reasons for the turnover. As referenced in **Chapter 3 – Managing Effectively,** turnover is a management problem and caused by management decisions and/or company direction.

If employee turnover is continuing at an accelerated rate impacting the quality of claim results and service, consider "over-staffing" until you can stabilize your staff resources. This will allow you to continue to handle claims without affecting claim quality. Over time, your staffing will come down to the budgetary level. This needs to be monitored closely in terms of the over-staffed employee count and the expense impact. In the end, the expense impact will be less if you are able to stabilize the operation, as employee turnover is very costly.

Another less desirable alternative is to hire temporary help until you are able stabilize the staffing due to continued turnover. Unfortunately, this could have negative consequences if you are not able to recruit experienced and qualified staff resources which may also increase your loss and expense costs.

As a cautionary note – do not over-load high performers on a long-term basis to manage employee turnover. Your high performers will become dissatisfied and be your next round of employee turnover.

Turnover will have a negative impact on the loss ratio with potential overpayments to resolve claims quicker (increasing average paids), inadequate case reserves, and increased ALAE costs with more claims going into litigation due to less engagement with claimant attorneys to settle claims. Get your arms around the issues affecting the turnover and manage staffing and workloads effectively.

# Budget Resource Allocation

As discussed in **Chapter 2 – Financial Operations** budgeting is a key function of claims management. The largest expense component of the claim budget are expenses associated with staff resources related to salary, benefits and payroll taxes.

Most companies refer to staff resource counts from a budget perspective as *Full Time Equivalents* (FTE) or *Personnel on Board* (POB). Approved staffing counts are established at the beginning of a budget period (e.g. 1/1/XX) which will provide the total number of approved staff members you are allocated for the budget period. The FTE count may not indicate the staff positions or roles – and be just a head count.

To fully understand the impact of expense on your claim budget, you need to know the total impact of salary and benefits for the total approved FTE count. If your proposed salary budget cannot support the FTE count, you will need to adjust the FTE count or the salary budget. This is an important concept in that the FTE count only provides an indication of the number of staff members, but the salary dollars are what impact the budget expenses (e.g. ULAE).

Each month, you may receive a *budget variance report* which will include variances (dollar and percentage) for all expense categories (e.g. salary and benefits) and the FTE count. Any negative budget variances exceeding a certain level may require an explanation to management.

It's important for the claim manager to monitor the monthly budget variance reports to be sure the budget vs. actual expenses are in order.

Achieving the balance between the budgeted staff vs. what you need may be a challenge. As indicated in prior chapters, the tradeoff in understaffing is improved ULAE savings against potentially poor-quality claim handling impacting the loss ratio – but you are responsible for both the loss ratio (impacted by poor quality claim handling) and the ULAE ratio (expense). Be proactive – don't wait to ask for more staff until the claim quality has suffered. Evaluate staffing regularly and submit staffing approval requests to senior management when needed with proper supporting documentation. Monitor premium growth and anticipate increased claim volume and the need for more staff.

Typically, the budget is prepared "top-down" meaning premium (revenue) is projected first for the upcoming budget year and then expenses are included to determine loss, expense and LAE ratios. If premium volume is down, and loss and expense remain constant, acceptable ratios become difficult to achieve because premium is the denominator in the ratio. Operational expenses may need to be adjusted downward and there may be a freeze on hiring and staffing levels, even if the prior calendar year had premium growth resulting in increased claim volume necessitating additional staffing in the current year. This is challenge, but if premium is down and expenses need to be reduced, you need to be prepared to do your share to get the company back on track. Remember, you are one department among others who all contribute to the expense allocations, and company profitability.

Staff the claim operation appropriately to achieve optimum quality claim outcomes, but don't have over-experienced claim staff handle low severity/low complexity claims – it will adversely impact your salary budget and prevent you from using those valuable salary dollars elsewhere.

Remember, people are your most important asset and your largest expense. Sometimes, claim managers decide to retain an employee who was not successful in their current role, placing them in a lower level role but not adjusting their salary level. The result is that the employee's salary is much higher than their peers and you are paying more for the position than warranted. This results in higher expense and may prevent you from hiring the additional staff needed in the claim operation. If you reduce an employee's role in an organization which changes the job grade, then the compensation for the new role should be adjusted if the salary ranges are materially different.

## Claim Workload Models

Most companies have claim workload models. These models include standards or guidelines for the volume of work a claim employee can handle. Generally, the models include a measurement of *new claims*, *reopened claims*, *closed claims*, *outstanding claims* and *closing ratio*. Some companies will also track *transferred claims*. Below is an explanation of each term:

- **New Claims:** New claims are all newly reported claims received by the company, counted during a specific time-period such as daily, weekly or monthly. New claims are a component of the *closing ratio* calculation.

- **Reopened Claims:** Reopened claims are all claims reopened and counted during a specific time-period such as daily, weekly or monthly. Reopened claims are a component of the *closing ratio* calculation.

- **Closed Claims:** Closed claims are all claims closed and counted during a specific time-period such as daily, weekly or monthly. Closed claims are a component of the *closing ratio* calculation.

- **Outstanding Claims:** Outstanding claims are all *open* claims counted during a specific time-period such as daily, weekly or monthly. To count the year-end outstanding or open claim count, you simply take the open claim count as of 12/31/XX. Outstanding claims are not a component of the *closing ratio* calculation.

- **Closing Ratio:** The closing ratio is the ratio of new and reopened claims to closed claims counted during a specific time-period such as daily, weekly or monthly. This closing ratio is calculated as closed claims divided by new claims + reopened claims. For example, if there are 714 new claims and 54 reopened claims, the total is 768. If we closed 731 claims during the same time-period, the closing ratio is 95.2% [731 / (714 + 54)].

- **Transferred Claims:** Transferred claims are all claims transferred from one adjuster to another adjuster during a specific time-period such as daily, weekly or monthly. These claims have already been recorded as a *new* or *reopened* claim at one point in time; therefore, should be excluded from your productivity analysis to avoid distorting the results.

The terms claim *exposure, feature, suffix, claimant* and *file* or *claim* counts are used in the context of claim workload and staffing models, with each having an impact on how productivity and workload should be calculated.

Below is an explanation of each in productivity terms:

- **Claim Exposure:** A *claim exposure* represents an exposure unit for a claimant or insured. For example, a liability claimant may have a bodily injury (BI) and medical payments (Med Pay) exposure on the same claim.

- **Claim Feature:** A *claim feature* is the same as a *claim exposure*.

- **Claim Suffix:** A *claim suffix* is the same as a *claim exposure*.

- **Claimant:** A *claimant* is a party to the loss who may have multiple exposures, features or suffixes. For example, an injured passenger or *claimant* in the insured vehicle may have a bodily injury (BI) and no fault (PIP) exposure on the same claim.

- **File or Claim:** A *file* or *claim* represents the entire claim, inclusive of all claimants, features and suffixes. This is the highest level in terms of productivity counts.

With these terms explained we can now review various claim *Workload Models* outlined below:

- **Claim Exposure Workload Model:** This model is used by many companies and is considered the most fair and equitable method to count adjuster productivity. In this model, all claim exposures or features are counted to determine productivity in each time-period, including new claims, reopened claims, closed claims, outstanding claims and the closing ratio. The claim counts represent claim exposures; therefore, one automobile accident could have multiple *claim exposures* such as collision, property damage, bodily injury and PIP. This model fairly contemplates the work necessary on each claim exposure to avoid misaligned or unfair adjuster workloads which are only counted as one file. Typically, this model is used in casualty claims (e.g. automobile, liability, etc.).

- **Claimant Workload Model**: This model is used by some insurance companies but is not considered a fair and equitable method in casualty claim, similar to the *Claim File Workload Model* (below). Since workloads are based on the number of claimants in one claim file, claim workloads and productivity may be distorted, if the claimants have multiple claim exposures or features. For example, a liability claimant may have a bodily injury and medical payments feature, or an automobile claimant may have a bodily injury and property damage feature. This model may be used in workers' compensation wherein claim workloads are based on one claimant to include an indemnity and medical claim feature.

- **Claim File Workload Model**: This model is used by some insurance companies but is not considered a fair and equitable method in casualty claims as indicated above. Since workloads are based on <u>all</u> claim exposures or features in one claim file, claim workloads and productivity may be distorted. This model may be used in certain lines of business such as property claims. If the insurance company does not want to separate the building, contents and time element exposures, they may use this method counting all property exposures as one claim file.

- **Hybrid Workload Model**: This model includes variations of the three models detailed above. For example, the *Claim Exposure Workload Model* may be used for casualty claims, the *Claimant Model* for workers' compensation claims and the *Claim File Model* for property claims. When using the hybrid model, it is important to reference or footnote its application when illustrating staffing and productivity.

# Claim Staffing Models

Establishing the basis for staffing is often a challenge considering all the *Various Impacts on Staffing & Workloads* discussed above.

The initial step in the development of a staffing model is to determine how you want to establish workloads by using workload and productivity standards. For example, you will need to develop workload and productivity standards by *claim role* to include both *new claims* and *outstanding claims*. The reason you include both is that an adjuster needs to close claims monthly to achieve a 1:1 or 100% closing ratio. If the adjuster does not close the required number of claims, then the outstanding claim volume will continue to increase, adversely affecting the adjuster's ability to achieve a quality work product on both new claims (e.g. initial investigations, evaluation, etc.) and outstanding open claims (e.g. reserve management, settlement disposition, litigation management, etc.). If the outstanding claim volume in the unit or department continues to grow you will eventually need additional staff.

The workloads will vary by claim role. A property damage adjuster can handle more new claims than a litigation adjuster because property damage claims require less handling activities and the claims have a shorter duration. A workers' compensation adjuster handling medical-only claims can handle more new claims than an indemnity adjuster also due to less claim activities and a shorter claim duration.

Illustrated below are examples of various desk adjuster workload standards based on the claim role or position in a P&C claim operation. This is an illustration only and will vary by company. Workload standards are also impacted by the lines of business and whether the claims are personal or commercial lines.

| WORKLOAD ILLUSTRATION BY P&C DESK ADJUSTER CLAIM ROLES BY EXPOSURE: EXHIBIT 7-C | | | |
|---|---|---|---|
| Claim Role | Claim Position | New Exposures Per Month | Pending Claim Exposures |
| Physical Damage Adjuster | CR I | 45 - 50 | 130 - 160 |
| Property Damage Adjuster | CR I or CR II | 45 - 50 | 130 - 160 |
| Bodily Injury Adjuster | CR II or CR III | 20 - 25 | 125 - 150 |
| Sr. Bodily Injury Adjuster | Claim Specialist | 15 - 20 | 125 - 150 |
| Complex Liability Adjuster | Claim Specialist | 10 - 15 | 90 - 110 |
| Litigation Adjuster | Litigation Specialist | 10 - 15 | 90 - 120 |
| Property Low Exposure Adj. | CR I or CR II | 30 - 40 | 100 - 130 |
| Property Medium Exposure Adj. | CR II or CR III | 20 - 30 | 95 - 110 |
| Property High Exposure Adjuster | CR III or Claim Spec. | 10 - 15 | 90 - 100 |
| WC Medical-Only Adjuster | CR I or CR II | 40 - 50 | 200 - 225 |
| WC Indemnity Adjuster | CR III or Claim Spec. | 18 - 22 | 100 - 125 |
| Subrogation Adjuster | CR III or Claim Spec. | 35 - 45 | 225- 250 |

When establishing workload and productivity standards, it is important to address the *Various Impacts on Staffing & Workloads* discussed above, to determine whether the workload standards need to be modified for specific roles.

Typically, staffing in a claim organization is based on claim workloads using a basis count of *new claim* and *reopened claim* volume, *outstanding claim* volume, or a combination of both in a specific time-period such as monthly. There are three *Staffing Models* which include:

- **New Claim Staffing Model:** This model focuses on productivity and staffing based on *new* and *reopened* claims handled within a specific time-period. The model contemplates that the adjusters will achieve a 100% closing ratio of new claims to closed claims. The model does not use *outstanding claim* volume as a primary metric in evaluating productivity and staffing.

- **Outstanding Claim Staffing Model:** This model focuses on *outstanding claim* or *pending claim* volume as the primary metric in evaluating productivity and staffing. The model does not use *new* and *reopened claim* volume as a primary metric; however, the outstanding claim volume will fluctuate with new and closed claim volume. The model contemplates that the adjusters will achieve a 100% closing ratio of new claims to closed claims to maintain an acceptable workload.

- **<u>Hybrid Staffing Model</u>**: This model focuses on both *new* and *reopened claim* volume and *outstanding claim* volume as the primary metric in evaluating productivity and staffing. It is considered the most prudent model in P&C claim staffing as it considers all work activities in the staffing model. For example, new claim handling activity may include different tasks than the tasks completed on outstanding or pending claims. By counting both you can measure the adjuster's ability to balance their workload tasks between the new losses (which are a priority) and outstanding losses. This model contemplates that the adjusters will achieve a 100% closing ratio of new claims to closed claims to maintain an acceptable workload (outstanding or pending claim volume).

The staffing model used may depend on the types of claims handled and may vary based on the claim role. For example, there should be more emphasis on new claim activity vs. outstanding claim volume for automobile physical damage, property damage and workers' compensation medical-only claims compared to claims which have a longer duration such as complex liability or litigation claims.

Some insurance companies have developed staffing models which incorporate *weightings* into the productivity calculation, based on the claim role and claim type. For example, a property damage adjuster may have more productivity emphasis on new claim activity vs. outstanding claim activity, as the former may be a better indicator of productivity.

Staffing models should include *capacity monitoring* which applies the workload standard, such as the basis count of new claim and reopened claim volume and outstanding claim volume, to the actual adjuster productivity. This provides claim management with an indicator of which adjusters have new assignment capacity vs. those adjusters who do not have capacity. The capacity monitoring metric should be used as a guide – don't overreact if an adjuster is slightly out of capacity which may only be temporary.

*Reopened* claims impact workloads due to the increased volume, but the reopened claim volume may be due to premature closing of claims (e.g. to meet the monthly closing ratio). The reopen claim metric should be monitored closely to be sure the reopen claim activity is kept at a minimum. Identify the adjusters with high reopened claim activity to determine the cause.

An effective method to balance workloads properly is to have an automated assignment process which includes *workload balancing*. Most modern architecture claim systems have automated assignment and workload balancing functionality. When the claim system is implemented, business rules are developed to classify certain types of claims which are handled by specific roles, adjusters or a group of adjusters. As the new claim is set up, the system will automatically assign the claim to the designated adjuster based on the predetermined business rules (e.g. type of claim, dollar value, injury, litigation, etc.). As the adjuster receives new assignments, the system will recognize predetermined workloads and "balance" the workloads by assigning a different adjuster once an adjuster has reached their predetermined capacity.

# <u>Productivity Reporting</u>

After we have selected the workload and staffing models, we can develop an appropriate *productivity reporting* methodology.

Productivity reporting is a management control and the key tool to monitor, control and manage claim productivity. Productivity goals for the adjuster and manager will typically be incorporated into employee performance management given the importance and impact on the organization. We use productivity reporting to manage productivity and evaluate staffing against our established workload standards. If claim workloads are either increasing or decreasing, we need to determine whether staff adjustments are necessary. We also use productivity reports to monitor staff productivity performance such as closing ratios and managing claim volume.

The type of productivity reporting available to the claim operation will depend on the organization's claim systems and reporting capability. For example, a company with a robust data warehouse will have high quality productivity reporting with the flexibility to modify reports based on need. Whether productivity reporting is developed using Excel® spreadsheets and the use of pivot tables, or system generated, the reports should include similiar information. At minmum, the productivity reporting should include the following detail:

- Adjuster Name
- Position/Role
- Time Period (e.g. monthly and rolling 12 months)
- New Claims
- Reopened Claims
- Outstanding Claims
- Closed Claims
- Closing Ratio
- Litigation Claims
- Average Metrics (new, reopened, closed, outstanding and closing ratio)

**Exhibit 7-D** below is an example of a basic productivity report. The productivity report provides an illustration of the current month and the prior rolling 12 month period. This type of report format can be built in Excel® using pivot tables to sort data. For example, the report could include a tab for the downloaded claim productivity data, and then allow for the use of *pivot tables* and *slicers* to sort and filter data in various categories.

| P&C CLAIM PRODUCTIVITY REPORTING (By Exposure): EXB. 7 - D | | | | | | | | | | |
|---|---|---|---|---|---|---|---|---|---|---|
| XYZ Productivity Activity: January 20XX | | | | | | Rolling 12 Month Average | | | | |
| Adjuster | Role | New | Reopen | Closed | Pending | Close Ratio | Avg New | Avg Reopen | Avg Closed | Avg O/S | Avg Close Ratio |
| Johnson, P. | CR I | 50 | 5 | 50 | 110 | 91% | 55 | 3 | 56 | 115 | 97% |
| Peterson, A. | CR II | 45 | 2 | 46 | 150 | 98% | 42 | 2 | 43 | 146 | 98% |
| McDonald, M. | CR III | 20 | 3 | 22 | 135 | 96% | 18 | 1 | 19 | 139 | 100% |
| Anderson, A. | CR III | 15 | 3 | 16 | 142 | 89% | 16 | 2 | 17 | 141 | 94% |
| Chamberlain, D. | Clm Spec | 12 | 1 | 13 | 98 | 100% | 13 | 1 | 14 | 100 | 100% |
| Cooper, S. | Lit Spec | 12 | 1 | 12 | 105 | 92% | 12 | 2 | 13 | 110 | 93% |
| Totals/Average: | | 154 | 15 | 159 | 740 | 94% | 156 | 11 | 162 | 751 | 97% |

Each claim employee should have productivity goals, and be accountable to achieve the established productivity goals during the designated performance period. On a monthly basis, productivity results should be discussed with each claim employee to monitor progress toward goal. When evaluating productivity don't over react to an occasional slippage in closing ratios, you want to look at productivity trends. If an adjuster has a manageable workload and a trending deteriorating closing ratio, you need to investigate the cause and take appropriate action.

Since we want to evaluate productivity trends, we need to evaluate performance using a rolling 12 month period. This will allow for an analysis of averages during specific time periods such as 3 months, 6 months and 12 months. The *average* analysis is a better metric as it evaluates results over time instead of focusing on a specific time period (e.g. monthly).

Modern architecture claim systems have built-in dashboard productivity reporting. It is very important that each adjuster receive or have access to their individual productivity report, at minmum on a monthly basis.

## Using Temporary Staff Resources

At times, either due to the unavailability of permanent staff or the inability to hire additional staff, we may need to use temporary staff resources. It is important that the temporary staff be appropriate for the work needed. Retaining temporary staff which end up mishandling claims will cause you more aggravation than overloading your staff temporarily until you are able to get the department back on track.

The key to retaining temporary staff resources effectively is to review their resume (not a job summary), request references from prior employers and conduct an interview. You want claim resources which have the knowledge and experience in the specific areas needed and will fit into your claim culture.

## Chapter Comments

In this chapter, we reviewed staffing and resource management in a claim operation. The financial management of staffing can be challenging for the claim manager in balancing the staff necessary to achieve quality claim outcomes and staying within the approved claim expense budget.

Lower workloads achieve higher quality results, favorable loss ratios, less adjuster stress, favorable employee retention and good customer service – but at a higher cost than your expense budget may be able to sustain. The opposite effect occurs with higher workloads – but at a lower cost favorably impacting your expense budget.

The claim operation has a budget for FTE counts and the associated salary and benefit expense for each employee, but the salary and benefit costs are most important given their financial impact on the claim budget.

Workload management is a key responsibility for the claim manager and requires monitoring workloads and staffing levels on a regular basis to be sure staffing levels are appropriate (upward or downward). Workload management is a challenge since there are many factors which impact staffing such as exposure vs. file counts, type of claim and line of business, complexity and severity, litigation and multi-jurisdictions, adjuster's knowledge and experience, claim authority levels, technology, compliance requirements and an organization's own claim handling requirements.

There are various *Claim Workload Models* which are used as the basis to develop workload and productivity standards. These models include the *Claim Exposure*, *Claimant*, *Claim File* and *Hybrid* workload models.

We use *Claim Staffing Models* to apply the workload standards to the claim operation and allocate staffing based on specific metrics such as new and reopened claim volume, outstanding or pending claims, or a combination of both. Staffing models include *New Claim*, *Outstanding Claim* and *Hybrid* staffing models.

Productivity reporting is an important management control and requires regular review to be sure the claim staff is meeting the productivity requirements (e.g. closing ratios). Productivity reporting formats will vary by organization depending on their IT resources and claim technology.

The most critical aspect of productivity management is to monitor adjuster capacity and the balancing of workloads.

# CHAPTER 8
# TECHNOLOGY & CLAIM SYSTEMS

This chapter is divided into three segments: claim technology & operations, new claim technology implementation and the future of claim technology.

- *Claim Technology & Operations* focuses on various aspects of claim technology and the impact on the claim operation, including technical claim handling, as well as, process and workflow. We also look at the *Modern Architecture Claim System* including its features and benefits.
- *New Claim Technology Implementation* provides a framework for the implementation of new claim systems, which may sometimes be underestimated in terms of both expense and resources.
- The *Future of Claim Technology* is changing rapidly. In this section we provide a glimpse into the future of the claims environment and how it will impact the claim operation of today.

## Claim Technology & Operations

The 21st century has brought about many insurance industry changes, including the work environment in P&C claims.

The industry has evolved – It wasn't too long ago that a claim supervisor's work effort was all driven by manual tasks and activities. Claim files were hard-copy and file notes were handwritten on memo paper and placed in the claim file folder. Diary management was limited to handwritten entries on a calendar. All information, inclusive of data, investigation, documents, notes, photographs, and legal pleadings were retained in a hard copy claim file.

Financial transactions were handwritten on multi-part paper forms and referred for batch data processing. Check payments were manually typed on a typewriter with a tissue copy of the issued check posted to the claim file folder. ISO ClaimSearch® (previously called CIB or Central Index Bureau) and other claim forms were manually typed, and letters and reports were dictated and then referred to a transcriptionist for typing. The availability of claim management reports was limited.

Claim files were piled up on the adjuster and supervisor's desk and matching incoming mail was an arduous process. If a telephone call was received, you had a 50/50 chance of being able to help the caller if you were lucky enough to locate the claim file in the office.

Fortunately, with the development of *Modern Architecture Claim Systems*, the claim environment has evolved into a robust electronic claim workstation eliminating many manual tasks. The claim supervisor's role has also changed – balancing the need for the staff to achieve a quality work product and working effectively in a fast-paced electronic claim environment.

Working in an electronic claim environment has its challenges and a claim supervisor must be well organized to use the claim system functionality effectively to manage the claim process. Do not let the system impede fundamental claim supervision – which sometimes requires discipline. As a claim supervisor you cannot look at everything, so you need to identify what requires your attention to provide oversight and supervision. Use the claim system management controls and be selectively involved in the claim files which require your attention.

Unfortunately, some insurance carriers and TPA's are still in a technology transition phase, having to work with diverse systems simultaneously – impeding productivity. This can be attributed to a variety of reasons including lack of financial resources and project priority constraints, as well as encountering application implementation and integration problems causing delays.

Technology which is only partially implemented or not fully integrated with other systems (e.g. policy administration, accounts payable, etc.) will negatively affect process, workflow and management reporting. Partial system implementation may be due to the lack of financial and/or project resources, or there are integration problems. For example, the core claim system may have been implemented, but only the financial transactional system is functional (which may be called Phase I), with another legacy system handling electronic notes and diary management, a separate system for medical bill review, a separate system for auto and property estimating, and yet another system for document management, claim forms and letter generation. The ultimate objective for Phase II is to interface all systems with full functional integration, yet this may take years to complete; and for some companies who take too long to transition, it may be impossible unless the original claim system is first upgraded.

When claim systems are not fully integrated, or only partially implemented, there is a "drag" on adjuster and claim support productivity, impacting claim quality and timeliness, and more importantly the ability to supervise effectively. Basically, it takes longer to get the job done using diverse systems (or combining existing manual tasks with systems) – including entry and review of electronic notes, reviewing and summarizing claim investigations, handling documents and attachments, managing the claim diary process, managing claim authority requests, handling and managing litigation claims, approving claim payments and processing reserve changes, generating forms and letters, and processing basic tasks such as ISO ClaimSearch®.

Tasks such as manually pasting emails and documents to the electronic file notes, indexing and matching mail, manually uploading attachments, or entering financial transactions such as reserve adjustments using separate or non-integrated systems, becomes time consuming and cumbersome for the claim support staff, adjuster and supervisor.

If adjusters or supervisors have a "drag" on their time, it will impact productivity and the quality of the work product. Most companies have workload standards outlining how many new claims and open pending claims an adjuster can handle monthly. If productivity is being impeded using diverse or legacy systems; adjusters and supervisors are being held accountable to manage to a productivity standard but with less available time. By using diverse systems an adjuster or supervisor's time can be potentially impacted by 15% - 20% each day. If your claim staff is operating at 80% capacity, and your claim salary and benefit costs are $6M annually, you may potentially have $1.2M in lost productivity dollars.

Equally problematic is the adverse impact on claim quality. Adjusters and supervisors may take shortcuts to get the job done which may cause *claim leakage*, due to inadequate claim investigations, poor settlement or reserve evaluations, improper reserve management (redundancy or deficiency), and poor settlement negotiations. Customer service will also be impacted due to adjuster time constraints resulting in not returning telephone calls timely, late issuance of claim payments and mistakes. This will all lead to a negative impact on the loss ratio and expense – loss ratio in terms of poor claim evaluations, overpayments and reserve redundancy or deficiency, and expense in terms of loss productivity.

Planning a claim system implementation is not an easy task and the implementation process will have a significant impact on the organization. As part of the assessment process, management needs to evaluate the impact on process and workflow, and not partially deploy systems which can result in a workflow slowdown or impede productivity and claim quality. Although not always possible, waiting for full deployment will yield a better result. Getting the business staff involved early on will also avoid some of these problems – system application implementation projects which are led by the business group historically have better results than led by an IT group.

## Modern Architecture Claim Systems

Today, many insurance carriers and TPAs have already implemented sophisticated claim systems or planning a future implementation. Others are still hanging on to their legacy systems not recognizing, or ignoring, the expense impact on the organization due to the need for more resources and lack of efficiency.

Modern architecture claim systems offer a host of features and benefits which can improve efficiency and productivity. These systems are modular and allow for ease of integration with existing and new systems (including policy administration systems), as well as integration with third party systems through *web services* (a web-based application integration standard) and other interfaces. The architecture allows for system configuration and modification with minimal adverse impact on future system upgrades.

With the advancement of modern architecture claim systems, many new features and benefits have been developed to enhance productivity, improve efficiency and reduce costs with the reduction of manual tasks.

It's important to conduct research before investing in a new claim system. Most claim systems will have similar core functionality such as processing financial transactions, electronic notes, attachments, and diary management. There is other functionality available in some newer systems which can have a material impact on process and workflow if properly implemented. This functionality may be available by the system vendor as an upgrade or require a modification. Do your homework – the upgrade or modification may seem too expensive, but if you do a *cost-benefit analysis* you may determine that it is well worth the investment.

Listed below are various *features and benefits* which are typically available with modern architecture claim systems, either within the core system product, or as an upgrade or modification. When we say "available" it does not necessarily mean "included" with the cost of base system.

## Web-Based Functionality

Current technology is web-based offering advanced functionality, ease of accessibility including remote access, speed and flexibility. External vendor applications are easily integrated allowing for increased functionality reducing manual entry.

Web-based systems provide an effective platform for deployment of computer tablets to the field adjuster and appraiser staff to improve efficiency and customer service.

## Adjuster-Intuitive Functionality

Claim personnel prefer a claim system which offers adjuster-intuitive functionality without having to access multiple screens for information, including the ability to refer to the last 5 – 10 claim records reviewed in a drop-down format without having to search.

Most new claim systems include base modules for various lines of business to tailor claim handling to specific types of claims. For example, the claim system may include modules for automobile, property, general liability and workers' compensation claims with claim-specific screens.

The system is structured the way an adjuster would handle their daily work activities to improve efficiency and productivity. Information is compartmentalized in various fields and screens, but the information is consolidated by commonality (e.g. new loss information, financials, litigation, subrogation, claim evaluation, etc.). Depending on the system, access to the various screens depends on the view of the information such as a "tabbed" view at the top of the screen or a hierarchical view to the left of the screen allowing for the expansion and contraction of screen detail.

New claim systems utilize more *structured data* (data in a fixed field selected by using a drop-down menu, radial button, etc.) to allow for increased reporting and analytics functionality. Having structured data eliminates the need to manually enter data in a free-form format which takes longer and is subject to human error, affecting downstream reporting.

## Flexible Business Rule Development

New claim systems have flexible business rule development which does not require advanced IT skills. Business rules are developed using complex decision logic which can use the system data to accelerate process and workflow, including the elimination of manual tasks.

For example, business rules may be developed around large loss reporting wherein a new reserve or reserve adjustment over a certain dollar threshold will automatically trigger emails to a predetermined recipient list and set a manager diary. Another example would be an automatic reserve established for certain exposures – e.g. when a PD exposure is set up, a reserve is automatically set at $1,500. Business rules can be developed for almost any system task – it requires a collaborative effort between the project business group and IT programmers.

## Dashboard Screen Views

Dashboards offer a screen view of summary information. For an adjuster the dashboard may include claim volume detail and productivity data (e.g. new, open, reopen and closed claim details), claim metrics such as closing ratios, claims by exposure type, number of litigation and large loss claims, a view of pending claims, current and late diaries, a calendar of important claim activities, access to the last 5 – 10 claims reviewed, links to other internal and external systems, etc.

For the claim supervisor, the dashboard is focused more on supervisory data and management controls including new claim assignments, claim productivity by adjuster (e.g. new, open, reopen and closed claim details), claim metrics such as closing ratios, late adjuster diaries, average paid loss and expense by exposure and expense type, average reserves and incurred losses, subrogation and salvage recovery summary, list of claims which meet large loss reporting criteria (with a link to the claim), list of claims which are open for a specified number of days, and the number of claims reviewed during the *claims quality review process* by adjuster.

The key to an effective dashboard is to not make it too cluttered with information not needed on a regular basis, which you can access from the report menu. Dashboards should be flexible with the ability to add and delete sections.

## Automated Adjuster Assignment

The automated adjuster assignment process assigns claims to specific adjusters, within certain business units based on predetermined assignment criteria. For example, the claim system may have 4 tiers of claim handling – simple, intermediate, complex and litigation. Within each tier are examples of the types of claims included in the tier. *Tier 1* may include automobile physical damage, property damage and medical payments; *Tier 2* may include bodily injury liability and general liability property damage; *Tier 3* may include serious and complex bodily injury or E&O claims; and *Tier 4* may include claims pending in litigation.

When claims are assigned, through business rule development, the claim system will recognize claim units and unit members (adjusters), and the tier level each unit member can handle. As new exposures are entered and set up, the claim system will automatically make the assignment based on the tier level of the claim and tier level qualifications for each adjuster. This process reduces the need for the supervisor to manually assign claims – the system can be programmed to add the supervisor diary at a future date for review, if needed.

Automated assignment will typically work in conjunction with *workload balancing*, as outlined below.

## Workload Balancing

Automated adjuster assignment features include *workload balancing*. As assignments are made to adjusters, the system will recognize the number of new claims which have been assigned to each adjuster and balance workloads in the unit. The system can also be programmed to not assign claims to adjusters who are out of the office (e.g. vacation, etc.), or have left the company.

Workload balancing is a great tool to maintain proper workloads and productivity standards. The key to developing an effective workload balancing tool is to be sure the tool is flexible to allow for making necessary changes or modifications without IT intervention.

## Productivity Reporting and Workload Management

Productivity and workload management has become sophisticated and most new systems offer these tools which are integrated into dashboards and management reporting tools. These tools provide metrics on new, reopen, and closed claim activity at the exposure level, as well as closing ratios to monitor closing production.

New claim systems monitor *claim capacity* to determine whether an adjuster is at the capacity standard based on predetermined criteria – for example monitoring the number of new claims assigned per month and open pending claim volume. Capacity standards are often developed using staffing models which also incorporate *weightings* into the productivity calculation, based on the claim role and claim type.

Productivity reporting should be able to generate on-demand reporting without having to wait until the end of the month. The reporting should be available in an Excel® format to include the underlying productivity data (e.g. claim file data), as well as productivity detail at the adjuster, unit and department level. Although a standard productivity format is recommended, *pivot tables* can be a useful tool to sort and filter productivity data based on need.

## Diary Management

It is important to have functionality which allows for multiple adjuster and supervisor diaries on a claim record and at the exposure level. For example, the claim record may need a separate diary for the subrogation adjuster or claim support, or separate diaries for the BI adjuster and the physical damage adjuster.

Additional functionality should include flexible label and classification of diaries with sort and filter functionality, claim file links to a diary entry, a diary list in a dashboard format with the ability to autoload the next diary upon diary review completion, and link to relevant attachments. There should be an historical file or log on past diaries for reference when needed. Diaries should be available for entry in a manual and automated format.

A supervisor should be able to access the adjuster's diary list and be notified by email if a diary is overdue after a certain number of days. There should be business rules which allow for automated diaries for certain claim events such as a supervisor diary triggered if the claim exceeds a certain incurred loss level or the claim is pending in litigation. Automated diaries should include adjuster and supervisor diaries at certain claim intervals, such as 15-day, 45-day, 90-day and every 180 days (for reserve reviews), and receipt of new claim mail or new attachments.

Diary management is a useful tool and it should be sophisticated but user-friendly.

## Electronic Notes

The electronic notes provide relevant information documented in the claim file. Typically, only those having the appropriate security credentials can enter an electronic note, and rarely can an electronic note be changed or modified without a higher security clearance. The electronic notes represent the investigation, claim handling and adjustment activities in the claim file. The notes are entered by the adjuster, supervisor, manager and claim support.

Electronic notes should have sort and filter functionality – for example being able to filter all supervisory, litigation, subrogation and investigation notes. Notes should also be able to link to documents or attachments, as well as flexible note label and classification. Business rules can also be developed to trigger brief electronic notes with certain claim activities such as payments, reserve transactions, medical bill review, ISO ClaimSearch®, etc.

## Financial Transactional Views

Sophisticated claim systems provide real-time financial transactional data including indemnity, loss, expense and recovery. The financial data can be displayed on a summary and detail level. The data can be sorted and filtered by claim, claimant, exposure, claim type, loss type, expense type, expense codes, recovery type (subrogation, salvage, deductible, etc.), paid transactions with payee name, check number, an indication if check has been cashed, and all reserve transactions with an historical view of reserve adjustments by date and user.

The financial transactional views should be integrated into other relevant claim screens. For example, the claim evaluation and litigation screens should display reserve and paid data for loss and expense. The physical damage screen should include paid loss and expense data (including rental reimbursement), as well as salvage and subrogation detail.

## Accounts Payable Integration

The methodology of issuing claim checks will depend on the claim system application and the carrier procedures. Some carriers require all claim payments to be processed in the accounting department, while others leave it with the claim department. Not all claim systems come with a built-in payment module to issue loss and expense payments. If the claim system does not come with an integrated accounts payable module, it will need to be interfaced with an external vendor product, with the payment data imported into the claim system financials.

There is various functionality needed for a claim payment to be processed: a reserve set up with a sufficient dollar amount of reserve to issue the payment, a pre-fillable screen using payee data previously entered at the claim set-up, security levels to approve and release the payment, a methodology to pass the payment to the next level if the amount exceeds the approver's authority, ability to see the issued check in the claim financials and determine if the check has been cashed with the date. Additionally, the ability to void and reissue checks from the claim system.

When reviewing payment modules, it is important to review the payment process and workflow, for example, when a payment has an attachment, or the payment needs to be sent via express mail. Although these are workflow issues it helps to understand the requirements in advance. Having to "re-do" programming is costly and impacts the project completion date.

Claim systems and vendor products will typically have an available *positive pay* integration module which is a tool used by banks to prevent fraud. The claims or accounting department provides a list of checks issued and authorized by the claim operation to the bank with the account number, check number and dollar amount. The bank then automatically matches the data to avoid unauthorized checks being paid. An exception report is then provided to the company listing checks which require further review before being released.

## Bulk Payment Functionality

Bulk payment functionality is important for the claim operation, particularly if the claim operation has a large volume of payments to the same vendor (e.g. adjuster firms, appraisal firms, law firms, medical bill review companies, etc.).

This functionality allows one check or one EFT transaction to be processed which may include all invoice payments to the same vendor, and then be able to allocate the individual invoice amounts to each claim record as an expense payment.

## Transactional & Activity Log

Transaction logs provide a documented "footprint" of all transactions in the claim system for security and operational reasons. The log includes the User ID, a brief note describing the details of the transaction (e.g. reserve increase, payment, etc.), the transaction type, and the date and time of the transaction.

Activity logs provide additional information such as electronic note entry and date, field changes, field updates, etc.

## Document Management

Document management systems will vary with most new systems having either integrated document management functionality within the claim application or a document management system provided by another vendor integrated with the claim system. The latter is the most common method, as many document management systems on the market are very sophisticated and often provide more functionality than a document management system within the claim application.

Document management is a broad term – and when we refer to document management it includes mail intake on new claims and pending claims (including FNOL, website loss reporting, mail, fax, etc.), opening new mail, scanning the documents to the system, attributing and attaching the documents to the claim record (determining the claim record number, adjuster name, categorizing and labeling the mail, etc.), and notification to the adjuster of receipt of new mail (in some systems, an automated diary indicating receipt of new mail).

Document management processes also include the mail received directly by the adjuster via the adjuster's desktop fax or email – which may be attributed and uploaded by the adjuster or forwarded to a document management support group for handling. It is important that the document management process and workflow be efficient and not impede the adjuster's job. Too much time spent on scanning, attributing and uploading of documents by the adjuster detracts from important adjuster activities.

Some companies have outsourced the entire document management process to a third-party vendor, including having mail sent directly to the third-party vendor location. Other companies have partially outsourced the document management process for medical bill review – by having all medical bills sent directly by the provider to the bill review vendor with the bill review vendor issuing payment with the EOB. Both the payment transaction and EOB are then returned and uploaded to the claim file.

## Integrated Form & Letter Generation

Integrated form and letter generation varies with most new systems having either internal functionality or a system provided by another vendor integrated with the claim system. This is one area which is often overlooked by those responsible for claim system implementations. There are sophisticated and integrated form and letter generation tools on the market – make sure you select a tool which best suits your needs. The claim staff needs a tool which is user friendly, easy to use, and can change or modify form letters and claim forms at the desktop (with proper security and not involve the IT department).

Modern architecture claim systems can easily generate letters which are professional looking, can add multiple attachments from the document management system, and have an electronic signature. If the form letters and claim forms have too many manual steps, or involve too much human intervention, you have selected the wrong product. These tools must not only integrate with the claim system, but also with other systems, process and workflow. For example, after the letters are processed from the claim system, with attachments, where are they printed and batched for mailing.

## Email Integration

Email is the primary communication method for the adjuster when communicating with parties to the claim. Email integration is probably one of the most overlooked functionality in most claim system implementations.

When selecting a new claim system, it is important to ask the vendor if the claim system provides email integration for both sending and receiving of emails. You want to see the process in a demonstration to be sure it is what you need. If the vendor indicates they will build the email integration, then provide the vendor with detailed requirements and ask for a *proof of concept* (demonstrating the product is feasible). Some new claims systems can only send emails – but often not acceptable because the sent email is not generated from the company secure email system.

Email integration has a substantial impact on adjuster productivity and should be a key focus in the claim system selection process. If possible, email integration should be with the company email system such as Outlook®, with the ability to send and receive emails to and from the claim system, including filing the email attachments in the document management system. Some companies may use an inefficient process to attribute the email to a claim record, similar to uploading a document attachment, which may require conversion of the email to a pdf document.

Some companies have integrated email with the claim system by linking the claim number in the subject line of the email for automatic filing as an attachment or have a drop-down screen or tab in the Email system which allows for attributing the email for attachment to the claim file record.

Email integration is expensive, but any costs incurred will be minimal compared to the lost productivity without it.

## First Report and Center Integration

The integration of the *First Notice of Loss* (FNOL) or *First Report of Injury* (FROI) with a call center and the claim record improves cycle time (report date to assignment), efficiency and customer service. This requires the development of a process and workflow around the business unit which takes first reports and the claim system functionality.

With this process, the FNOL/FROI report and documents are integrated into the claim record, with automatic assignment to the adjuster. The claim file record will have a copy of the FNOL or FROI, or a summary report screen for review by the adjuster.

## Claim Detail & Summary Screens

These screens provide detail and summary level claim information at the claim, party (e.g. insured or claimant) or exposure level. The screens include a claim overview and basic loss details such as date of loss, time of loss, date reported, date received, claims made (Y/N), loss location, brief accident description, loss causation, parties to the claim and contact information (claimant, insured, agent, attorneys, underwriter, vendors, etc.).

Additional information may include a summary of financial information (exposures, reserves and paid transactions), suit indicator, complex claim and/or large loss indicator, claim status (open, closed and reopen), exposures, most recent notes, claim metrics such as days open, days since last view, activities past due, number of reserve changes, comparative negligence fault rating on claimant, insured and third parties (%), catastrophe number and peril, claim jurisdiction, witness names and addresses, police and fire report info, complete vehicle information, detailed property information, SIU detail and referral info, and special claim handling details.

For workers' compensation claims additional screen detail may include a summary of type of benefits paid and reserved, claim details on lost time, work status, wages, dependents, jurisdictional factors, average weekly wage (AWW), type of indemnity (TTD, TPD, PPD, etc.) and transactional data, paid benefits by week, waiting periods, retroactive periods, EDI reporting, reserve adjustments, total case value, negotiations, FROI details, MMI (maximum medical improvement) detail, Medical Case Management detail, Utilization Review detail, Medical Bill Review detail, Pharmacy Management detail, comorbidity information, diagnosis, prognosis, IME details, medical and hospital providers, etc.

The key to screen development is to be sure you are capturing the information needed and that the information is organized properly by fields and screens for easy access. Links from one screen to another improve efficiency.

## Plan of Action (POA) Screens

Action plan screens reduce redundancy in the electronic file notes. The action plan screen provides fillable detail with both structured and unstructured data and the ability to update the action plan as the claim progresses.

Most claim organizations use some type of action plan. Automate the process to the extent possible and integrate it with the diary management process using business rules. For example, if action plans are required at certain time intervals (e.g. 60 or 90 days) create an automatic diary for the 60-day or 90-day period.

When the adjuster clicks on the diary, it will bring them to a blank *action plan* screen. After completion of the action plan screen, a summary is automatically posted as an electronic note, and the supervisor is notified that an action plan has been completed and available for review.

## Policy Detail & Coverage Screens

These screens provide integrated coverage detail and verification directly from the policy administration system including the named insured, additional insureds, loss payees and mortgagees, listed driver names, locations covered, vehicles insured, policy number, policy period, insured address, agent information, applicable coverage forms, policy limits, deductibles (1st and 3rd party), retroactive dates, replacement cost vs. actual cash value, co-insurance applicability, aggregate limit tracking, SIC codes, etc.

Added functionality may include a link to the policy file including the declaration page and policy forms and endorsements.

## Litigation Management Screens

Litigation management screens provide the ability to manage litigation effectively within the claim system including tracking incoming law suit activity, date served, answer due date, extension of time to answer date, discovery due dates, date suit referred to defense counsel, date of defense counsel acknowledgement, date answer filed by defense counsel, etc.

Litigation screens provide relevant detail such as parties to the litigation, who we are defending, defense counsel and plaintiff counsel information, suit referral document to defense counsel, litigation plan and legal budget, defense counsels' evaluation, adjuster's evaluation, pretrial and trial information, date excess letter(s) were sent (if applicable), and if there are coverage issues.

By integrating litigation management into the claim system, you improve efficiency and have better control of the litigation process. There are vendor products on the market which can integrate with the claim system and provide similar information as outlined above, combined with a legal document repository for all documents generated by defense counsel, and a legal budget submission and approval process.

## Subrogation Management Screens

Subrogation screens provide detailed information for the subrogation adjuster to manage subrogation separate from the underlying claim but have access to the entire claim record and all its functionality (e.g. diary management, electronic notes, etc.).

The subrogation screen may include the matter name, responsible party(s) information and address, responsible party carrier detail and coverage limits, statute of limitations, statute of repose, date third party placed on notice, projected recovery dollar amount, % of negligence on all parties, if applicable, any expert information and report, promissory note detail, collections data, and the date recovery was open and closed. It will also include relevant detail on any referral to a collections agency or attorney to assist in the recovery effort.

## Claim Evaluation Screens

Claim evaluation screens can be used in all lines of business and provide a detailed methodology for the evaluation of liability, compensability and damages. Claim evaluation screens provide a methodology to document the claim evaluation (reserve and settlement) without having to scroll through electronic claim notes.

For liability claims, the evaluation screen will include damage detail (bodily injury, property damage, etc.), itemized *general damages* such as pain and suffering, permanency, loss of consortium, etc., itemized *special damages* by category (e.g. medical, hospital, diagnostic, wage loss, etc.), a calculated *gross* damage exposure, and liability percentages on all parties to the claim to arrive at a *net* claim value. Strengths and weaknesses can be listed, as well as a settlement range and a record of settlement offers and demands. The screens should include negotiations strategy including planned first offer and target settlement amount.

Similar evaluation screens can be developed for other lines of business (e.g. property, workers' compensation, etc.)

## Automobile Claim Screens

Automobile claim screens make the automobile physical damage and property damage claim handling more efficient with a consolidated view of the relevant claim details.

Automobile claim screens provide relevant vehicle information such as vehicle make, model and year, vehicle identification number, deductible, damages, repair estimates, appraisal detail with link to the appraisal report attachment, total loss evaluation with link to the total loss report attachment, and link to salvage detail screen where the projected salvage dollar amount is indicated along with the salvage facility detail and dollar return.

The screens also include automobile rental and loss of use claim detail including daily and maximum limits (1st party), number of days approved, payments to date, and rental company information. With system modifications, a link or interface can be established with the rental company's system to avoid having to work in two separate systems.

The automobile claim screens may also include a view of the claim evaluation for property damage liability claims with application of comparative negligence

## Salvage Management Screens

Salvage management screens provide detailed information for the automobile adjuster to manage the salvage process. The screen will include a link from the automobile screen when a vehicle has been declared a total loss.

The details included in the salvage screen will vary but typically include the salvage arrangement type (e.g. vehicle salvage retained by owner, sale through a salvage bid process, or referral to a salvage facility for an auction sale) and the projected salvage amount.

If an auction facility is involved, information on the facility will be indicated along with the date notified of the total loss and salvage, date referred to the salvage facility, status at the salvage facility (e.g. awaiting sale, pending vehicle title, pending lien release, etc.), date salvage proceeds received, salvage expense, and net salvage dollar amount.

## Property Claim Screens

Property claim screens provide relevant first party property and third-party general liability property detail including property description and property location.

First party property claim screens include coverage summary, property locations, property values, co-insurance applicability, limits and deductibles, scheduled items, scope and damages (ACV and RCV), repair estimates, appraisal detail with link to the attached appraisal and photographs, *Insurance to Value* (ITV) calculations, third-party vendors (e.g. asbestos removal company, water mitigation company, cause & origin, engineer, etc.) and salvage detail where the projected salvage dollar amount is indicated along with the salvage facility detail.

Third-party general liability property claim screens will provide similar detail as indicated above but on a third-party basis (e.g. ACV damages, repair estimates, appraisal with photographs, salvage, etc.), as well as an analysis of liability.

## Debit Card & EFT Functionality

This functionality allows for debit cards to be issued in lieu claim checks, for example, debit cards being issued during a catastrophe loss or for workers' compensation indemnity benefits. EFT functionality allows transfer of the claim payment directly into the claimant or insured's bank account.

## Integrated Automated ISO ClaimSearch®

The full integration of ISO ClaimSearch® with the claim system for all lines of business is essential and included as an option with most new claim systems.

With this integration, the ISO ClaimSearch® record is automatically processed when the claim record is setup and automatically updated as the claim detail or attributes change. The ISO results are posted to the claim file record as attachments for review by the adjuster, with some systems providing diary notification with receipt of new relevant information.

Full automation of the ISO ClaimSearch® improves efficiency in the claim process and reduces manual effort such as entering the ISO record at the vendor website and pasting over pdf documents to the document management system.

## Integrated OFAC Compliance Checks

This functionality integrates with the Federal Government's *Specially Designated Nationals and Blocked Persons List* (SDN) to facilitate OFAC compliance by running each claim payment against the SDN list. The process is automatic reducing manual entry and improving accuracy.

If there is a match to the SDN list, the check is placed on hold pending further review. There are also vendor products which can integrate with claim systems, providing a similar service.

## Integrated Medical Bill Review

The *Medical Bill Review* (MBR) process should be integrated with the claim system and is typically integrated with an external medical bill review vendor. The process varies by company, but the typical process is for the claim operation to export data from the claim system to the MBR vendor (e.g. nightly) which includes all medical and hospital bills referred by the adjuster for bill review.

The MBR vendor re-prices each bill and provides a data file with an EOB (explanation of benefits) and bill review invoice for each claim record. The data is then imported into the claim system with the re-priced medical bill and EOB posted to the claim file record. The MBR invoices are individually allocated to each claim record using a *bulk bill payment* process. The check with EOB then appears in the adjuster's payable approval file for release, printing and mailing. Some MBR vendors offer a payment service wherein the vendor issues the payments (via a loss fund account) and EOB on behalf of the company, which is very efficient.

Being able to print the EOB with the check is functionality not always available in claim systems. If the support staff must manually match the medical payment check with the EOB for mailing, it is inefficient and costly.

## Integrated Pharmacy Benefit Management

The *Pharmacy Benefit Management* (PBM) process should be integrated with the claim system and is typically integrated with an external PBM vendor. The claimant is provided with a *pharmacy debit card* to allow for payment of the prescriptions at the local pharmacy.

All prescriptions are processed through the PBM vendor which receives the prescription data from retail pharmacies for review and payment processing. The claim operation is provided with prescription data records and payment data which are allocated to each claim record. The adjuster controls issuance and cancellation of the *pharmacy debit card*.

## Integrated Estimating Functionality (Auto and Property)

Many property and automobile estimating companies provide web portals used to view field appraisals by internal or external adjusting or appraisal staff.

Some carriers have integrated the process into their own systems. For example, the claim operation may use XYZ estimating software, requiring all their internal and/or external adjusting (or appraisal) staff to use the same software. This allows the claim operation to utilize the vendor web portal to review all activities involving their claims and have access to comprehensive reporting and analytics across all claims. It improves efficiency and cycle time.

Some new claim systems also offer full integration with the estimating software vendor's web portal providing a view of the data in claim screens.

Automobile carriers have integrated the estimating software process with their *Direct Repair Programs* (DRP), by requiring the body shop or repair facility to use their automobile estimating software to write their repair estimates. This provides consistency in the DRP process, as well as comprehensive reporting and analytics.

## Integrated Reserve Evaluation

Some carriers have integrated automated case reserve evaluations with the claim system reserve transaction functionality (e.g. workers' compensation).

Case reserves are automated using relevant claim data and sophisticated algorithms. The case reserves are then updated based on changes or additions to the claim attributes, including data on injuries, treatment, diagnosis, etc.

## EDI Reporting (WC) Functionality

EDI or *Electronic Data Interchange* is an automated method to electronically transmit *First Report of Injury* (FROI) and *Subsequent Report of Injury* (SROI) data to state workers' compensation jurisdictions.

By interfacing the EDI process with the claim system, the reporting process becomes simplified and efficient, reducing manual tasks.

## Integrated Legal & Independent Adjuster Bill Audit

There are vendors which provide web-based bill review services for legal and independent adjuster bills. Business rules and algorithms are established for the bill review process with each bill run through the process, with non-compliance billing entries rejected or adjusted.

These processes can be integrated into the claim system to approve the bill with automated payment processing, as well as budgeting.

## Integrated DMV & Official Reporting

Claim systems can be integrated for official reports and motor vehicle report requests, to allow for online requests from the claim system with receipt of the report attached to the document management system, triggering a diary that the report has been received. The invoices are paid using a bulk payment process.

## Integrated Recorded Statement Functionality

Many companies use integrated *Voice Over IP* (VOIP) telephone systems. These systems are then integrated with either internal or external recording system functionality to provide the claim staff with the ability to take recorded statements by telephone.

The statement is taken by telephone and the recording or link to the recording is filed in the claim record. The location of the recording or link may be within a designated *recorded statement summary screen*.

## Single Sign-On Capability

Single Sign-On (SSO) is an authentication process that allows a user to access multiple applications with the same login credentials.

Single Sign-On is essential when you are working in a multi-system application environment. For example, the adjuster may be accessing the primary claim system, the document management system and a claim audit system. If the adjuster needs to have separate sign-on credentials for each system, it slows down the adjuster and impacts productivity. The solution is to have single sign-on functionality.

## Reporting & Analytics

The extent of the reporting and analytics functionality will depend on the system and whether the organization has an integrated *data warehouse* serving all functional departments.

Most modern architecture claim systems have built in *dashboard* functionality which includes the ability to generate claim management reports at the desktop. Additionally, a report menu provides basic standard and *ad-hoc* reporting of claim and financial data.

A data warehouse provides for more comprehensive reporting (including analytics) by integrating all application system data into one database (e.g. underwriting, policy administration, claims, finance and accounting, etc.), with the ability to establish separate "cubes" for each functional area or department. Typically, a database reporting tool interfaces with the data warehouse to retrieve data and allow for customized reporting.

We will further discuss claim management reporting in **Chapter 9 – Claim Management Reports**.

# New Claim Technology Implementation

There are two critical challenges we encounter with implementation of new claim technology. First, the claim operation can be critically impacted when system technology has only been partially implemented or integrated with existing systems. Second, whether the system implementation has met the original investment objectives yielding expense reduction, improvement in productivity and efficiency, and having a positive impact on loss costs with improvements in the quality of claim handling. The latter being critical to executive management on the decision to purchase the new claim system.

Before embarking on a new system implementation project executive management may request a financial analysis to determine whether the cost is worth the investment. This may be in the form of a cost-benefit analysis or *Return on Investment* (ROI) analysis.

The implementation of new claim technology can be a daunting task for any organization. It involves a comprehensive process and will include the dedication of a substantial amount of your staff resources.

It is recommended that you retain a consultant from the outset to assist you through the entire technology implementation process. The consultant will guide you through the requirements, proposal and selection process.

An experienced *consultant* will assist with the following:

## Budget

Developing a *budget* is important and one of the first steps in the system implementation process. You will need to know the total budget for the project including both *capitalized*[23] and *non-capitalized*[24] costs. The cost of the software and some of the implementation costs may be capitalized, which means the cost is not expensed up front when incurred – the cost will be spread over time based on a depreciation or amortization schedule.

Remember, the expense is not always all paid up front – it could take a couple of years to pay the full cost of the implementation. Work with the finance department to develop a detailed budget in advance of the selection process. You need to know how much you can spend so you do not waste your time looking at systems which are over your budget

Build in *contingencies* into the total cost projections – you will need the additional funds as most system implementations cost more than initially projected.

## Project Team & Structure

To successfully implement a new claim system, you will need establish a project team, which should include experienced project managers and subject matter experts (SMEs), as well as members of the application software vendor and system integration firm.

Identify the proposed project team, including the project manager, subject matter experts (business and IT SMEs), executive sponsor and the steering committee. The project structure should have rigor including the development of a business case, statement of work, project charter, project management plan, a risk analysis, detailed budget, and status reports. Effective and organized project management fosters interactions among the team members with a minimum amount of disruptions, overlaps and conflict.

---

[23] **Capitalized Expenses** are recorded as a *fixed asset* on the balance sheet written off as depreciation expense over a specific period instead of being expensed in the same year of purchase.
[24] **Non-Capitalized Expenses** are typically coded as an operating expense.

The project team will include 15% - 20% of your staff particularly during the initial vendor presentations, system demonstrations, implementation and testing. Be prepared to dedicate some of your staff 100% to the project – not dedicating enough staff resources to system implementations is one of the primary causes of system implementation failures.

Keep in mind that some system implementations can take up to two plus years – it is distracting and has a material impact on staffing and productivity. Many organizations experience "organizational fatigue" if the system implementation takes too long or is delayed

## Business Requirements

Consultants help you understand your claim system *business requirements*. Sounds easy but is often a challenging task for most claim organizations.

The business requirements are primary and should be a comprehensive list of all operational, financial and user requirements at a very granular level. The requirements list will be very helpful when meeting with system vendors to evaluate their products and services to determine if there is compatibility and synergy. Developing business requirements includes your "wish list" of features and benefits. It also involves avoiding the development of requirements exclusively around the current legacy system functionality, instead of looking to adapt to new system (modern architecture) functionality which may be more efficient and cost-effective, but unfamiliar to the staff.

You will never find the perfect application software which is why you will need to make modifications. Look to use the new system base functionality to the extent possible – and not take your current operational functionality and overlay it on the new system, which will be very costly and inefficient.

Look for a modern architecture and flexible system configuration allowing for modification with minimal adverse impact on future system upgrades.

## IT System Platform

Determine the appropriate IT system platform. Will the claim system be internal to the organization or hosted by the software application vendor or other vendor externally?

Web-based systems are now preferred by many organizations adapting to cloud computing. This discussion will include hardware and servers, web services and integration points, personal computers and peripherals. It will also include the use of tablets and other devices used by field personnel.

## System Integration Requirements

Determine integration requirements including *web services* with various external business partners. This step should involve schematics or diagrams of the various integration points and who will be responsible to develop and manage the system integrations.

It is important to include the system application vendor in these discussions to be sure the software application includes the appropriate functionality to integrate or interface with other external vendor applications.

## Data Conversion Requirements

If you are moving from an existing system, you need to consider what type of *data conversion* you will need.

Data conversion is the process of converting existing legacy data from your current system and moving it into the new system to capture historical data for a specified period. Some companies will convert 5 – 7 years of open and closed claim data for the new system. For the prior years, the data may be moved to a data warehouse where it can be accessed for reporting purposes by the actuaries or others in the organization using analytics software or reporting tools.

Do not underestimate the complexity and cost of a data conversion project. It is expensive and should be done by a professional. It is important to confirm in writing the details and requirements of the data conversion project with all parties to the project.

## Request for Proposal (RFP)

The consultant will assist in the development of a *Request for Proposal* (RFP) to be sent to a select number of vendors – it can be a complicated process to prepare a quality RFP document.

The consultant will match your business requirements with select known vendors saving you time trying to determine the best vendor and application for your organization. The consultant will also select vendors which will be aligned with the proposed pricing structure, compatible with the company's operations and the budget.

RFP documents will be sent to each vendor, but not sent to vendors which do not meet the base system or business requirements. The RFP should be clear and concise on the needs of the organization. If the vendor does not respond to specific RFP questions, or is ambiguous with their response(s), there needs to be a request for clarification in writing.

If you intend to integrate the claim application with other functional areas or systems (e.g. underwriting, policy administration, accounting, etc.) it is important to request written confirmation that the products can be integrated and verification that it has been done successfully in the past.

## Vendor Interviews & System Demonstrations

After receipt of the RFP responses, vendor interviews and system demonstrations are completed.

Conducting vendor interviews and system demonstrations is a complicated process which requires time and staff resources. Interviews and system demonstrations are essential to the selection process. The vendor interviews should be extensive and involve multiple vendor representatives (software and hardware) including the system software/hardware architect and *subject matter experts* (SME) from the business and IT areas. The claim SME knows the business requirements and can communicate the requirements to the vendor and ask appropriate questions during the system demonstration. The IT expert knows the existing systems and integration points to provide relevant and essential information which will impact implementation costs.

This step may also involve the vendor developing "proof of concepts" to illustrate how the system will handle proposed customized system functionality. Some unscrupulous system vendors may indicate that the system has functionality which is not included or a very expensive add-on. It is important to request written confirmation of functionality and a clarification as to whether the functionality is standard and included in the base price or a custom modification with increased cost. Make sure the vendor understands your needs and acknowledges all discussions in writing.

## Checking References

References are critical to the selection process. It is important that references be provided and contacted by the project team upon receipt of the RFP response.

It is recommended that specific and consistent questions be asked by the person checking references so that the same questions are asked of each vendor, with the detailed responses documented in the project documents.

## Proposal & Pricing Review

After the proposals are received and interviews are completed the consultant will assist in reviewing each proposal and work with each vendor to resolve any questions or other issues. Clarification on pricing will be discussed which includes the total cost of the software application, implementation, integration, testing, training and any proposed modifications discussed during the vendor interviews and system demonstration process.

Review pricing carefully – what is the base price for the software application and the implementation and integration process. Who will be responsible to implement and integrate the product(s) – the software application vendor or a third-party integrator? What is the total projected cost for the integration?

A *fixed bid* is preferable in system implementation projects. A fixed-pricing methodology is easier to budget for the project, but you need to understand what is included in the cost structure. The software application which may include a purchase or annual lease arrangement, additional hosting fees, software modifications, software upgrades, system implementation by the application software vendor or a third-party software integrator, testing by your staff or a third-party vendor, the development of various interfaces and web services, data conversion costs, and hardware and peripherals.

The consultant will use various techniques and methodologies such as a *Pugh Analysis* or *Decision Matrix* to facilitate the selection process and present the recommendations to senior management.

# The Future of Claim Technology

The claim business model is evolving rapidly with advancements in technology and the industry's customer focus. Policyholders want to be connected electronically with self-service functionality to improve the claim customer experience and service.

Policyholder retention and leveraging data are critical in a technology-driven organization. To survive in a very competitive industry insurance companies are making effective use of mobile applications, advanced analytics and sophisticated core claim system applications.

With advancements in technology, claim systems continue to evolve including the use of predictive analytics, improving efficiency, productivity and claim outcomes. Advancements in claim technology will change the way we manage a claim operation, but we should not lose sight of fundamental claim handling concepts which are the basis for quality claim results.

Insurance industry claim technology is rapidly changing, providing new and more efficient ways to handle and manage claims at a reduced cost. Some examples of advanced technology are listed below.

## Auto-Adjudication of Claims

Insurance companies are using the power of analytics and have adapted analytical models which are integrated with claim system to *auto-adjudicate* claims. For example, some insurance companies are auto adjudicating workers' compensation medical-only and extended warranty claims.

Auto-adjudication identifies claim attributes and predicts claim outcomes in low-dollar claims using predictive analytics based on historical paid amounts with similar claim attributes without human intervention. The analytics program determines which claims can be auto-adjudicated and if the claim attributes meet the predetermined criteria. If the claim attributes do not meet the predetermined criteria, it is considered anomalistic and referred for manual adjudication by an adjuster.

Predictive analytics models can predict frequency and severity, as well as early identification of potential fraudulent claims

## Mobile Technology

Smartphones and tablets are everywhere and integrated with many of our daily activities. Mobile applications are common in many industries and have become routine and expected – customers want to see similar functionality from insurance companies. Customers want responsive online claim services including FNOL reporting and expedited settlement of claims using mobile devices.

The ability to access claim data using mobile applications is critical and changing the claim environment. Customers want access to claim records for statuses and payments. FNOL reporting is becoming more sophisticated with photo and video upload of accident scene details and vehicles by the customer.

The damage inspection process has significantly changed for automobile and property claims, as well as handling catastrophe losses, using mobile technology. Computer tablets are being deployed to field adjusters and appraisers, with estimating software and system access using mobile technology. Desk adjusters can now receive damage estimates, video and photograph uploads from the loss location to assist in the appraisal and adjustment process – changing the "business model" we have relied on for many years.

## Telematics and UBI

The use of *Telematics* (data collection devices) and *Usage Based Insurance* (UBI) has changed the insurance industry. It provides more accurate pricing using driver behavior to develop automobile insurance rates and encourages policyholders to drive responsibly to maintain the reduced premium rate.

The claim process will continue to transform with vehicles using telematics integration and transmitting data to the company. Using sophisticated systems to determine accident responsibility will change the way we do business and reduce litigation costs with the ability to confirm liability early in the claim process.

We may be faced with some challenges including potential privacy issues using telematics data during a claim investigation, as well as the potential for data cyber-attacks. Our claim investigations will transition from automobile liability due to the driver's actions to the manufacturer's product liability for faulty vehicle systems.

This innovative technology will change the adjuster of the future – wherein technology and claim skills will be required to adjudicate and manage claims.

## Advanced Vehicle Technology

Many new vehicles are equipped with advanced technology to correct human error, including technology which can self-park vehicles, warn or detect potential accidents with the use of emergency braking systems, and avoidance technology such as warning the driver when changing lanes, or veering, without signaling, all potentially reducing accident frequency and severity.

*Autonomous Vehicle Technology* (AVT) or driverless vehicles are already on the market, but insurance companies will be challenged in how to handle the claim process using this innovative technology. Auto-pilot vehicles will prevent auto accidents caused by human error, but the technology still needs to be refined. We will eventually see a reduction in automobile accidents, and enhanced technology-causation claim investigations.

The new *technology-adjuster* of the future will require a different skill-set. Adjusters will need to be trained in vehicle technology and causation – developing advanced claim and technology expertise.

## Drone Technology

The use of *Unmanned Aerial Vehicles* (UAVs) or "Drones" have become very common with the military, businesses and consumers. Drones can be used for package delivery, as well as taking photographs and streaming remote live video. Sophisticated drones have auto landing features, high definition cameras, video equipment and advanced navigation systems.

Drone technology has had a positive impact on claim handling, being used to inspect damages in areas with restrictive access such as roofs, or claims which are remotely located, providing photos and video to the field and desk adjuster. Drones are used to survey damages after a catastrophe loss such as a hurricane or tornado, and to conduct surveillance on claimants with photographs and live video.

The use of drones in the insurance industry continues to evolve and has become very common, particularly with the larger carriers and adjustment firms. We will continue to see more regulations on the use of drones, and the requirements to be certified as a drone pilot.

## Predictive Analytics

Predictive analytics has become more common in the claim operation either through an internal analytics group or using a third-party vendor product. Predictive analytics is a type of advanced analytics that uses new and historical data to predict future activity such as claim trends. It includes various statistical techniques such a predictive modeling, machine learning and data mining.

Claim data provides valuable insights and we use technology tools to analyze the data to improve the quality of claim handling and outcomes. With predictive analytics we can use data to manage claims more effectively, including the ability to predict future outcomes.

It is important to note that predictive models do not make decisions, they point to areas where people make decisions.

## Machine Learning & Robotics

Machine learning uses algorithms and historical data to predict current or future outcomes. Machine learning will change the future of insurance operations by applying artificial intelligence to insurance data. Advances in machine learning and artificial intelligence within the claim operation will change staffing requirements and the use of humans in insurance operations.

Machine learning will enhance claim processes with a significant reduction in the time necessary to complete tasks and identify claim leakage during the initial stages of the claims process.

Robotics can be described as using programming software to make decisions on multi-step tasks, including the automation of repetitive tasks. Robotics will have a significant impact on efficiency improvement in the future claim operation including a reduction in claim costs.

The industry has evolved, and technology is advancing rapidly. Insurer's need to focus on developing a technology-enabled organization to remain competitive.

## Chapter Comments

In this chapter we reviewed claim technology and systems. The claim supervisor or manager can work very effectively in an electronic environment, but they must be well organized and not lose sight of their primary function to achieve a quality claim work product by providing high quality supervision and oversight.

Modern architecture claim systems offer many features and benefits which can improve productivity and efficiency. Spend the necessary time and effort to identify the product best suited for the claim operation. Remember, you will never find the perfect solution and you will need to make some modifications, which are costly. Look to use the base functionality in the new claim system as much as possible and avoid trying to modify the new system functionality to handle your current legacy process and workflow.

Consider retaining a consultant to assist with the system selection and implementation process – it will save the company time and money. Consultants have a lot of experience in system implementations and will know the vendors which will be suitable for the organization. They will protect your interests and help with all phases of the process.

System implementations are time consuming and require dedicated resources for the vendor selection process, vendor interviews, system demonstrations, the implementation phase and testing. Consider the human resource impact on the organization before you get started – and have a plan in place to avoid a shortage of staff to maintain a quality claim operation and customer service.

Technology is changing very rapidly with auto-adjudication of claims, mobile technology, telematics and UBI, advance vehicle technology including autonomous vehicle technology (AVT), drone technology, predictive analytics, machine learning and robotics. The future claim operation will be very different for both the adjuster and supervisor.

There will be a need to develop a new *technology-adjuster* with a different skill set including having both claim and advanced technology skills.

# CHAPTER 9
# CLAIM MANAGEMENT REPORTS

Management reports are critical to the claim operation, providing claim management with the ability to analyze data to gain insight into the claim operation, control loss and expense costs, identify claim trends, review financial transactions, monitor performance, and manage productivity and workloads.

The types of management reports available in a claim operation will vary depending on the organization, and may include *standard* reports (daily, monthly and weekly), *dashboard reports* and *ad hoc* reports which can be customized to specific needs.

*Standard Reports* are reports available on a report menu either within the claim system or data warehouse. The reports are preformatted and require minimal input by the requestor other than the date range, and a sort and filter selection. These reports may be available in different formats but are usually distributed in a pdf format. The reports may also be sent automatically to claim management by email at various predetermined intervals with new system technology.

*Dashboard Reports* are available from the claim system dashboard. Typically, the claim system dashboard report menu will only provide a select number of reports which are used regularly. As with the standard reports, the report data will be preformatted and require minimal input by the requestor other than the date range, and a sort and filter selection. Examples of these reports may include diary management reports, productivity and workload management reports, large loss reports, litigation and suit reports, and average paid/reserve reports. These reports are integrated with the claim system and the data will typically come from the claim system database directly. These reports may be available in different formats including Excel® and pdf.

*Ad Hoc* reports are available from the claim system or a data warehouse. These reports are more sophisticated and require more input by the requestor. Ad hoc reports can be described as "on demand" reports, wherein the requestor develops their own report format using a specific dataset. For example, the requestor may create a customized outstanding claim reserve report for certain exposures, within a specific dollar amount and date range. The report may include a dataset in Excel® with integrated pivot tables (a powerful data extraction and analytics tool) with the ability to sort and filter the data yielding the desired results.

The key to effective management reports is to be sure the reports include the necessary information on a detail and summary level, are easily accessible and useful. Management reports can provide detailed information, metrics results or analytics reporting. The most useful reports are reports in an Excel® format inclusive of pivot tables.

Management reports can be categorized as *Financial Reports* (financial transactions) and *Operational Reports* inclusive of production reports (workload management), dashboard reports and metrics reports (e.g. cycle time reports).

# Financial Reports

The following reports are considered claim *financial reports* typically used by the claim operation or other functional departments (e.g. underwriting, accounting, etc.). These reports provide important and relevant claim transactional detail required in a claim operation.

## Loss Run Report - Detail and Summary Level

The *Loss Run Report* is available in a variety of formats and the content will vary by organization, depending on the purpose of the report.

Typically, the loss run report includes a list of open, closed and reopen claims inclusive of various header column information (depending on the need and recipient of the loss run) such as claim office, claim manager, adjuster, claim number, policy number, effective dates, date of loss, date reported, date received, claim status (e.g. open, closed or reopen), suit (Y/N), insured name, claimant name, line of business, state, exposure, paid loss and expense, loss and expense reserves, incurred claim activity, and recovery at the claim exposure or claim occurrence level.

The report should be available by date range and in real time. If provided in Excel® including a tab for the detailed dataset, the use of *pivot tables* allows for this report to be used to analyze many claim issues by customizing the report fields and data views.

Loss runs are used by the claims and underwriting staff, providing comprehensive detailed information on claim volume, financial transactions and claim activity. Policyholders and agents will request loss runs at the policy renewal period to evaluate loss history.

Loss runs can also be tailored to provide a report listing *Outstanding Reserves* and *Claim History Reports* for policyholders.

## Average Reserve Report – By Line of Business

The *Average Reserve Report* provides a list of average dollar reserves on a detail and summary level (loss or expense) by claim number, line of business, exposure, reserve range, claim type, adjuster, business unit, state, date range and analysis year (e.g. Calendar Year, Policy Year or Accident Year).

This report is used by the claims and underwriting staff to monitor average reserve claim activity to determine if there are fluctuations in average reserves. If average reserves are increasing, it will have a negative effect on the loss ratio and should be investigated further.

If management determines there is *trend* in increased average reserves, it will be necessary to conduct a *root cause analysis* to identify the cause(s). Some causes may be attributed to an overall increase in severity due to underwriting and risk selection, claim staff experience or new hires establishing higher case reserves than warranted, improper claim evaluations, a change in reserve philosophy by the claim staff, or the impact of large losses during the period being analyzed.

## Average Paid Loss Reports - By Exposure

The *Average Paid Loss Report – By Exposure* provides a list of average paid losses on a detail and summary level by line of business, exposure, paid range, claim type, adjuster, business unit, state, date range and analysis year (e.g. Calendar Year, Policy Year or Accident Year).

This report is used by the claims and underwriting staff to monitor average paid loss activity to determine if there are fluctuations in average paids. If average paids are increasing, it will have a negative effect on the loss ratio and should be investigated further.

If management determines there is *trend* in increased average paid losses, it will be necessary to conduct a *root cause analysis* to identify the cause(s). Some causes may be attributed to an overall increase in severity due to underwriting and risk selection, the impact of large loss payments during the period being analyzed, potential claim overpayments, improper claim evaluations, or a lack of understanding or change in the settlement philosophy.

For example, if the claim operation is undergoing extensive staff turnover, adjusters may become overloaded with claims, and pay more on claim settlements to reduce their workloads, or due to high workloads the claim investigations may be incomplete yielding improper claim evaluations and ultimately overpayments.

## Open with Zero Reserves

The *Open with Zero Reserves* report provides a list of claim exposures with zero-dollar reserves and the claim record is statistically open. The report may include the claim number, line of business, exposure, reserve, claim type, adjuster, business unit, date of loss, date reported, date received, and the date range being reviewed.

This report will identify claims which may be open on an adjuster's pending claim count, yet the claim exposure has zero reserves, which can either be closed or requires a reserve adjustment.

## Open with Minimal Reserves

The *Open with Minimal Reserves* report provides a list of claim exposures with low dollar (e.g. under $100) reserves and statistically open. The report may include the claim number, line of business, exposure, reserve, claim type, adjuster, business unit, date of loss, date reported, date received, and the date range being reviewed.

This report will identify claims which may be open on an adjuster's pending claim count with minimal reserves, which can either be closed or require a reserve adjustment.

## Open with Negative Reserves

The *Open with Negative Reserves* report provides a list of claim exposures with negative dollar reserves and statistically open. The report may include the claim number, line of business, exposure, reserve, claim type, adjuster, business unit, date of loss, date reported, date received, and the date range being reviewed.

This report will identify claims which may be open on an adjuster's pending claim count with negative reserves, which can either be closed or require a reserve adjustment.

## Claim Reopen Reserve Report

The *Claim Reopen Reserve Report* provides a list of claim exposures which have a reopened reserve. The report may include the claim number, line of business, exposure, reopened reserve, claim type, adjuster, business unit, date of loss, date reported, date received, date of closure, date reopened, and the date range being reviewed.

The report can provide data on the reopened claims to determine whether claims are being closed prematurely. With monthly productivity goals (e.g. closing ratios), adjusters may prematurely close claim exposures which may then need to be reopened later. This distorts closing ratios and productivity.

## Reserve Transaction Report

The *Reserve Transaction Report* provides a list of claim reserve transactions on a detail and summary level including new, reopen, closed and reserve adjustments for both loss and expense – by claim number, line of business, exposure, claim type, adjuster, business unit, reserve transaction type (new, reopen, closed and adjustments), reserve dollar amounts and date range.

This report provides critical information for management to monitor reserve transactions, particularly new reserves and reserve adjustments.

## Reserve Redundancy & Deficiency

The *Reserve Redundancy & Deficiency* report provides a list of claim payment transactions on a detail and summary level compared against the outstanding claim reserve at the time of payment. The report includes loss and expense, by claim number, line of business, exposure, reserve at payment, payment amount, claim type, adjuster, business unit, payment transaction type (partial or final), date range and analysis year (e.g. Calendar Year, Policy Year or Accident Year).

The report should also highlight claim payment transactions on a detail level compared against the outstanding claim reserve at time of payment, wherein the reserve was adjusted within 30 days of the claim payment. This is important as it provides information on claims with reserves which may have been deficient within 30 days of the payment but only recognized with further analysis.

Payments below the outstanding claim reserve at the time of payment will appear in the redundancy section and payments over the outstanding claim reserve at time of payment will appear in the deficiency section.

This report is important to monitor reserve adequacy, with management being able to match claim payments against outstanding reserves at the time of payment – evaluating reserve redundancy and deficiency. When reviewing this report, it is important to determine redundancy and deficiency on an aggregate level by exposure type, adjuster, unit, etc. as an indicator of overall reserve adequacy.

## Paid Loss Detail & Summary Report

The *Paid Loss Detail & Summary Report* provides a list of paid losses ($) on a detail and summary level by claim number, line of business, exposure, claim type, adjuster, business unit and date range.

This report allows management to monitor claim payment activity, including payments within a certain paid loss threshold and date range.

## Supplemental Payment Report

The *Supplemental Payment Report* provides a list of claim supplemental payments on a detail and summary level by payment amount, claim number, line of business, exposure, claim type, adjuster, business unit and date range.

The report can provide data on the number supplemental payments and average supplemental payments. It is a useful tool to determine whether claims are being closed prematurely, resulting in the need for supplemental payments.

## Incurred Loss Excess of $ Amount

The *Incurred Loss Excess of $ Amount* report provides a list of incurred loss activity excess of a certain dollar value, by claim number, line of business, exposure, reserve, payments, recovery, claim type, adjuster, business unit, and date range, with the ability to filter by incurred loss dollar levels.

This is an excellent report to identify claims with high incurred loss activity (e.g. large losses) which may need reporting to home office or the reinsurer. It is also a useful tool to identify claims which may need reassignment to another adjuster based on the incurred loss level.

## Paid Expense Detail & Summary Report

The *Paid Expense Detail & Summary Report* provides a list of paid expenses on a detail and summary level by claim number, line of business, exposure, expense amount, claim type, expense category (e.g. ALAE), expense type (attorney, adjuster, expert), adjuster, business unit and date range.

This report is used to monitor claim expenses and identify expenses in certain expense categories and expense types wherein LAE is being impacted.

## Average Paid Expense Report

The *Average Paid Expense Report* provides a list of average paid ALAE expenses on a detail and summary level by line of business, exposure, expense type, claim type, adjuster, business unit, date range and analysis year (e.g. Calendar Year, Policy Year or Accident Year).

This report is used by claims management to monitor average paid expense activity to determine if there are fluctuations in average paids. If average paids are increasing, it will have a negative impact on the LAE ratio.

If management determines there is *trend* in increased average paid expenses, it will be necessary to conduct a *root cause analysis* to identify the cause(s). Some causes may be attributed to an increase in litigation activity, not controlling legal expenses effectively, or receipt of an unexpected number of large legal expense bills on serious or complex litigation claims.

## ALAE Expense Report

The *ALAE Expense Report* provides a list of paid ALAE expenses on a detail and summary level by line of business, exposure, expense type, claim type, adjuster, business unit, date range and analysis year (e.g. Calendar Year, Policy Year or Accident Year).

The report includes expenses such as legal, attorney, adjuster, experts, official reports, and some medical bill review expenses. The report provides a breakdown of each expense type inclusive of the dollar amount and as a percentage of the total expense for the review period.

## ULAE Expense Report

The *ULAE Expense Report* provides a list of paid ULAE expenses on a detail and summary level by business unit, department, expense type and date range.

The report includes expenses such the cost of the claim operations and certain claim file expenses (e.g. coverage counsel) and provides a breakdown of each expense type inclusive of the dollar amount and as a percentage of the total expense for the review period.

## Expense by Vendor Name & Type

The *Expense by Vendor Name & Type* report provides a list of vendor names and the vendor type in each classification.

The vendor types include attorney, court reporter, medical provider, adjuster, appraiser, expert, etc. The report includes full vendor name and details including the Tax ID Number.

## 1099 Tax ID Report

The *1099 Tax ID Report* provides relevant vendor information by Tax ID number, including vendor name, vendor type, and vendor code. This report is used as the basis for filing year-end 1099's with state and federal tax authorities.

It is important that the vendor provide a signed W-9 form to verify the vendor Tax ID number for accounting to send the vendor a *1099 Miscellaneous Income Form* at year-end.

## Recovery by Type Report

The *Recovery by Type Report* provides a detail and summary list of recovery transactions by recovery type including subrogation, salvage, and loss refund by claim number, line of business, exposure, amount, claim type, recovery type, payee, adjuster, claim status (open/closed), business unit, and date range, with the ability to filter by dollar levels.

This is a useful tool for the claim manager and recovery claim supervisor to monitor recovery transactions.

## Average Recovery by Recovery Type

The *Average Recovery by Recovery Type* provides a list of average recovery returns by subrogation, salvage, loss refund and other recovery transactions by recovery type on a detail and summary level by line of business, exposure, claim type, adjuster, business unit and date range.

This is a useful tool for the claim manager and recovery claim supervisor to monitor recovery returns to evaluate averages in various recovery categories. Any decline in the average returns should involve further analysis.

## Outstanding Subrogation Report

The *Outstanding Subrogation Report* provides a list of projected open subrogation recovery returns (e.g. recovery reserve) with projected dollar amounts on a detail and summary level by line of business, exposure, claim type, claim number, adjuster, business unit and date range.

This is a useful tool for the claim manager and recovery claim supervisor to monitor projected subrogation returns, by requiring entry of a projected dollar recovery amount for each pending subrogation claim in the claim system for tracking purposes.

## Third-Party Deductible Report

The *Third-Party Deductible Report* provides a detail and summary list of third party deductible transactions outstanding (or billed) and received by policy number, policy effective dates, insured name, claim number, line of business, exposure, claim type, deductible amount, received amount, date billed, date received, payee, check or transaction number, adjuster, business unit, and date range, with the ability to sort and filter.

This is a useful tool for the claim manager and recovery claim supervisor to monitor third party deductible transactions.

## Check Register

The *Check Register* provides a list of claim checks – loss and expense payments – on a detail and summary level, by payee name, check number, check date, check amount, payment type, claim number, adjuster, agent name, date of loss, insured name, etc.

This report is used by claims and accounting to monitor outgoing check payments.

## Recovery Receipts Register

The *Recovery Receipts Register* provides a list of claim recovery checks received – loss and expense recoveries, on a detail and summary level, for subrogation, salvage or loss refund by payee name, check number, check date, check amount, recovery type, claim number, date of loss, insured name, adjuster, etc.

This report is used by claims and accounting to monitor receipt of incoming recovery checks.

## Stop Payment Register

The *Stop Payment Register* provides a list of claim checks which have a stop payment processed – loss and expense payments, on a detail and summary level, by payee name, check number, check date, check amount, payment type, claim number, date of loss, insured name, stop payment date, adjuster, etc.

This report is used by claims and accounting to monitor the volume of stop payment transactions. If the claim staff has too many stop payment transactions, it may be due to not researching the proper payee before issuing payment, e.g. excluding the mortgagee, loss payee, public adjuster, attorney, etc.

## Check Reissuance Register

The *Check Reissuance Register* provides a list of claim checks on a detail and summary level which have been reissued – loss and expense payments by payee name, check number, check reissuance date, check amount, payment type, claim number, date of loss, insured name, original payee name, original check amount, original check number and original check date.

## Claim Escheatment Report

The *Claim Escheatment* report provides a list of claim checks on a detail level which have not been cashed. These checks must be reissued to the original payee or referred to the state as unclaimed property.

The report will include the payee name, address, check number, check amount, check date, payment type, claim number, etc.

## Aging Incurred Losses (Loss Triangle)

The *Aging Incurred Losses* report is a *loss triangle*[25] report which provides a comparison of *incurred loss* activity in various exposure categories (e.g. automobile BI) over specific time periods. *Incurred losses* are case reserves <u>plus</u> paid losses <u>less</u> recoveries.

For example, comparing incurred losses by accident year over a 48-month period at every 6-month interval. This report will illustrate how long accident year claims are pending and provide critical feedback on whether the incurred activity is increasing or decreasing over a specified period. It will also provide an indication as to whether claims are closing within an appropriate time, open too long, or have adverse reserve development.

To illustrate, if we are analyzing accident year 20XX, which was 4 years ago, we will see how long it takes to reduce the incurred claim activity in future calendar years for all claims which occurred in 20XX. If the incurred activity is increasing in the third and fourth year, then it may be due to adverse reserve development. The analysis provides an "aged" view of claims at each review interval (e.g. 6 months).

---

[25] A **loss triangle** is a method used by actuaries to analyze claim data. Data is displayed in a triangle format to illustrate how claim activity is developing over a specific time-period.

The report should have the flexibility to select the line of business, exposure type, business unit or company, accident year, calendar year or policy year, and the comparison periods with specific intervals.

## Aging Outstanding Reserves (Loss Triangle)

This the same loss triangle report as the *Aging Incurred Losses* report but provides an analysis of outstanding reserves (losses).

This report will illustrate how long claims are pending and provide critical feedback on whether reserves are increasing or decreasing over a specified period. It will also provide an indication as to whether claims are closing within an appropriate time, open too long, or have adverse reserve development.

## Aging Average Paid Losses (Loss Triangle)

The *Aging Average Paid Losses* report is a *loss triangle* report which provides a comparison of *average paid losses* in various exposure categories (e.g. workers' compensation indemnity) over specific time periods.

For example, comparing average paid losses over a 48-month period at every 6-month interval. This report will illustrate whether average paid losses are stable or increasing or decreasing over a specified period. The report provides important feedback on average paid loss trends which impact the loss ratio.

The report should have the flexibility to select by line of business, exposure type, business unit or company, accident year, calendar year or policy year, and the comparison periods with specific intervals.

## Aging Claim Volume Analysis (Loss Triangle)

The *Aging Claim Volume Analysis* report is similar to the other loss triangle reports but analyzes the claim volume over specific periods of time.

This report illustrates fluctuations in claim volume activity and provides critical feedback on claim volume at specific time periods or intervals. For example, comparing the number of new, open or closed claim exposures over a 48-month period at every 6-month interval.

The report is very useful to understand claim volume activity over specific periods of time and can be used as a tool to project future staffing needs and evaluate whether claims are being closed on a timely basis.

The report should have the flexibility to select by line of business, exposure type, business unit or company, accident year, calendar year or policy year, and the comparison periods with specific intervals.

## Reinsurance Transaction Reports

*Reinsurance Transaction Reports* provide a detailed list of claims with reinsurance transactions which include the gross and net claim transaction, as well as the ceded transaction. The *gross* transaction is the total transaction amount (e.g. reserve or payment) and the *net* transaction is the amount after reinsurance has been applied. The difference between the gross and net transaction is the reinsurance ceded transaction.

For example, if the pro-rata reinsurance agreement indicates all losses are reinsured at 40% of each loss, and there is a $100,000 loss, then the gross transaction is $100,000. The net transaction to the carrier is $60,000 with the balance of $40,000 being *ceded* or transferred to the reinsurer

The report would include the reinsurer name, reinsurance contract number, contract year, date reported to reinsurer, policy number, claim number, insured name, claimant name, date of loss, date reported, line of business, claim type, exposure, gross transactions, net transactions (reserves, paids and recovery) and ceded transactions, etc.

These reports are used by claims and reinsurance accounting to monitor ceding transactions and receipt of reinsurance recoverables.

# Operational Reports

The following reports are considered claim operational reports typically used by the claim operation. These reports provide important and relevant claim operational information and data.

## FNOL Reporting

*First Notice of Loss* (FNOL) or *First Report of Injury* (FROI) summary reports provide detailed information on new loss reporting activity – including the number and volume of new losses by line of business, exposure, state, agent name, date of loss, and date reported with the ability to analyze new loss activity reported within specific time periods.

The report should be available by adjuster, claim manager, unit, etc.

## Medicare Management Reports

Many companies have outsourced Medicare reporting to a third-party vendor due to its complexity and the need to be in full compliance.

*Medicare Management Reports* are either provided internally by a special unit or a partner vendor. Medicare reporting is complex and requires timely reporting. Often, there are reporting errors which need to be resolved such as claims with missing data elements, incorrect coding, or not identifying Medicare eligibility. Having the availability of management reports helps to maintain compliance and timely reporting.

## Diary Management Reports

*Diary Management Reports* provide diary management information on a summary and detail basis by adjuster and manager inclusive of the current volume of open or closed diaries, by diary type or diary category, overdue diaries (by # of days), open diaries by date, or by date range. The report should include the adjuster name, manager name, claim file number, type of diary, number of days overdue, etc.

Diary management is a valuable tool for the adjuster and manager in managing claims and various activities on a timely basis. There should be established guidelines on what is considered an acceptable number of days late beyond the actual diary due date (e.g. 3 – 5 days). Diaries should not be consistently late – if they are you may need to review workloads and/or consider a performance plan if the adjuster is habitually late with diary management.

## Adjuster Productivity Reports

The *Adjuster Productivity Report* provides adjuster productivity data on a summary and detail basis at the claim or exposure level, by adjuster and unit, by month and on a rolling 12-month period. The report will typically include new, open/pending, reassigned/transferred and closed claim activity (with closing ratios).

This report should be provided to the adjuster every month, be available by adjuster, claim manager, unit, etc. and be able to capture both current (real-time) data and data in the past by specific date range.

Some productivity reports may include information on adjuster *capacity* (i.e. what percentage of capacity is the adjuster at based on established maximum workloads) and *weightings* to adjust workloads based on the type and complexity/severity of claims being handled (e.g. BI vs. PD).

As indicated in other chapters productivity reporting is critical in managing workloads, performance and ULAE expense (e.g. staffing costs).

## Detail Exposure List by Adjuster

The *Detail Exposure List by Adjuster* report provides a detailed list of claim exposures by adjuster in the following productivity categories: new, open/pending, reassigned/transferred and closed claim exposures.

This report provides the detail behind the productivity report referenced above. The claim list includes the claim number, line of business, claim type, insured, claimant, exposure, assigned adjuster, date of loss, date reported, date received, date assigned, productivity category (new, open/pending, etc.), reserves, payments and recoveries.

The report should be available by adjuster, claim manager, unit, etc. and should capture both current data and a date range in the past.

## Detail Claim List by Adjuster

The *Detail Claim List by Adjuster* report is the same report as the *Detail Exposure List by Adjuster*, but on a claim basis (inclusive of all claimants and exposures).

## Recovery Adjuster Productivity Report

The *Recovery Adjuster Productivity Report* provides recovery productivity on a summary and detail exposure level (including subrogation and salvage) by adjuster monthly and on a rolling 12-months inclusive of new, reopened and closed recovery claims (with closing ratios).

This report should be provided to the recovery adjuster monthly. The report should be available by adjuster, claim manager, unit, and recovery category, capturing both current data and a date range in the past.

## Detail Exposure List by Recovery Adjuster

The *Detail Exposure List by Recovery Adjuster* report provides a detailed list of recovery claim exposures (subrogation and salvage) by adjuster including new and closed recovery claims.

This report provides the detail behind the recovery productivity report above. The claim lists include the claim number, claim type, exposure, recovery type, recovery adjuster, date of loss, date reported, date recovery assigned, date recovery closed, recovery productivity category (new, closed, or reopen), reserves, payments and dollar recovery (detail and summary).

## Staff Appraiser Productivity Report

The *Staff Appraiser Productivity Report* provides appraiser productivity on a summary and detail level by staff appraiser and exposure monthly and on a rolling 12-months, inclusive of newly assigned inspections, current open/pending inspections, closed inspections (with closing ratios) and the number of supplemental appraisals and total losses.

The report may also include average appraisal and supplemental appraisal dollar values, average total loss values and cycle time reporting (e.g. assignment date to inspection, inspection to completion, etc.).

This report should also be provided to the appraiser monthly. The report should be available by appraiser, claim manager, unit, etc. and capture both current data and a date range in the past.

## Staff Appraiser Detailed Assignment Report

The *Staff Appraiser Detailed Assignment Report* provides the detail behind the staff appraiser productivity report indicated above.

The report includes the claim number, claim type, exposure, assigned appraiser, date of loss, date reported, date received, date inspection assigned, date inspection completed, appraisal amount, total loss (Y/N), total loss values, supplemental (Y/N), supplemental amounts and productivity category (e.g. new, open, closed).

## Total Loss & Salvage Reports

The *Total Loss & Salvage Report* tracks vehicle total losses handled by the claim staff and the timeliness of salvage management.

Many companies use salvage vendors to pick up vehicle salvage and auction the vehicles, remitting the proceeds to the company less the vendor and storage fees. If salvage vehicles are not picked up timely or left at the salvage facility too long incurring additional storage charges, there are increased costs.

These reports provide important tracking information to monitor and control the vehicle salvage process including the claim number, claim type, exposure, adjuster, appraiser, claimant/insured name, total loss amount, salvage $ projection, date of loss, date reported, date salvage picked up by salvor, date salvage auctioned and sold, salvage expenses, net salvage proceeds, and pending remarks (e.g. awaiting vehicle title, lien release, etc.).

These reports are typically provided by the salvage vendor or available in an accessible web portal provided by the vendor.

## Rental & Loss of Use Report

The *Rental & Loss of Use Report* provides relevant information on 1st and 3rd party automobile rental claims. The report may include the claim number, claim type, exposure, adjuster, manager, date of loss, date reported, date received, insured name, claimant name, appraisal $ amount, rental company name, first day of rental, last day of rental, number of rental days[26], rental $ paid per day, total rental dollars paid and average paids.

---

[26] As a general guideline, the ratio between repair time (hours) and rental usage should be approximately (4+) hours of repair time per rental day. On smaller estimates, an extra day may need to be included. This is an important concept as it provides the framework to determine the number of reasonable rental days for both 1st and 3rd party rental claims. To calculate the ratio between the repair time and rental usage, the adjuster should review the damage appraisal to determine the total number of repair hours and divide it by 4 (hours). For example, if the repair time is indicated as 20 hours then a reasonable number

This report is used to manage the costs associated with the vehicle rental process. Many claim departments have high claim leakage due to the lack of rental claim management.

## Claim Cycle Time Reports

*Claim Cycle Time Reports* provide a series of cycle time metrics comparing date of loss to date reported; date reported to date received; date reported to date assigned; date assigned to date of first contact; date of appraisal assignment to date completed; date of payment from date assigned; date open to date closed, etc.

Cycle time reports can be used in many different areas in the claim process to evaluate compliance with *best practices* and customer service impact

## Litigation Claim Reports

*Litigation Claim Reports* provide a report of litigation activity on a summary and detail basis of all litigation claims (open and closed) inclusive of claim number, docket number, court, venue, date suit open, date suit closed, current loss and expense reserves, paid loss and expense, line of business, exposure, claim type, plaintiff, insured, defense counsel, plaintiff attorney, adjuster and manager.

These reports are also referred to as a *suit list report* or *matter report* and can be automated with functionality available in new claim systems.

## Legal Bill Review Reports

Companies are outsourcing the review of legal bills to control costs. This process includes defense counsel submitting a legal budget, and then submitting legal bills to the vendor's portal for review and re-pricing.

Legal bill review vendors can provide comprehensive reporting on the number of legal bills submitted (by defense firm), the original legal bill dollar value, the re-priced legal bill amount, the fees associated with the service and the *gross* (without vendor fees) and *net* (net of vendor fees) savings.

---

of rental days would be 5 (20 Labor Hours / 4 Hours = 5 Rental Days). Additional days may be needed if the repair is between a weekend (add 2 days), if there are supplementals (using the same methodology for the number of hours on the supplemental repair), or if the vehicle parts are on order by the shop. Under normal circumstances, if the vehicle is deemed a total loss, seven (7) days should be a reasonable amount of time to provide a rental vehicle once the settlement offer has been extended.

## Suit Log Report

The *Suit Log Report* is a litigation report which lists all incoming and outgoing lawsuit activity as a management control to avoid a *default judgment* (missing the date due for an answer and appearance to the Summons & Complaint).

The report includes a detailed list of all newly received litigation inclusive of the claim number, date of loss, date reported, docket number, court, venue, date suit open, answer due date, extension of time to answer (Y/N and date), date referred to defense counsel, answer date, plaintiff, insured, defense counsel, plaintiff attorney, line of business, exposure, claim type, adjuster and manager name. This report should allow for sorting and filtering by data field.

The *Suit Log Report* is critical in any claim operation which handles litigation claims and can also be automated with functionality available in new claim systems.

## Medical Bill Review Reports

*Medical Bill Review Reports* provide relevant and detailed information on the medical bill review process (e.g. workers' compensation).

Whether the medical bill review is handled internally or outsourced to a vendor, detailed information should be provided monthly to evaluate the effectiveness of the process. For example, reporting should include the period reviewed (e.g. monthly, annually, etc.), medical bill count, total charges, total bill reductions, PPO reductions, allowances, gross savings, total fees, net savings and turnaround time (days).

## Inter-Company Arbitration Reports

If your company is a member of *Arbitration Forums, Inc.,* you should have access to their arbitration management reports which include the number of claims filed in arbitration as *Applicant* and *Respondent*, with the status and results, by office, unit, adjuster and program (e.g. Auto, Property, etc.).

These reports are a valuable tool. Utilization of arbitration is a cost-effective method to resolve liability and damage issues between carriers. By reviewing the management reports you can identify the volume of arbitration claims by applicant and respondent, success rates, total and average returns by program, etc.

## SIU Production Report

The *Special Investigative Unit (SIU) Production Report* provides summary and detail information on SIU production inclusive of new, open/pending and closed SIU matters.

The report should include the claim number, SIU investigator name, adjuster, manager, claim type, exposure, insured, claimant, date of SIU assignment, date assignment closed, date of loss, date reported, work completed by the SIU investigator and the disposition.

## Catastrophe (CAT) Reports

*Catastrophe (CAT) Reports* include catastrophe production details such as CAT ID number, peril, exposure, date range, claim volume activity (new, reopen and closed), territory affected, adjusters assigned, loss and expense detail with averages (reserves and payments) and future projections.

The extent of available CAT loss reporting in an organization will depend on the claim system and sophistication of reporting. Insurance companies with high CAT claim volume have invested in sophisticated reporting platforms or developed their own platforms internally.

## Large Loss Report Lists

*Large Loss Report Lists* provide a list of large loss claims (e.g. over a certain dollar threshold) by line of business, exposure, claim type, claim number, claimant, insured, date of loss, date reported, reserves and payments, incurred loss and expense, adjuster, claim manager, business unit, and date range – with the ability to filter by incurred loss dollar levels (paid, reserves and recovery).

Large loss lists are used to identify large loss exposure claims for reporting purposes.

## Home Office Reporting Claim List

The *Home Office Reporting Claim List* provides a list of files which qualify for home office reporting. The file list will include the exposure, claim type, claim number, claimant, insured, adjuster, HO Claim Manager, business unit, date of loss, date reported, financial details (reserves and payments) and date referred to home office.

This report assists the claim manager in identifying new and pending claims referred to home office claims, and those claims which need to be reported.

## P&L Budget Variance Report

The claim departmental *P&L Budget Variance Report* includes month-to-date (MTD) and year-to-date (YTD) financial data by budget expense category with variance reporting and a comparison of MTD and YTD for prior years.

Variance reporting provides the ability to measure actual vs. budget progress on a detail and summary level. This report is a useful tool to monitor claim department budget expenses (ULAE)

# Chapter Comments

In this chapter we reviewed a sampling of the various claim management reports available to the claim operation, which include both financial and operational reports.

Management reports are a tool we use to monitor claim activity and various trends – a *management control* for the claim supervisor or manager. The types of claim management report you use, or have access to, will depend on your level in the organization. The higher your level in the organization the more you will depend on claim management reports to be effective.

To properly manage a claim unit or claim department, management reports need to be relevant and useful. Management reports may point to an issue or problem, but you may need to dig deeper to find the answer either in the claim file or through your claim staff. Don't waste your time looking at management reports which are not useful or helpful. If you don't understand the report content or how to interpret the data get some help! If the report(s) you are using exclude data you need, then ask for the report to be modified.

Lastly, don't completely manage the claim operation by using management reports. You need review claims to understand technical claim quality and performance issues, especially at the claim supervisor or claim manager level.

Remember, the reports do not tell you everything. You are working with people – you need to get out of your office and know what is going on in the claim operation!

# Bibliography

American Educational Institute. *Senior Claim Law Associate (SCLA)*. 2016. 10 May 2017. <https://www.aeiclaimslaw.com/designations-overview>.

American Institute for Chartered Property Casualty Underwriters. *Associate in Claims (AIC™)*. 2017. 10 May 2017. <https://www.theinstitutes.org/program/associate-claims-aic?cid=PS_GGL_AIC_Gen_Ex_2&ads_cmpid=652962950&ads_adid=31394417405&ads_matchtype=e&ads_network=g&ads_creative=177355427437&utm_term=associate%20in%20claims&ads_targetid=kwd-1153506757&utm_campaign=&>.

—. *Chartered Property Casualty Underwriter (CPCU®)*. 2017. 10 May 2017. <https://www.theinstitutes.org/guide/designations/chartered-property-casualty-underwriter-cpcu>.

—. *The Canons, Rules, and Guidelines of the CPCU Code of Professional Conduct*. 2nd. Vol. 1st Printing. Malverne, February 2016. 21 April 2017. <http://www.theinstitutes.org/doc/canons.pdf>.

Cardinal, Rosalind. "6 Management Styles and When to Use Them." *TheHuffingtonPost.com, The Blog*. 13 January 2015. 24 April 2017. <http://www.huffingtonpost.com/rosalind-cardinal/6-management-styles-and-when-to-use-them_b_6446960.html>.

Department of the Treasury. *Office of Foreign Assets Control (OFAC)*. Washington DC, n.d. 5 October 2017. <https://www.treasury.gov/about/organizational-structure/offices/Pages/Office-of-Foreign-Assets-Control.aspx>.

Murdock, Michael T. "Choosing the Right P&C System." *The Nolan Company - Spotlight Publication*. Simsbury, 23 June 2013. 25 May 2017. <http://archive.constantcontact.com/fs166/1101062399246/archive/1112222719361.html>.

—. *Claim Operations: A Practical Guide*. 1st. Dallas: International Risk Management Institute, Inc., 2010.

—. "Getting Claim Costs Under Control: Improve Your Loss Ratio Using These Proven Fundamentals." *Claims Jounrnal* 1 March 2016. 27 April 2017. <http://www.claimsjournal.com/news/national/2016/03/01/269155.htm>.

—. "Impact of Reserve Redundancy and Deficiency on Results." *Claims Management Magazine (CLM)* 30 November 2012. 2 May 2017. <ttp://clmmag.theclm.org/home/article/Impact-of-Reserve-Redundancy-and-Deficiency-on-Results>.

—. "Improving the Financial Performance of your Claims Organization ." *The Nolan Company - Spotlight Publication*. Simsbury, June 2013. 27 May 2017. <http://archive.constantcontact.com/fs166/1101062399246/archive/1113798235846.html>.

—. "Setting It Aside: The Science and Art of Liability Case Reserve Management." *Claims Management Magazine (CLM)* 28 November 2012. 22 April 2017. <http://clmmag.theclm.org/home/article/Claims-Liability-Case-Reserve-Management>.

National Associaion of Insurance Commissioners (NAIC). *Statutory Accounting Principles (SAP) - NAIC Accounting Practices and Procedures Manual (AP&P Manual)*. Washington, n.d. 12 April 2017. <http://www.naic.org/cipr_topics/topic_statutory_accounting_principles.htm>.

The Merriam-Webster Online Dictionary. *Delegation*. n.d. 18 April 2017. <https://www.merriam-webster.com/dictionary/delegation>.

—. *Leadership*. n.d. 18 April 2017. <https://www.merriam-webster.com/dictionary/leadership>.

U.S. Centers for Medicare & Medicaid Services. "Mandatory Insurer Reporting (NGHP) ." *CMS.Gov, Centers for Medicare & Medicaid Services*. Baltimore, n.d. 5 October 2017. <https://www.cms.gov/Medicare/Coordination-of-Benefits-and-Recovery/Mandatory-Insurer-Reporting-For-Non-Group-Health-Plans/Overview.html>.

—. *Workers' Compensation Medicare Set Aside Arrangements*. 18 April 2016. 28 April 2017. <https://www.cms.gov/Medicare/Coordination-of-Benefits-and-Recovery/Workers-Compensation-Medicare-Set-Aside-Arrangements/WCMSA-Overview.html >.

Verisk Analytics, Inc. | Verisk Analytics® | ISO ClaimSearch®. *ISO ClaimSearch® - ISO Claims Solutions*. Jersey City, n.d. 18 April 2017. <http://www.verisk.com/iso/claimsearch/iso-claims-solutions.html>.

Verisk Analytics, Inc. | Verisk Analytics®. *ISO ClaimSearch® Database Segments*. Jersey City, n.d. 26 April 2017. <http://www.verisk.com/iso/claimsearch/database-segments.html>.

Web Finance, Inc. "PEST Analysis." *Business Dictionary*. 2017. 9 May 2017. <http://www.businessdictionary.com/definition/PEST-analysis.html, >.

—. "SWOT Analysis." *Business Dictionary*. 2017. 10 May 2017. <http://www.businessdictionary.com/definition/SWOT-analysis.html>.

Wickert, Gary. "Understanding Comparative Fault, Contributory Negligence and Joint & Several Liability." *Claims Journal*. 5 September 2013. 28 April 2017. <http://www.claimsjournal.com/news/national/2013/09/05/235755.htm>.

# Index

turnover, 62, 73–74, 78, 82, 88–90, 210